Political Analysis:
AN INTRODUCTION

Political Analysis:

AN INTRODUCTION

M. Margaret Conway
UNIVERSITY OF MARYLAND

Frank B. Feigert
STATE UNIVERSITY OF NEW YORK, BROCKPORT

Allyn and Bacon, Inc.
BOSTON

Library of Congress Catalog Card Number: 73–182592

Third printing . . . March, 1973

Contents

Group-Level Analysis   *144*
7

Decision-Making   *169*
8

Systems Analysis   *193*
9

Communications   *221*
10

Theory and Politics   *244*
11

Index   *277*

List of Illustrations
1

8

9

11

Preface

A major focus of modern political science has been the development of explanatory theory. While that goal is far from achieved, a number of approaches to theory are now being used within political science. One purpose of this book is to examine the underlying assumptions and the logic of the methods used to develop that type of theory. A second is to explore the basic concepts employed within selected theoretical approaches. A third is to present some of the generalizations about politics developed within each of the theoretical approaches examined. Both theories focusing on individual behavior (micro–theory) and theories accenting the behavior of collectivities, groups, nations, or the international system (macro-theory) are examined.

The first two chapters examine the context within which increased attention to problems of political theory has been developed, and the logic and assumptions of methods used to develop explanatory political theory. The next four chapters examine four approaches to the study of individual political behavior. Chapters Seven through Ten consider approaches which have been and are currently being used in the study of politics at the system or collectivities level. We conclude with a chapter which relates empirical political analysis to the practical requirements of the real world.

In a sense, this work constitutes a critical essay on the major works and concepts of modern political science. We have therefore chosen to omit a bibliographic essay for any of the given topics, as each chapter is essentially just that. We have attempted to cover a great range of works in a relatively short space, and suggest to interested students that the works we reference may be used as a starting point for further readings.

Betty Zisk and Lyman Kellstedt provided thorough and highly useful comments on the entire manuscript. We also wish to acknowledge the critical reading given earlier drafts by A. Jay Stevens and Robert J. Alperin. Roman Hedges and James Strouse also read selected chapters, and we have benefitted from their comments as well. The interpretations of the literature we have reviewed have varied widely, and we must therefore absolve them from any errors of omission or commission which remain. Also acknowledged are the assistance of Linda L. Pagelson, research assistant; Lillian Valoris and Dorothy Lukens, secretaries; and our typists, Linda Allen, Melody Davis, Barbara W. Hedges, Wendy Axelroth, Pamela Slade, Lea Chartock, and Maureen Eby. The cooperation and encouragement offered us by Louise Sullivan, Robert J. Patterson, and H. David Snook of Allyn & Bacon has also helped immeasurably.

Finally, the assistance of Fran Feigert in preparing the index and in ensuring the cooperation of Ben and Danny is voluntarily and gratefully acknowledged.

M.M.C.   *F.B.F.*
College Park, Md.   *Brockport, N.Y.*

Political Analysis:

AN INTRODUCTION

Part One

Approaches to Political Analysis

1

WHAT IS POLITICAL SCIENCE?

On June 5, 1968, the victorious primary candidate spoke to his cheering supporters in the crowded ballroom of the Los Angeles Ambassador Hotel. Leaving the ballroom, he walked through a narrow passageway; shots rang out, and Bobby Kennedy slumped to the floor, fatally wounded. The assassination, one of many in the decade of the 1960's, prompted the president of the United States to appoint a National Commission on the Causes and Prevention of Violence, charged with utilizing all means possible to determine why all too frequently the United States had experienced violent outbursts of both an individual and mass nature. Hearings, investigations, and research reports generated numerous documents and publications; many questions were raised. What are the historical patterns of violence in America? Did the frontier tradition of our development cause Americans to be more violence prone than citizens of other countries? Were patterns of violence in the 1960's significantly different from historical patterns of working class or racial violence in the United States? Was our experience with violence significantly different from that of other countries in the 1960's? What are the different kinds of civil strife which nations have been experiencing? Is it possible to develop a theory of civil violence? What are the sources of domestic violence, and what are their effects on political processes and political structures? Is there any relationship between patterns of domestic violence and patterns of international conflict? Many political scientists, along with other social scientists, focused attention and research efforts on finding answers to questions such as these. Are these typical of subjects which political scientists study? By what means can political scientists find answers to relevant questions such as these?

What subjects do political scientists study? One focus has been on legal governments,[1] but is political science anything more than that? If this were to be the limit, we would focus on the formal structure and decision-making processes and on the processes of controlling the legal institutions by such means as elections and the activities of political parties. Other subjects permissible under such a definition would include the study of policy outputs of the legal governments, and, perhaps, the relationships between the society and the legal institutions. A more extended definition of the proper scope of political science draws on a traditional concern of political science with values, or the goals which political systems and individual political activity should seek to maximize.

A more recent statement of the subject matter of political science is that it is the study of the authoritative allocation of values for a society.[2] Some critics have charged that this definition creates too large a task for political scientists, as values can be authoritatively allocated by a number of social institutions, such as the family, a religious organization, and the education system of a nation.

Another definition that has been suggested is that political analysis focuses on the study of power, authority, or rule.[3] This expands the subject matter beyond legal governments, and is subject to the same criticisms raised previously; that it sets too large a task for political science. Other definitions could be offered, but let us summarize by stating that in practice the subject matter of political science has been any and all things which either directly or indirectly might be related to politics.

---

[1] For discussions of possible definitions of the scope of political science, see Charles S. Hyneman, *The Study of Politics* (Urbana: University of Illinois Press, 1959) and David Easton, *The Political System* (New York: Alfred A. Knopf, 1959).

[2] David Easton, *op. cit.*, pp. 129-31; *A Framework for Political Analysis* (Englewood Cliffs, N.J.: Prentice Hall, 1965), p. 50; *A Systems Analysis of Political Life* (New York: John Wiley and Sons, 1965), pp. 21-22.

[3] Robert A. Dahl, *Modern Political Analysis* (Englewood Cliffs, N.J.: Prentice Hall, Inc., 1963), p. 7.

Hence, we find political scientists studying such subjects as domestic violence, patterns of revolution, political modernization, and the relationship of domestic violence to international conflict, as well as the more traditional subjects usually associated with political science, such as constitutional law and history, political parties, legislatures, and political philosophy.

Another way of distinguishing political science concerns is by the varieties of theory which are the central focus of political scientists. The term "theory" has several meanings. Commonly but incorrectly it is used to mean a hypothesis or conjecture. More appropriately, it refers to analysis of the interrelationships between ideas or variables or objects. One distinction is between speculative and non-speculative theory. Speculative theory can be defined as that which examines different relationships and aspects of a subject without sufficient evidence being presented to support the conclusions advanced. A second distinction is between empirical and normative theory. Empirical theory is theory derived from a careful consideration of experience and observation of recurring events. Normative theory is concerned with moral imperatives of behavior, values, or goals prescribed for an individual, group, or society. From the distinctions between speculative and non-speculative theory and between normative and empirical theory we can construct the following typology:

	Speculative	Non-speculative
Empirical	+	+
Normative	+	−

Is it possible for normative theory to be non-speculative? Probably not, for by its very nature it deals with questions resolvable only through value judgments. Can empirical theory be speculative? Technically, the answer would be no, but practically, much of what is claimed to be empirical theory is speculative in the sense that an exhaustive consideration of the evidence has not been completed and probably cannot be, because of the time, energy, and access to the subject required by such an exhaustive study. Generally, we can say that the recent and current theoretical concerns of political scientists are and have been speculative normative theory, and speculative and non-speculative empirical theory.

What we shall discuss in this book are the research methods and theoretical approaches which are being used to develop empirical theories. These theoretical approaches, which make possible description and explanation of political and social problems, are the basis for developing solutions to domestic and foreign policy problems. In order to understand these policy problems and to evaluate critically the solutions proposed for them, knowledge of the methods used to derive the explanations of the problems' causes and consequences is essential. Equally essential is an understanding of the theoretical approaches on which analyses are based. The development of empirical theories results in accurate and extensive description of political and social behavior, explains that behavior, and therefore makes possible the understanding of what conditions result in a particular political problem.

Thus, the boundaries of the subject matter of political science are quite all-encompassing. Social problems lead to demands for political action and public policy. If air is polluted or people hungry or tornado damage extensive or inflation rampant or safety of air travel diminished, demands arise for government action. Where disputes exist between groups or interests in society, that interest which believes government action will favor it demands government intervention in the conflict. Government is viewed as the solver of problems and the resolver of conflicts, and political science takes as its boundaries the study of the activities of government and the related political processes.

The result has been the increased interrelationship between political science and other behavioral science disciplines such as sociology, psychology and economics. What we study is human behavior in politically relevant situations or activities. Hence, the theories which generally describe and explain human behavior are useful in understanding human behavior in a political context.

THEORIES AND METHODS: STABILITY AND CHANGE

Early in the 1950's advocates of the development of systematic, rigorous, non-speculative empirical theory became the protagonists in a controversy about the appropriate subject matter and research methods for political science. Labelled "the behavioral approach," the focus of political science should be, according to its advocates, "to discover the extent and nature of uniformities in the actual behavior of men and groups of men in the political process."[4] Robert Dahl, in a discussion

[4] Samuel J. Eldersveld, Alexander Heard, Samuel P. Huntington, Morris Janowitz, Avery Leiserson, Dayton D. MacKean, and David B. Truman, "Research in Political Behavior," in S. Sidney Ulmer (ed.), *Introductory Readings in Political Behavior* (Chicago: Rand McNally and Company, 1961), p. 8.

of the development of the behavioral approach, stated it somewhat differently:

> . . . the behavioral approach is an attempt to improve our understanding of politics by seeking to explain the empirical aspects of political life by means of methods, theories, and criteria of proof that are acceptable according to the canons, conventions, and assumptions of modern empirical science.[5]

Dahl posed the question of whether or not this relatively new political behavior approach was ever more than a protest movement by a dissident wing of the political science discipline. This dissident wing shared skepticism about the supposed prior accomplishments of political science and also shared a sympathy toward scientific methods of research and the possibilities of creating a more soundly based knowledge of political processes. Is the behavioral approach any more than this; sharing beliefs, assumptions, methods, or topics? He concludes that the behavioral approach is an attempt to make political science more scientific in its empirical content; an orientation "which aims at stating all the phenomena of government in terms of the observed and observable behavior of men."[6] In other words political behavior was viewed as *not a field of study* within political science but as *a means of studying all fields* of political science.

In summary, a minimal definition of the goal of political science which might be acceptable to most participants in the study of politics is the development of "a body of systematic and orderly thinking about a determinate subject matter."[7] Regardless of the particular problem of interest, the aim is the development of systematic, empirical theories of politics which will make it possible for us both to explain and to predict human behavior in the political arena. To accomplish this goal of developing empirical theories, emphasis has also been placed on developing or adapting from other academic disciplines new methods of observation in order to ascertain the nature of political reality. Generally agreement exists on the need for new units of analysis,[8] as those previously predominant in the study of politics are not adequate for the development of the desired theories. For example, variations in political moti-

---

[5] Robert Dahl, "The Behavioral Approach in Political Science: Epitaph for a Monument to a Successful Protest," *American Political Science Review*, LV (December, 1961), 767.

[6] *Ibid.*, p. 766.

[7] David B. Truman, *Items* (Social Science Research Council), December, 1951.

[8] Heinz Eulau, *The Behavioral Persuasion* (New York: Random House, 1963), pp. 14-19; Eldersveld *et al, op. cit.*, p. 8; Karl Deutsch, *The Nerves of Government* (New York: The Free Press, 1963), pp. 22-50.

vation and incentive systems, role performance, or attitudes associated with patterns of traditional or innovative political participation cannot be adequately evaluated using institutional concepts. In addition, the units of analysis must be useful in describing and generalizing about political behavior in non-western as well as western political systems. For example, what are the similarities in the political revolutions in the American colonies in 1776, France in 1789, Mexico in 1911, Russia in 1918, and those occurring in Latin American and African nations today? How can we explain the patterns of domestic political violence found in both politically developed and politically modernizing societies? How does domestic violence relate to patterns of international conflict? The development of theories of politics requires units of analysis which can be used to evaluate similar patterns of behavior or events occurring in different cultures and in different historical periods; only then can we develop political theories of significant scope. In other words, we search for the communalities of what may otherwise be considered unique events, situations, or processes. Together with psychology, anthropology, sociology, and economics, political science focuses on the behavior of men in social settings.[9] The boundaries between these academic disciplines have been drawn by distinctions between different roles; economics focuses on behavior relevant to the production of goods and services, while sociology examines man in a number of different social roles, such as a member of a family, a religious unit, or other social group. The distinctions are based on abstracting certain elements of an individual's behavior from other elements; however, we cannot deny that these elements coexist and exert mutual influence. For example, parents in the processes of exercising authority over their children create in children patterns of expectations about the behavior of wielders of power which may influence the children's later reactions to political authorities.[10] Each of the other social sciences can contribute to a better understanding of politics through application of theories of human behavior developed in them. For example, a general theory of motivation developed by psychologists and used in the study of cycles of economic productivity can help us understand patterns of motivation for different types of political participation, such as party organization work versus candidacy for public office, or for the patterns of political development in emerging nations. Thus, the study of politics has become in a sense interdisciplinary in that it utilizes the units of analyses and theories of other behavioral

[9] See Dahl, *American Political Science Review, op. cit.*, p. 769.

[10] For discussion of the evidence for this, see Robert Hess and Judith Torney, *The Development of Political Attitudes in Children* (Chicago: Aldine Publishing Company, 1967), pp. 99-101; Fred I. Greenstein, *Children and Politics* (New Haven: Yale University Press, 1965), pp. 50-51; Dean Jaros, "Children's Attitudes toward the President," *Journal of Politics*, XXIX (May, 1967), pp. 368-87.

sciences in an attempt to understand social, psychological, and cultural influences on behavior in the political realm.

Much emphasis has been placed by recent political science research on methodological problems.[11] If political science is to develop valid generalizations, more precise methods of making observations, categorizing observed phenomena, and measuring variables are required. Some critics mistakenly perceived this concern with better tools of observation, categorization, and measurement to be the sole aim of many innovative researchers. The need for better methods of measurement and observation has led political scientists to learn and apply observational techniques developed in other academic disciplines, such as content analysis,[12] attitude scaling,[13] and sociometric or interaction analysis.[14] Additionally, many political scientists have sought to develop their knowledge of statistics and mathematics in order to describe more systematically and to draw inferences more correctly about the phenomena they observe.[15] It must be remembered that the ultimate aim reflected in these concerns with units of analysis, better tools of observation, measurement and categorization, and knowledge developed in other disciplines is the development of empirical political theory.

Among the predominant characteristics of political science as it existed in the pre-World War II period the following have been enumerated by various political scientists:[16]

[11] Albert Somit and Joseph Tannenhaus, The Development of Political Science (Boston: Allyn and Bacon, 1967), p. 179; Dahl, op. cit.

[12] Robert C. North, Ole Holsti, M. George Zaninovich, and Dina Zinnes, Content Analysis (Evanston: Northwestern University Press, 1963).

[13] Basic works on attitude scaling include William S. Torgeson, Theory and Method of Scaling (New York: John Wiley and Sons, 1958); Allen L. Edwards, Techniques of Attitude Scale Construction (New York: Appleton-Century-Crofts, 1957).

[14] For examples of attitude measures, see John P. Robinson, Jerrold G. Rusk, and Kendra Head, Measures of Political Attitudes (Ann Arbor: Institute for Social Research, September, 1968).

[15] Several works have been published which focus on statistical measures of use to political scientists. They include the following: V. O. Key, Jr., Statistics for Political Scientists (New York: Thomas Y. Crowell Company, 1954); Hubert M. Blalock, Jr., Social Statistics (New York: McGraw-Hill Book Company, 1960); Linton C. Freeman, Elementary Applied Statistics for Students in Behavioral Science (New York: John Wiley and Sons, 1965); Sidney Siegel, Nonparametric Statistics for the Behavioral Sciences (New York: McGraw-Hill Book Company, 1956); Celeste McCullough and Loche Van Atta, Statistical Concepts: A Program for Self Instruction (New York: McGraw-Hill Book Company, 1963); William Hays, Statistics for Psychologists (New York: Holt, Rinehart, and Winston, 1963).

[16] For critiques of political science theory and methodology, see Roy Macridis, The Study of Comparative Government (New York: Random House, 1955), pp. 7-22; Richard Snyder, "A Decision-Making Approach to the Study of Political Phenomena," in Approaches to the Study of Politics, ed. Roland Young (Evanston: Northwestern University Press, 1958), pp. 3-15; David Easton, The Political System, op. cit.

1. an emphasis on the study of institutions to the exclusion of political processes;
2. the neglect of the study of non-American political systems; where studied, the focus was largely on Western European systems;
3. a very strong tendency toward description of existing institutions rather than analysis and development of systematic generalizations about political behavior which would account adequately for similarities, differences, and changes in political processes;
4. a fascination with institutions or political patterns perceived by the researchers as unique, and consequently a failure to consider adequately the premise of uniqueness as well as to develop generalizations, which cannot, of course, be derived from the study of phenomena conceived of as unique;
5. a tendency to take the characteristics of the polity for granted, thereby ignoring changes in the political system or differences in rates of change either over time within one system or between different political systems;
6. a view of science as raw empiricism, rather than as the development of systematic theories through the thoughtful gathering of data and analysis in order to test specific hypotheses;
7. a strong reformist tendency, with emphasis on value judgments specifying what ought to be the nature of political structures and institutions, occasionally accompanied by polemics for the adoption of the author's preferred reforms of the political system;
8. a neglect of the findings of other social science disciplines which would contribute to the understanding of political behavior.

David B. Truman has suggested that political scientists in the period from the 1880's to the 1930's generally held a common set of beliefs about both the problems and the research methods appropriate to the discipline; he perceives the features of this predominant agreement as being:

1. an unconcern with political systems as such, including the American system, which amounted in most cases to taking their properties and requirements for granted;
2. an unexamined and mostly implicit conception of political change and development that was blandly optimistic and unreflectively reformist;
3. an almost total neglect of theory in any meaningful sense of the term;
4. a consequent enthusiasm for a conception of 'science' that rarely went beyond raw empiricism;

5. a strongly parochial preoccupation with things American that stunted the development of an effective comparative method; and

6. the establishment of a confining commitment to concrete description.[17]

Truman, writing in 1965, believed that a new consensus about the nature of the discipline was evolving in political science. Among the factors contributing to the development of this consensus were a concern with the political system as such, examining the interrelationships which persist in a recurring pattern and resulting in a convergence of the theoretical interests operating in discrete sub-fields of the discipline.[18] Thus we would expect to find greater congruence between theoretical developments in the study of political participation in the United States and in the study of political participation in other countries. Also evolving was a revival of interest in political theory and a concern with the relationship between empirical theory and empirical investigation.[19] Theory guides research through indication of what concepts are relevant and what facts are therefore relevant. A third contributor to the evolution of a new consensus about the scope of political science was, according to Truman, a recommitment to the goal of science.[20]

ORIGINS OF NEW APPROACHES

Several factors which contributed to the development of new approaches to the study of political science can be enumerated. In the United States, several persons stimulated interest in an alternative method of studying the traditional subject matter of political science. Arthur Bentley, a sociologist and journalist writing in 1908, argued that political science should focus on human behavior in political situations as the object of its attention, emphasizing group relationships and activities in the political process.[21] Charles Merriam, chairman of the political science department at the University of Chicago and a practitioner in the maze of Chicago politics, advocated to his students and throughout the discipline greater attention to psychological factors in political be-

[17] David B. Truman, "Disillusion and Regeneration: The Quest for a Discipline," *American Political Science Review*, LIX (December, 1965), p. 866.
[18] *Ibid.*, p. 869.
[19] *Ibid.*, p. 870.
[20] *Ibid.*, p. 871.
[21] Arthur F. Bentley, *The Process of Government* (Evanston: Principia Press, 1939). First published in 1908.

havior.[22] One of Merriam's colleagues, Harold Lasswell, utilized psychological concepts in his research, and greatly influenced the use of a variety of variables and analytic techniques in political science research.[23]

A second influence was the writing and later the teaching in American universities of a number of European scholars. For example, Englishman Graham Wallas advocated attention to psychological factors which affect individual political behavior in a book first published in 1908.[24] Herbert Tingsten, a Swede, published in 1937 an analysis of European political behavior which received considerable attention in this country.[25]

In addition, the crisis in Europe during the 1930's brought to this country a number of scholars strongly influenced in their approach to political analysis by European sociologists. The writings of Max Weber, Pareto, Michels, and Mosca received wider exposure through the teaching and research of the refugee scholars.[26]

Another factor was undoubtedly the tasks assigned to a large number of political scientists during the Second World War.[27] Political scientists descended from the ivory towers to assume a variety of responsibilities in the federal government. Some who were assigned to administrative functions realized that an emphasis on legal and formal subjects resulted in much of the political process being ignored, and the answers to important questions could not be provided by such an approach. Secondly, many were assigned to inter-disciplinary research responsibilities which brought them into contact with the concepts, previous findings, and research methods of sociology, economics, and psychology.

Several other factors, perhaps peculiar to the American environment, have exerted influence and provided support for changes in the study of politics. One was the establishment by the Social Science Research Council in 1945 of a Committee on Political Behavior.[28] The

[22] Charles Merriam, New Aspects of Politics (Chicago: University of Chicago Press, 1925), p. 11.

[23] Harold Lasswell, Psychopathology and Politics (New York: The Viking Press, 1960). First published in 1930.

[24] Graham Wallas, Human Nature in Politics (Lincoln: University of Nebraska Press, 1962). First published in 1908.

[25] Herbert Tingsten, Political Behavior: Studies in Election Statistics (London: P. S. Kind and Son, Ltd., 1937).

[26] Max Weber, Theory of Economic and Social Organizations, trans. Talcott Parsons (New York: Free Press, 1947); Vilfredo Pareto, Selections, ed. Joseph Lopreato (New York: Thomas Y. Crowell Company, 1965); Gaetano Mosca, The Ruling Class, trans. Hannah Kahn (New York: McGraw-Hill, 1939).

[27] For a discussion of this influence, see Robert A. Dahl, "The Behavioral Approach in Political Science: Epitaph for a Monument to a Successful Protest," op. cit.

[28] Ibid.

committee, through sponsoring conferences and granting research support, stimulated the growth of the behavioral movement within political science. A second committee of the Social Science Research Council, the Committee on Comparative Politics, stimulated new theoretical and methodological approaches to the study of comparative politics.

Another important factor has been the existence of philanthropic foundations such as Ford, Carnegie, and Rockefeller, which have made large contributions to frequently very expensive research projects. They have had, by their selection of certain research proposals to finance, a significant effect on the direction of the discipline, both in terms of subject foci and research methods. Additionally, a number of agencies of the federal government have financed research aimed at the description of political processes, the development of empirical political theories, or the development of new methods of research. For example, such topics as patterns of international conflict and alliances, nation-building, and conditions conducive to the outbreak of domestic violence have been the subject of research financed by Department of Defense agencies. The National Science Foundation has also contributed to the development of empirical theory and research methodology and the training of political scientists in research techniques.

A number of assumptions are made in developing empirical theories of politics.[29] We are first assuming that there are discoverable uniformities in human behavior in politics; this means we believe that behavior is not random, that men behave in a regularized or recurring fashion when engaged in political acts, such as when citizens vote in a presidential election or when Congress enacts legislation or when judges decide on the constitutionality of laws passed by Congress.

Is the assumption of uniformities or regularities in patterns of behavior one that can be accepted? While the people who are casting their votes at the ballot box or in the legislature or handing down decisions in the courtroom change over time, the act is the same kind of act. Problems, issues, and demands change but continuities in patterns of behavior can be discerned. For example, legislators are subjected to pressures from different clienteles, such as interest groups, party organization units, and officials in the executive branch; both the nature of the pressures and the characteristics of the clienteles can be analyzed and patterns of pressures from certain types of clienteles can be studied at different points in time and in different political systems. In addition,

[29] For further discussions of the assumptions made in social science research and their validity, see John Kemeny, A Philosopher Looks at Science (Princeton: Van Nostrand and Company, 1959), Ch. 15; Ernest Nagel, The Structure of Science (London: Routledge and Kegan Paul, 1961), Ch. 13 and 14.

the relationship between voting behavior of individual legislators and significant cue givers inside the legislative chamber, such as committee chairmen, caucus chairman, party floor leader, or state or county delegation dean, can be examined and patterns of relationship found. What we are assuming is not that the same problem or issue is present or that the same person must remain in office, but that human behavior in political situations is not random, but patterned, and that these patterns can be observed.

We further are assuming that these regularities can be expressed in generalizations which approximate the universality of a scientific law or theory in the natural sciences. However, the universality itself of these uniformities or regularities in political behavior is not assumed; it is established through the procedures of scientific investigation by careful observation of the behavior patterns. If we are to observe behavior carefully, then we must pay attention to the development of criteria and techniques for the observation and measurement of behavior.

It is also assumed that one can study political happenings and arrive at generalizations which are not influenced or biased by the observer's personal values. A political scientist can both assert value judgments and present empirical explanations, but it is possible and equally necessary to keep the two distinct and separate. We can study values, and we can assert value judgments, but we cannot assert the validity of the value judgments through use of scientific methods.

Generally it is agreed that research not guided by theoretical concerns contributes inadequately to the development of our knowledge about the political activities of men, and similarly, adequate theories to explain politics can be developed only through empirical research.

The emphasis on development of empirical theory has been institutionalized within the discipline in a number of ways. One is the development of data archives and multi-university research methodology training programs. The most prominent example is the creation and growth of the Inter-University Consortium for Political Research. The consortium is a co-operative arrangement between the Political Behavior program of the Survey Research Center, University of Michigan, and political science departments in approximately 150 American and foreign universities and colleges. It collects and disseminates upon request to member departments various sets of political science data, such as past election results from the United States and other countries, congressional roll call data, and data obtained from survey research on significant aspects of political behavior. The consortium also operates summer training programs for faculty and students from member departments. Through consortium efforts greater sophistication in research techniques is promoted and data are made more readily available. A number of individual universities have also developed data archives specializing in particular regions of the world or in a particular aspect of political science.[30]

Other indications of the institutionalization of the focus on developing empirical theory can be found in the recent advent of specialized journals which focus either on specific types of political problems or on interdisciplinary research. These include such journals as *The Journal of Conflict Resolution, Administrative Science Quarterly, Comparative Political Studies, Comparative Politics, Urban Affairs Quarterly, Public Choice, Behavioral Science,* and *American Behavioral Scientist.*

Another indication of the widespread acceptance of the changes in political science is found in the predominance of articles oriented toward empirical research in the political science journals. Commercial textbook and monograph publishers also appear to have found a favorable response to new approaches within the discipline, as their lists of publications would indicate. Still another indicator is found among the courses required of both undergraduate and graduate students in many political science departments. Increasingly, courses which introduce students to empirical theory and to sophisticated research methodology are required of students majoring in political science. To summarize, political science has, in the period since World War II, experienced extensive changes in the types of subjects studied, research methods used, and stated goals of the discipline.

However, the emphasis on the development of non-speculative empirical theory led to a counter-movement within American political science in the late 1960's which demanded a direct concern with an emphasis on policy outcomes. To some of the "post-behavioralists" this extended to selecting research problems because of their immediate policy relevance, advocating the selection of a particular solution of the policy problem within the context of one's research, and involving the national and regional organizations of political scientists through both resolutions and actions in the advocacy of particular public policy alternatives.

In the chapters which follow we will examine components of the post-World War II change in how we study politics. In Chapter Two we examine the nature of science, the characteristics of scientific meth-

---

[30] Information about the archives at various institutions can be obtained from the Council of Social Science Data Archives, whose administrative offices are located at the University of Pittsburgh.

od, and possible problems in using scientific method to develop empirical theories of politics. We also discuss principles of observation, measurement, and inference used in gathering and analyzing data about politics. In subsequent chapters we shall discuss a number of conceptual approaches utilizing a variety of units of analysis and consider their potential for contributing to the development of empirical political theory.

Political Science as Science

2

INTRODUCTION

One approach that political scientists have used to increase our understanding of political processes is that of scientific method, applying to the study of politics the criteria for theory building developed and employed in the natural and behavioral sciences. Scientists observe what happens, manipulating things when possible in order to examine what happens under different conditions.[1] The function of science is generally perceived as being the establishment of general laws or theories which explain the behavior with which the particular discipline is concerned.[2] For political science, the subject is political behavior in all its manifestations, which includes the behavior of individuals, institutions, and nations. If we can develop empirical theories, we can understand the common characteristics of individual events and make predictions about the character and occurrence of various types of political behavior.

[1] Gustav Bergmann, *Philosophy of Science* (Madison: University of Wisconsin Press, 1957), p. 3.
[2] R. B. Braithwaite, *Scientific Explanation* (New York: Harper Torchbooks, 1960), p. 1.

Thus, any science has two major objectives, the description of phenomena, in this case political behavior, and the establishment of general principles by which that behavior can be explained and predicted.[3]

These, then, are two of the defining characteristics of the scientific enterprise: description of the properties of and relationships among phenomena, and the development of explanations of these relationships. Three other qualities denote the nature of science. First, these descriptions and explanations are based on empirical evidence. Secondly, concern with the facts is unaffected by an individual's definition of what is good or what would be the preferable condition. In other words, science in the statement of facts and relationships is value-free. Finally, objectivity prevails in that nothing in the environment of scientific inquiry prevents the basing of statements on the empirical evidence.[4]

Kerlinger points out that there are two views as to what it is that scientists do. The static view is that science is a form of activity which contributes systematized information to the world. People who engage in the scientific enterprise discover new facts and seek to explain them. The dynamic view regards science as the development of theories and of conceptual frameworks which promote the discovery of facts and their relationship.[5]

The basic purpose of political science is dynamic, to form theories which will explain the facts of the political universe. For a good scientific explanation, we must have well established general theories, and we must be in possession of facts known independently of the phenomena to be explained. The phenomena to be explained must be a logical consequence of the general theories and known facts.[6] We could say, therefore, that the aim and defining characteristics of science are to discover "what the facts truly are"[7] and to explain their existence through theories and laws. Now we must deal with the question, "what is a fact?" A number of definitions abound in the writings of philosophers of science and of political scientists. David Easton defines a fact as "a particular ordering of reality in terms of a theoretical interest."[8] An-

[3] Carl G. Hempel, *Fundamentals of Concept Formation in Empirical Science*, International Encyclopedia of Unified Science, Vol. II (Chicago: University of Chicago Press, 1952), p. 1.

[4] Quentin Gibson, *The Logic of Social Inquiry* (London: Routledge and Kegan Paul, 1960), p. 3.

[5] Fred Kerlinger, *Foundations of Behavioral Research* (New York: Holt, Rinehart and Winston, 1965), p. 9.

[6] John Kemeny, *A Philosopher Looks at Science* (Princeton: D. Van Nostrand Company, 1959), Ch. 9.

[7] Morris Cohen and Ernest Nagel, *An Introduction to Logic and Scientific Method* (London: Routledge and Kegan Paul, 1934), p. 391.

[8] David Easton, *The Political System* (New York: Alfred A. Knopf, 1959).

other definition is that a fact is "an empirically verifiable observation."[9] Vernon Van Dyke defines a fact as a finding or statement about the nature of reality in which universal agreement is achievable, at least in principle.[10] Another definition is that facts are propositions about known and particular phenomena for which there is considerable evidence.[11] In this we can contrast fact with theory; a theory is a universal statement which we can never know to be entirely true. For example, to say that the sun "rose" today is a fact. To say that the sun "rises" every 24 hours would be a theoretical statement.

SCIENTIFIC METHOD

We start in science with curiosity or puzzlement, aware of an unexplained phenomenon which can be stated as a problem for investigation. Among the types of problems which might be of concern to political scientists are the following: 1) Why do some countries have several major political parties, others have two major political parties, and still others have only one? The development of political parties is a relatively recent phenomenon; why did they develop? Do all political parties perform the same functions in the governing of a nation? 2) Some of the countries created after the Second World War have had relatively stable governmental systems, while others have been relatively unstable. Why has this occurred? What contributes to governmental instability? 3) Why do some legislators consistently support liberal domestic programs, others consistently oppose them, and still others vary in their support of these programs? Does the nature of the constituency, the personality of the legislator, his position in various power systems in the legislative system, the various role orientations which he holds, or his personal values influence his voting behavior? These three represent a sample of the types of problems with which political scientists have been concerned.

The analysis of all these problems can be handled under the same method. That method is the logic of science. We can consider it to be a cycle or a process in which we start with facts and end up with facts. We have a set of facts for which we wish to account; these facts are a

[9] William J. Goode and Paul K. Hatt, *Methods in Social Research* (New York: McGraw-Hill Book Company, 1952), p. 8.
[10] Vernon Van Dyke, *Political Science: A Philosophical Analysis* (Stanford: Stanford University Press, 1960), p. 56.
[11] Kemeny, *op. cit.*, p. 91.

statement of the problem. For example, certain countries have stable governments; others are very unstable, or some legislators support liberal domestic programs while others oppose these programs.

We have facts, such as a government and legislators; these are specific entities. If we want to develop generalizations, we must concern ourselves with a class of objects sharing certain specified characteristics. In designating this class of objects we have used a concept. The term concept has been variously defined as "a word that expresses an abstraction formed by generalization from particulars,"[12] a name given to any general element in one's experience,"[13] and "a shorthand representation of a variety of facts. Its purpose is to simplify thinking by subsuming a number of events under one general heading."[14] For example, concepts used in our previous examples included "stable governments" and "liberal domestic programs."

The first stage in scientific method is the inductive stage, the process by which hypotheses are formed to fit the observed facts to be explained. One goes from the particular facts or observed phenomena to a general statement which is conjectural, a tentative statement about the relationship between two or more observed phenomena. For any set of phenomena there are probably several hypotheses which could be formulated to express the relationship between them. One is selected to be tested. Hypotheses are formulated on the basis of one's previous knowledge of the subject; hence the basic requirement for scientific research is an encyclopedic knowledge of previous research and findings in the field. Hypotheses can also be generated on the basis of knowledge of other subject matter which shows a similar structure or nature, such as the use of knowledge of physics and biology to develop hypotheses about communication patterns within formal and informal organizations. Hypotheses are general statements, suggestions of the connections between concepts. How does one determine which of several possible hypotheses to select for testing? One rule is to select that which is simplest in its formulation of the connections between the variables. A second is to select that which appears most probable. A necessary requirement is that the hypotheses will make possible the explanation of or accounting for all the known facts.

The second step in scientific method is that of deduction. One deduces the logical consequences of the hypothesis; these are in the form of observable facts. We deduce what particular facts would be present

---

[12] Kerlinger, op. cit., p. 31.
[13] Van Dyke, op. cit., p. 62.
[14] David Clarence McClelland, *Personality* (New York: William Sloane Associates, Inc., 1951).

if our hypothesis about the relationship between the concepts stated in the hypothesis is valid.

The third step of scientific method is to check to see if the facts we deduced from our hypothesis are present. If they are, we fail to reject the hypothesis as incorrect. This step of scientific method is the verification step. What we have verified, however, is not the hypothesis itself, but the logical consequences of the hypothesis. What we have done is test the relationship expressed by the hypothesis by examining to see if other facts which would be expected to occur if the hypothesis were not invalid actually did occur.

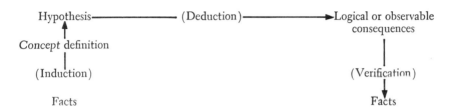

Figure 1   The Steps of Scientific Method *

Sometimes the third step is referred to as the "falsification" step, as we are trying to reject the hypothesis. In addition, we never completely test any hypothesis, as all possible occurrences of the relationship specified in the hypothesis cannot be tested because of time and observation limitations. While a hypothesis can be rejected because the predicted relationships are not found, we cannot prove a hypothesis; not only can we not test for all possible occurrences of the predicted relationships, our observations or measurements are at best only approximations.

Usually in scientific research, what is actually tested is the obverse of the specified hypothesis, a hypothesis of no relationship. Such a hypothesis, called the *null hypothesis*, states that no relationship exists between the concepts. One rejects the null hypothesis and fails to reject the positive hypothesis only if the relationships found were very unlikely to have occurred by chance. For example, it is common practice to reject the null hypothesis and accept the research hypothesis only if the relationship is likely to occur only five times out of one hundred on a random chance basis. It is for these reasons that this third step can also

* This diagram is a modification and elaboration of one found in Kemeny, *op. cit.*, p. 86.

be referred to as *falsification*. In effect, we can never completely verify a hypothesis, but we can invalidate or reject it.

Let us consider a problem in political analysis. For example, we observe that a friend who considers himself to have little influence on political events rarely votes, while another perceives himself to be politically effective and always votes in elections. From this set of facts we establish a hypothesis: individuals who believe themselves to be politically effective are more likely to vote than individuals who do not believe themselves to be politically effective. The logical consequences which we deduce are that those who are politically effective (self-perceived) will vote and those not perceiving themselves to be politically effective will not vote in a particular election. We then can observe by interviewing a sample of the potential electorate after an election has been held, asking questions designed to measure the presence and perhaps the degree of political effectiveness, and finding out whether or not the individuals voted. We can then, on the basis of our observations, either reject (falsify) our hypothesis or not reject it.

The actual outcome of previous research on this question is that there is a tendency for those who are more politically efficacious to vote with greater frequency, but there is not a perfect relationship between degree of political efficacy and voting turnout. Therefore we modify our hypothesis to account for the discrepancies, perhaps adding such additional possible influencing variables as the individual's degree of interest in the election outcome, his belief that the outcome of the election will make a difference to him, his strength of commitment to a political party, his concern with campaign issues, and his reaction to the candidates in the election. The modified hypothesis, in turn, should now be tested for validity and inclusiveness.

The building blocks or key terms in the hypotheses are concepts. Examples of concepts used in political science are: authority, power, class, influence, society, conflict, legitimacy, political system and political efficacy. Generally, concepts must have two characteristics to be useful in any scientific study. The first is that a concept must have a clear empirical referent. When using ordinary language, we unconsciously accept this requirement; the process of learning a language is in part the process of associating the name for a class of objects with the objects, such as the concept "tree" with the type of object to which the concept refers. A second requirement for a concept is that it must be useable in the formulation of a theory.[15]

---

[15] Hempel, *op. cit.*, p. 39. A distinction can be made between concepts and constructs. A construct is a concept deliberately created for use in scientific research and theorizing. The term "party cohesion," used in studying the unity of a political party in voting in a legislative body, is an example of a construct.

One of the characteristics of a well developed science is the existence of a number of concepts for which a common set of definitions has been agreed on and accepted by those in the scientific discipline. A science still in its infancy, such as political science, must struggle to develop a set of these commonly defined units of analysis. How can concepts be defined?

A basic distinction must be made between two methods of defining concepts. Philosophers seek real definitions of concepts, that is, their essential characteristics. A political philosopher, for example, would seek to identify the essential characteristics of the thing we call *justice*. This is a concern with the analysis of meaning, or *analytic definition*, without recourse to empirical analysis. The other type of definition provides meaning by stipulation and is called *nominal definition*. We name the set of characteristics which constitute the concept; this is the type of definition with which science is concerned. There are two ways of doing this. One way, that of a *constitutive definition*, is to define a concept in terms of other words or concepts. The second method of defining is called *operational definition*. One can provide either measured or experimental operational definitions. When a concept is given a measured definition, we define the concept by describing the procedures used to measure its existence in the subject studied. If, for example, we wish to study the existence of authoritarian attitudes among residents of a particular country, a measured definition of authoritarianism would be a statement or presentation of the attitude question or set of questions used to measure the presence of authoritarianism. An experimental definition of a concept is provided by a statement of the operations or manipulations performed by the researcher to induce or activate the existence or effect of the concept.

Experimental operational definitions take the form of *if* . . ., *then* . . . statements. Each specifies the operation to be performed; if it is performed successfully, then an instance of the concept has occurred.

If . . . operation ———————▶ Successful result ———————▶ then . . . concept
                                   (meeting of conditions)
     (O)   (R)   (C)

For example, we say that if a substance is placed in water and the substance dissolves, then the substance is soluble. This is an operational definition of solubility, providing a test for the presence or absence of the concept.

As yet political science lacks a set of concepts or units of analysis for which generally accepted definitions of either a constitutive or operational type have been developed. Any science in such a state is handicapped, in that those who are dealing with a particular aspect of politics are really talking about precisely the same thing. For example, the inability of those working with the concept of power to agree on a common meaning for the concept has led other political scientists to suggest that it cannot be useful in building empirical political theories.

Concepts can be categorized by various characteristics. Some are merely *classificatory*, denoting the class of objects to which a thing belongs. In this sense they are a set of "either-or" labels to apply to the object. For example, we can refer to voters by their party identification as Republican, Democrat, or Independent. This broad-gauge labeling, however, may be too gross. We may wish to elaborate a set of concepts which take account of the degrees of a certain quality which are present in the objects we are studying. We can do this by specifying concepts which indicate degrees of rank order variation, or *comparative* degrees of a quality, which are present in the objects. For example, we can establish categories of "Strong Democrat," "Weak Democrat," "Independent," "Strong Republican," and "Weak Republican," This set of concepts is comparative — more than mere labeling. A further refinement would be to specify *quantitatively* through the concepts we use precisely to what degree a quality is present in an object, as if, for example, we could specify someone as a 99.44 per cent Democrat. Usually, in political science, concepts are either merely classificatory or comparative.

The set of concepts we use in our analysis we can label a conceptual scheme. Any conceptual scheme should meet the following criteria: the concepts should be appropriate for the problem studied, collectively exhaustive and mutually exclusive. Thus, for example, in a study of voters' self-perceived party affiliation we would have, at a minimum, the categories of Republican, Democrat, Independent and Other. If we left any one of them out, the set would not be exhaustive. If we have a category, "Republican-Democrat," the set would not consist of mutually exclusive categories.

SCIENTIFIC LAWS AND THEORIES

Obviously, the development of scientific knowledge follows from the development or creation of theories. We must examine more closely the nature of scientific theories and the process by which they are formed. One definition of theory and its relationship to scientific laws has been presented by Gustav Bergmann:

> A theory is a group of laws, usually rather few, from which others, usually a larger number, have actually been deduced and from which one expects to deduce still further ones. The laws that serve as the premises of these deductions are called the axioms of the theory; those which appear as conclusions are called its theorems.[16]

Bergmann has also characterized the differences between scientific laws and theories in this fashion: "Statements of individual fact are explained by laws; laws are explained by theories."[17] Kemeny contrasts theory and fact thus: "Facts are known and particular (refer to a single event), whereas theories are universal and hence can never be known to be entirely true."[18]

Three different interpretations can be made of what it is a theory represents, these three being labeled *descriptive, instrumental* and *realist.*[19] According to the realist view, a theory is either true or false. Thus one evaluates a theory in terms of the success of efforts to falsify it, or more accurately, to falsify deductions from the theory. Thus scientific theories, like hypotheses, cannot be directly verified. The logical consequences deduced from a theory can be tested by observation; if the conclusions are rejected, then the theory itself is not accepted. However, even if not rejected by falsifying the consequences through repeated testing, theories are accepted only tentatively, because we have not tested all possible occurrences of the consequences and, furthermore, such testing is an impossibility. Obviously, no theory contains within itself the test or proof of its own axioms; however, by formalizing a theory (converting its verbal or descriptive statements into mathematical statements), one can test the logical correctness of the deductions made within the theory.[20]

The second view of theory is that a theory is not and cannot be considered in terms of its accuracy in describing reality. This instrumentalist interpretation views a theory as a means of organizing one's perceptions of reality. As such it provides rules for organizing and inference-making. Thus, it can be evaluated in terms of its usefulness in doing that. The third interpretation views theory as descriptive, that is, theories are not true or false, but describe in a simplified fashion aspects of

---

[16] Bergmann, *op. cit.,* pp. 31-32.

[17] *Ibid.,* p. 17.

[18] Kemeny, *op. cit.,* p. 91.

[19] See Ernest Nagel, *The Structure of Science* (London: Routledge and Kegan Paul, 1961), Ch. 6 *passim.*

[20] Abraham Kaplan, *The Conduct of Inquiry* (San Francisco: Chandler Publications, 1964), pp. 295-98.

reality. A concomitant aspect of this descriptive view is that theories do not explain.

To summarize, theories are not tested directly, and hence always involve some degree of uncertainty. A scientist tests the logical consequences deduced from a hypothesis; he observes to see if the facts which are predicted as logical consequences of the hypothesis do indeed occur. A hypothesis tested many times and not rejected is accorded the status of a scientific law, and laws are associated by theories.

We have not made any distinction in types of empirical theory. Some philosophers of science make a distinction between universal and statistical laws, or universal and statistical theories. The distinctions refer to the degree of probability assigned to the generalization. In statistical generalizations, less than 100 per cent probability in specifying the outcome of the designated conditions is obtained. For example, we say that if conditions A, B and C occur, then the probability of X occuring is .85. In contrast, in a universal generalization, we can state that when conditions A, B and C occur, the probability of X occurring is 1.00. Our aim is to develop universal generalizations, and most social scientists work on the assumption that ultimately universal generalizations can be achieved in all the social sciences.

Several other distinctions in types of theories can be made. Individualistic theory has as its basic units of analysis concepts which refer to aspects of individual behavior. Supporters of this philosophical position argue that all behavior, even of groups and regardless of the size or character of the group, can be explained in terms of units of analysis which refer to individual behavior. The opposing view, referred to as *holism*, argues that a group, be it the AFL-CIO, the United States Senate or the United States of America, is more than the total of the characteristics of the individuals who compose the group. In other words, the group characteristics cannot be reduced to the units of analysis appropriate for analyzing individual behavior, and different concepts and theories are necessary for adequate explanation.

Another distinction which is sometimes made is between theory and meta theory. Robert Merton distinguishes meta theory as middle range theory, which focuses on limited sets of data and is of limited scope. These theories of the middle range "consolidate otherwise segregated hypotheses and empirical uniformities."[21] A theory then incorporates a wider range of data and a broader set of generalizations. One can question if such a distinction between theory and meta theory serves any useful analytical purpose.

[21] Robert K. Merton, *Social Theory and Social Structure*, revised edition (Glencoe: The Free Press, 1957), p. 280.

The discussion has implied a progression from hypothesis to law to theory. One must remember, however, that developments in science do not always follow such a progression. For example, from a theory we can deduce certain other relationships for whose existence we can test; as a result we can either confirm the deduced relationships or reject them. If we reject them, we are forced to modify the theory so that it is not in conflict with our observations. Hence, instead of a simple progression from hypotheses to law to theory, scientific knowledge also can develop from an existing theory to deduced proposition or hypothesis to law, further extending or developing that theory.

Thus, theories guide the research process as well as result from that process. They indicate the nature of the data to be examined; formulation of new or expanded theories indicates by deductive processes new relationships. These are capable of being tested indirectly, thereby resulting in either the further extension or the revision of the theory. In effect, a theory contains criteria of relevance, which indicate the nature of the data to be used to test the propositions or tentative generalizations deducible from the theory.

The basic aim of political science is to form theories which can explain the facts of the political universe. Explanations in science require the following. First, one must have laws or theories which are well established. Second, one must be in possession of facts known independently of the facts to be explained. Explanation occurs when the facts to be explained can be deduced as a logical consequence of the laws or theory and the other known facts. An example of explanation of physical phenomena can illustrate the nature of scientific explanations. In cold weather water in a car radiator is frozen. We can explain this occurrence by reference to a general theory and other known facts. The general theory specifies that substances change their form with certain changes in temperature. The freezing point for water is 32°F. We also know that the temperature has declined below 32°F. Combining the general theory of the freezing of substances with the knowledge that the temperature dropped below 32°F, we can deduce that the water in the car radiator would freeze. We have explained the facts by bringing them under a general theory. This is the nature of scientific explanation; an occurrence or set of facts is explained when it can be deduced from a law or theory.[22] If our generalizations are only statistical, limits are placed on the development of theory. If we do not have universal gen-

---

[22] For more extensive discussions of explanation in science, see Kemeny, *op. cit.*, Ch. 9; Kaplan, *op. cit.*, pp. 327-69; Bergmann, *op. cit.*, pp. 75-84; Van Dyke, *op. cit.*, Ch. 3; Eugene J. Meehan, *The Theory and Method of Political Analysis* (Homewood: Dorsey Press, 1965), Chs. 4 and 5.

eralizations, we cannot have deductively connected theory. As we have indicated previously, an event (set of facts) is explained when it can be deduced from a theory and other facts known independently of the facts to be explained. If we have only statistical generalizations, explanation in that sense cannot occur.

What is the difference between explanation and prediction? Explanation refers to accounting for the facts after their occurrence; in prediction we are specifying the general law and other facts which, when combined, will be followed by the particular facts to be explained. In other words, the difference between explanation and prediction relates to the time of occurrence. Prediction must be distinguished from forecasting. Forecasting implies stating a specific time and place when an event will occur, such as the statement that a hurricane will exist in the Atlantic off Puerto Rico six months from today. Prediction, in contrast, is the statement that under certain combinations of climatic conditions a type of weather condition we have designated as the concept "hurricane" will come into existence. Prediction does not specify a particular time and place; it merely is a statement of conditions which are accompanied by some other condition, the specification being made possible by the existence of general laws and knowledge of necessary conditions.

Much confusion in science arises from the use of the term "law." That sort of confusion is likely to occur whenever we use a word which can have several possible meanings. Law is understood by many people to imply either a moral imperative (an "ought" of behavior), or determinism, in the sense that if an aspect of the behavior of individuals is covered or described by a scientific law, the individuals do not have free will to determine their own behavior.

This confusion can be eliminated by clarifying several points. First, remember that a scientific law serves as a description of the connection between facts. Therefore, scientific laws do not determine anything; they merely serve to describe what has been observed to exist within limits of probability or chance. However, if the theories which deductively relate laws can be used to predict events, is not then free will abrogated? Let us phrase it this way — what is necessary for perfect predictability? We would have to have a complete set of theories covering every possible form and type of human behavior, knowledge of all the relevant facts, sufficient mental capabilities to evaluate the facts and laws, and adequate time in which to do computations. Just listing these requirements indicates that perfect predictability, while logically possible, actually is highly improbable. But even if we could have perfect predictability, individuals still have a choice or free will. All we would be saying is that individuals exercise that choice in predictable, *i.e.*, regular, patterns.

VALUES IN THE STUDY OF POLITICS

We have yet to deal with certain other questions which must be raised. One of these is the problem of values. Some accuse political scientists of treating all value statements as being of equal merit. This would imply, for example, that a communist or fascist political system is equal in merit to a democratic system. However, the charge that researchers assert all things are equally valued is unfounded. The problem is that no value in itself can be proven superior by means of scientific method. One can use scientific method in means-ends analysis, where the end has been selected on the basis of criteria other than scientific method. One can then use scientific method to evaluate the alternative means available for the achievement of that end. Much governmental decision-making is of this type. For example, once the Congress declared it to be the policy of the United States to promote through public resources and laws full employment of all persons desiring to work, social scientists using scientific method could indicate to government officials the alternative means of achieving that goal and their various possible effects. However, the decision to promote full employment as expressed in the Full Employment Act of 1946 was a value judgment, and grounded in ethical and moral considerations, not in science.

Donald Searing has argued that value-free political science is impossible, but *value laden* does not mean *biased* political science. Is that a contradiction? According to Searing, bias is an "instance where an investigator's values have, in fact, led to mis-perceptions in descriptions, or to attributing unwarranted validity to generalizations."[23] Value judgment is defined as "statements which assert that something is good or desirable."[24]

Philosophers of science generally agree that the researcher's values may enter into research in several different ways. Certainly one is the selection of a research subject or problem. This, however, would not necessarily result in biased research results. One can select a problem, such as the nature of prejudice, the relationship between domestic in-

[23] Donald Searing, "Values in Empirical Research; A Behavioralist Response," *Midwest Journal of Political Science*, 14 (February, 1970), p. 74.
[24] *Ibid.*, p. 75.

stability and international conflict and violence, or the process of political modernization in developing countries and its relationship to economic development, because in some way one's personal values are related to or affected by that problem. The research can be conducted without having the conclusions biased by one's values, if one follows the prescribed, generally accepted methods of research, and makes clear the processes by which conclusions are reached. In that manner, others can check and criticize the appropriateness of the conclusions drawn from the evidence.

There are other ways in which values can affect research results other than in selection of the problem to be studied or the drawing of conclusions from the research. One is in the selection of the facts to be studied. For example, if one were to study the treatment of citizens by the police and ignore the use of certain kinds of language in police-minority group member interactions, he would be neglecting to study what minority group members regard as a type of police brutality, derogatory or disrespectful language. His values would be acting as a perceptual screen, leading him to disregard this as a particular aspect of police mistreatment of citizens.

Values may also lead one to biased conclusions through the incorrect assessment of the facts or evidence for a particular hypothesis. For example, if one were to study police brutality, what level of police physical or verbal mistreatment of citizens would constitute high incidence of police mistreatment? Would five instances out of 1000, or would 25 out of 1000, or would 75 out of 1000 be the lower limit for the category, "high incidence of police brutality"?

At several other points in the research process values could influence results. One of these is in the definition of concepts. While a definition indicates the relevant characteristics of a concept, an element of valuation may be attached to the concept in the statement of those characteristics, if care is not taken in their specification. Much criticism has been directed at some elements of structural-functional analysis for just this reason. In this kind of analysis, we ask what institutional structures perform what political functions: for example, we would consider how interests of various groups in society are aggregated in the political system and communicated to political decision makers. A major concern is with how these processes work to maintain the political system. It is argued that such a focus on system stability or on system maintenance represents a bias against change by the researchers. The dependent variable we wish to study would have to be defined as a concept and operationally measured in such a way as to preclude introduction of bias.

Underlying this concept definition problem is a second problem, that of values entering through the underlying theory on which the research is based and which the research is designed to test or elaborate. Because we lack well developed theories in political science, values are more likely to create problems. Donald Searing has pointed out that:

> When axioms are introduced in social research as unstated or poorly formulated assumptions they are easily shaped by the investigator's values, and can become untenable characterizations of individual or social systems.[25]

Searing points out another aspect of research where values might enter into the research process, that is in the interpretation of data. The extreme position which can be taken on this problem is that all objects and situations are both selectively perceived and selectively interpreted, and because of this it would be impossible to have value-free research of any kind, scientific or otherwise. The reply is that a science develops agreed-upon patterns of perceiving and interpreting data. In other words, the theories and methods of a scientific discipline create and impose generally accepted patterns of observing and interpreting phenomena.

Some of these problems can be illustrated by examining the controversies growing out of the studies of local community decision making and the distribution of power in local communities. (These topics are examined in much greater detail in Chapter Eight.)

The sociologists who have studied community power have started from a different theoretical basis than the political scientists, with stratification or social class theories underlying much of their work. Political scientists have attacked this as being an inadequate theoretical perspective, ignoring the characteristics of the political processes and groups in the political process. Some have argued for research more directly based on decision theory.

The early studies tended to ask a general question: "Who makes decisions in this community, or who has power?" That was criticized for its lack of focus. For example, Robert Dahl argued that one can test for the existence of a power elite only if one examined a representative sample of key decisions and evaluated patterns found in that representative sample of key decisions.[26]

Two crucial problems in concept formation are also at the center of the controversy: How should "decision" be defined? How should "power" be defined? In part because researchers have defined these concepts differently, they have reached different conclusions about how power is distributed and who influences decisions.

[25] *Ibid.*, p. 95.
[26] Robert A. Dahl, "A Critique of the Ruling Elite Model," *American Political Science Review*, 52 (June, 1958), pp. 463-69.

Polsby has pointed out that indices of power in various studies have included: "(1) who participate in decision making, (2) who prevail in decision making."[27] According to Polsby, power can be assessed by the capability of an individual to change the relative probability of outcomes A and B by acting on others in the situation.[28]

Distinctions can be made among power, influence, authority and manipulation, and this conceptual refinement could contribute to a clarification of the nature of community power and decision making.

Definitions of decision have also varied among various researchers. Robert Dahl has defined a decision as "a set of actions related to and including the choice of one alternative rather than another."[29] A second definition is a "policy involving severe sanctions (deprivations)."[30] The latter indicates decisions exist only when sanctions have been or could be involved. Other aspects of the definition of decisions have been commented on by critics. E. E. Schattschneider has pointed out that the way in which lines of conflict are drawn in the society as well as political structures and processes limits the political outcomes possible. This "mobilization of bias" which operates in a systemic fashion to favor some and not others is sustained by non-decision making. According to Bachrach and Baratz, a non-decision is "a decision that results in suppression or thwarting of a latent or manifest challenge to the values or interests of the decision-maker."[31] Demands for allocative changes are inhibited from being made; access to the decision-making process is denied.[32] Critics argue that both sociologists and political scientists who have studied community power have ignored these non-decisions. This, according to the critics, is a function of bias created by the researchers' values which have affected the theoretical base, definition of concepts, data selection, and data interpretation in the studies.

Among the channels by which values can influence research on community power structures is the process through which one selects the decisions to be studied, with the procedures for ensuring the representativeness of decisions and non-decisions being very important. Secondly, if one says that only certain kinds of issues are those in which

[27] Nelson Polsby, Community Power and Political Theory (New Haven: Yale University Press, 1963), p. 4.

[28] Ibid., p. 5.

[29] Robert A. Dahl, "The Analysis of Influence in Local Communities," in Social Science and Community Action, ed. Charles Adrian (East Lansing: Michigan State University Press, 1960), p. 26.

[30] Harold D. Lasswell and Abraham Kaplan, Power and Society (New Haven: Yale University Press, 1950), p. 74.

[31] Peter Bachrach and Morton S. Baratz, Power and Poverty (New York: Oxford University Press, 1970), p. 44.

[32] Ibid.

the key decisions are made, by specification of those issues one's values can enter the study.

Problems also arise when we evaluate the influence of individuals' values on their political behavior; we must accurately measure the nature and intensity of relevant values and correctly infer their influence on political behavior. Fortunately, advances in research techniques both in political science and in other disciplines such as sociology and psychology have increased the ease with which this can be done.

In summary, although the development of empirical theories and laws of politics will probably not be easy, there is nothing in the subject matter of political science which will prevent that goal from being pursued and ultimately accomplished. The method of science is the same for all fields of scholarly study and can be applied in the study of politics as it has been in the study of the natural sciences as well as in economics, psychology, sociology, and anthropology. Theoretical developments in political science will be promoted by a conscious and constant concern for the appropriateness of the concepts and the research techniques we use in our studies of political behavior.

SCIENTIFIC REVOLUTIONS

In any discipline at a specific time in history certain assumptions are made which limit and direct the nature of theorizing and research. These include beliefs about the basic units of the subject matter, the patterns of interrelationships possible among them, and the research techniques and procedure by which they may be investigated. As Thomas S. Kuhn states it, "Normal science, the activity in which most scientists inevitably spend almost all their time, is predicated on the assumption that the scientific community knows what the world is like."[33] Landmarks in the development of a discipline, which Kuhn labels scientific revolutions, are accompanied by the rejection of one scientific theory in favor of another. Discussing scientific revolutions, Kuhn states:

> Each produced a consequent shift in the problems available
> for scientific scrutiny and in the standards by which the
> profession determined what should count as an admissible
> problem or as a legitimate problem-solution. And each trans-
> formed the scientific imagination in ways that we shall ulti-
> mately need to describe as a transformation of the world

[33] Thomas Kuhn, *The Structure of Scientific Revolutions* (Chicago: Phoenix, University of Chicago Press, 1964), p. 5.

within which scientific work was done. Such changes, together with the controversies which always accompany them, are the defining characteristics of scientific revolutions.[34]

The replacement of an old theory by a new one requires the reconstruction of prior knowledge. Theoretical achievements which are capable of attracting advocates from existing theories, which are unprecedented, which are foundations for future research, and which do not foreclose further development and expansion are labeled *paradigms* by Kuhn. A scientific or theoretical revolution occurs when one paradigm replaces another. The basic characteristic of a mature science is the existence of a paradigm or paradigms which guide and shape research.

Kuhn argues that paradigms gain their significance because they are more capable of resolving the set of problems with which scientists are most concerned at that time. The aims of normal science are to describe the facts, match facts with theory, and elaborate existing theory, not the development of new theory with a new focus and different conceptual framework. A new paradigm or theory usually will meet with considerable opposition, as adherents of the old paradigm defend it against onslaughts of the new. However, as anomalies have become apparent in the existing paradigm, a crisis has been generated, and eventually a new paradigm is generated, largely as a creative act. Thus a new conceptual structure is produced to replace the older; the battle is drawn between adherents of the old and the new, and the outcome largely influenced by the relative capabilities of the two paradigms to focus on significant questions, explain anomalies, and thus serve as a vehicle for the conduct of what Kuhn calls normal science.

David Truman has argued that political science is still in search of a paradigm to replace that dominant up to World War II.[35] What follows in the remaining chapters of this book are several alternative conceptual approaches which have been suggested as the basis for a new paradigm for political science. As Kuhn points out,

> . . . paradigms differ in more than substance, for they are
> directed not only to nature but also back upon the science
> that produced them. They are the sources of the methods,
> problem-field, and standards of solution accepted by any
> mature scientific community at any given time.[36]

It might be appropriate to say that political science experienced one scientific revolution when the discipline began to focus on the relative merits of the use of the scientific approach in the study of politics. More

[34] *Ibid.*, p. 6.
[35] David Truman, "Disillusion and Regeneration: The Quest for a Discipline," *American Political Science Review*, LIX (December, 1965), 865-73.
[36] Kuhn, *op. cit.*, p. 102.

recent criticisms may constitute a second questioning of the utility of the scientific approach.

Is there a paradigm which guides political science? We can suggest that there are several candidates for paradigms, in various stages of elaboration and development. It is our task to evaluate several of those candidates. All of them are based on the use of scientific method for their elaboration. They vary in their units of analysis, conceptual elaboration, focus on problems with which they are centrally concerned.

If we accept the meaning of theory as being simply a set of empirically tested generalizations — not a set of deductively structured generalizations — then we have theories in political science.

By what criteria can we evaluate theories? Quite simply, they can be evaluated in terms of their capability to account for those things we wish to explain. This is a functional criterion of evaluation. If one theory is better able to explain a set of events, it will be accepted more readily.

A second criterion is the logical consistency of the theory. As we have pointed out, this is possible when the theory is in the form of universal generalizations.

A third criterion is the ability of the theory to lead us to other suggested generalizations which can be deduced from the theory. These generalizations can then be tested and contribute to the further elaboration of the theory.

Another criterion in evaluating theory is the ease with which key terms can be operationalized. This is not to say that all concepts in a theory must be capable of being defined operationally.

An additional criterion is the extent of testing of the generalizations which are contained in the theory and the quality of the data base upon which they are tested. Extensive testing of a rigorous nature using sound sets of data carefully collected for explicit hypothesis testing constitutes a more reassuring basis for accepting a theory.

In science, argument is also made in favor of parsimony. If one has a choice between two theories which are equally satisfactory as explanations, preference is generally given to the simpler and less complicated of the two.

HYPOTHESIS TESTING

We have indicated that knowledge in a discipline accumulates through careful and repeated testing of hypotheses, which ultimately leads to the development of theories. How does one test a hypothesis? What criteria can we use to evaluate these research efforts? A number of research procedures exist for the collection and evaluation of observations necessary for the checking of the predicted consequences of hypotheses.

We will discuss two types of evaluations which are found with some frequency in political analysis, these being the degree to which two or more variables are associated (vary together) and the likelihood of the distribution of observations occurring in that pattern by chance in the population from which the sample of observations was taken. The first of these is referred to as *association* or *correlation* while the second evaluative criteria is labeled a "test of significance."

In association we ask to what degree do two variables vary together. For example, if a blue collar worker is a union member, is he more likely to be a Democrat than a worker who is not a union member? We are asking to what degree, if any, is there association between union membership and support of the Democratic Party. A formal statement of the hypothesis would read:

> If a blue collar worker is a member of a labor union, then he
> is more likely to be a Democrat than a blue collar worker who
> is not a union member.

In order to make observations, we would have to define the concepts *blue collar worker, union member* and *Democrat*. Let us define them as follows:

> Blue collar worker: anyone employed or seeking employment
>   in an unskilled, semi-skilled, or skilled labor category as
>   defined by the U. S. Bureau of the Census.
> Union member: an individual who pays dues to any local or
>   national labor organization which engages in collective
>   bargaining.
> Democrat: any individual who in response to a survey question indicates that he considers himself to be a Democrat.

Ideally, our hypothesis should be tested on a national sample, but limitations of time and money may make that difficult. Secondly, our hypothesis should be tested a number of times in order to ensure that the level of relationship found is relatively constant over time, and not a function of variations in the sample drawn or peculiar to certain other conditions present at that time which we have not considered.

Suppose we obtain the following results from three different groups of blue collar workers.

Quite obviously, the results of Samples I, II, and III are very different. One way of stating the different patterns of association is through a statistical measure of association which is comparable for all three samples. What measure shall we use? We must digress for a moment

	Sample I Union Member	
	Yes	No
Democrat Yes	50%	50%
Democrat No	50	50
Total	100%	100%
N	500	500

$X^2 = 0, p > 0, C = 0$

	Sample II Union Member	
	Yes	No
Democrat Yes	80%	70%
Democrat No	20	30
Total	100%	100%
N	500	500

$X^2 = 13.332, p < .001, C = .115$

	Sample III Union Member	
	Yes	No
Democrat Yes	70%	30%
Democrat No	30	70
Total	100%	100%
N	500	500

$X^2 = 160.0, p < .001, C = .372$

to talk about levels of measurement, for there are different measures of association for each level of measurement.

Regardless of the source of data, we refer to several levels by which political data may be classified for purposes of analysis.

The first level of measurement is described as *nominal-scale*, and is analogous to the classificatory concept. Numbers may be used to describe persons, events or other categories of analysis in a classificatory sense. Thus, people may be Democrats or Republicans, voters or nonvoters, or some other dichotomy. Similarly, they may have a range of occupations, such as doctors, craftsman, clerks, and so forth. In nominal-scale situations, there is no underlying continuum, and the various classifications used are described as mutually exclusive.

Ordinal-scale data, corresponding to the comparative concept, suggests an underlying and continuous distribution of some given quality. Thus a person may describe himself as a Strong Democrat or Republican, a Weak Democrat or Republican, or an Independent Democrat or Republican (the examples chosen here are used by the Survey Research Center to augment the traditional self-classification of individuals as Democrat, Republican, or other). The classification of voters may then follow some continuum, such as Strong Democrat, Weak Democrat, Independent Democrat, Independent, Independent Republican, Weak Republican and Strong Republican. An ordinal scale for categories of low, medium and high education may operationally define these by the number of grades completed, such as 0—8, 9—12, and education beyond high school.

Interval scale data carries the classification process a step further. It corresponds roughly to the quantitative concept, although we have already shown that numbers may be used to implement the lower-level nominal and ordinal scales. It assumes, like the ordinal scale, an underlying continuum, but has the additional property of having equal intervals or distances between the classifications. The example we used above for ordinal classification of education would therefore require modification to meet interval-scale requirements. We might set up a scale based upon an equal interval of four years of education, such as 1st—4th grades, 5th—8th, 9th—12th, and completion of college. Income may be classified as $0—$2,999, $3,000—$5,999, $6,000—$8,999, and so forth. There is an equal interval built into the categorization of education and income in these examples. Given these qualities, it is possible to assign numbers "with the positions of the objects on an interval scale so that the operations of arithmetic may be meaningfully performed on the *differences* between these numbers."[37] This type of data is rarely seen in behavioral political science, inasmuch as it is difficult to establish a "common and constant unit of measurement."[38] A fourth level is *ratio-scale*. This type of scale requires a true zero point and is notable in that the ratio between any two intervals on the scale is constant and independent of the measurement unit.

Both concepts we are dealing with in the hypothesis about union membership and Democratic party affiliation are measured at the nominal level. We have merely classified individuals as union members or non-members and as Democrats or non-Democrats. One statistical measure of association appropriate for such data is the Coefficient of Contingency, C. If we calculate C for each of the three samples, we obtain the following results:

Sample I   C = 0, no association
Sample II   C = .115, very little association
Sample III   C = .372, moderate association

Thus, the degree of association or relationship between being a blue

---

[37] Sidney Siegel, *Nonparametric Statistics for the Behavioral Sciences* (New York: McGraw-Hill Book Company, Inc., 1956), p. 28.
[38] *Ibid.*, p. 26.

collar worker and Democratic party affiliation varies considerably among the three groups, and using C we can compare the level of association present in the three samples.

Another method for testing hypotheses involves making inferences about the population based on observations from a sample of the universe or population. There are two types of inferences. One, generally labeled *estimation*, involves estimating the true value of a population characteristic (called a *parameter*) from the estimate based on the sample data. For example, we take a random sample of three thousand members of the voting age population. From the responses of individuals to the question of which party's candidate each will support in the ensuing election, we estimate the population characteristic's value from observations based on a random or probability sample.

The second type of inference statistics involves *hypothesis testing* A research hypothesis is stated, for example, indicating that association exists between two concepts in the population about which we wish to generalize. An alternative hypothesis is then stated; this null hypothesis posits that no relationship exists between the variables in the population we want to study. A statistical test appropriate to the level of measurement is selected, and the size of the sample of the population to be used is determined. Generally, the larger the sample size, the lower the error or the more accurate the results obtained. A level of significance is set, and a generally accepted level is .05. This means that if the distribution of our observations is so improbable as to have occurred in only five out of every 100 samples, then we will reject the null hypothesis. Of course, in order to apply such a test the sampling distribution of results associated with the particular statistic must be known. A sampling distribution would indicate the probability of obtaining each of the possible outcomes; for example, we could develop a sampling distribution for obtaining from ten heads and no tails to no heads and ten tails on the flip of a coin. Morrison and Henkel characterize tests of significance in the following manner:

> First and foremost, a test of significance is a formal procedure for making a decision between two hypotheses about some characteristic of a population (parameter) on the basis of knowledge obtained from a sample (sample statistic) of that population. Typically, one of these hypotheses, the hypothesis tested, is termed the "null hypothesis," and the other is termed the alternative.[39]

[93] Denton E. Morrison and Ramon E. Henkel, "Significance Tests Reconsidered," *The American Sociologist*, 4 (May, 1969), p. 133.

Testing for significance involves a comparison of the differences between the sample statistic and the parameter specified by the null hypothesis with a theoretically determined
sampling distribution. This comparison allows estimation of
how often such a difference would occur if the difference
were due to random errors in the sample selection process
(sample error). The significance level that results from the
comparison gives the relative frequency (probability) with
which a sample statistic of the obtained size or more extreme
size would be expected to occur over repeated trials (samples)
utilizing the same probability sampling method on the same
population if the hypothesized value for the population pa-
ramater (null hypothesis) were true.[40]

The null hypothesis is rejected if the probability of obtaining the
statistic of that size by chance is sufficiently small. At what level of
probability should the rejection of the null hypothesis be set? That is a
function of the risks involved in making a wrong decision. Can one
afford to reject the hypothesis of no association when it is in fact correct
ten times out of one hundred, or only five times out of one hundred, or
only one time out of one hundred? That is a function of the subject
under consideration and the hypothesis being tested, and is up to the
judgment of the researcher to evaluate. This is one point in the research
where the investigator's values may enter.

Referring to our previous example, we state the hypothesis in the
null (H_0) form: there is no significant difference between union and
non-union members in the rate of Democratic party affiliation. We may
now apply a test to measure the statistical significance of the distribu-
tio which is observed. One such test is called chi square (χ^2), and is
frequently used in political science research. For samples 2 and 3, we
reject the null hypothesis and conclude that there is a significant difference between union and non-union members in regard to the frequency
of being a Democrat. In both samples 2 and 3 the probability of obtaining that distribution by chance is less than one in a thousand. By rejecting the null hypothesis we run the risk of rejecting H_0 when it is true.
On the other hand, if statistical significance had been lacking, we might
have committed the opposite error, accepting the null hypothesis when
it is false. Since statistics is a matter of chance and probability, we must
accept these risks. However, we can now state to some measure of
precision — again running a risk — that the distribution is statistically significant. We have provided a commonly accepted base for the examination of the distribution, by employing a test which is appropriate to

[40] *Ibid.*, p. 132.

that end rather than indulging in unsubstantiated guesses that the distribution is significant.

There is a distinction between analytical and statistical significance, a point which commonly eludes those who are new to empirical research. While our sample distribution has proven to be statistically significant according to an established criterion, it may or may not be analytically significant to the political scientist. Suppose, for instance, that the question asked of the workers is of a variety which has no relevance to our hypothesis in any way, and might have bearing only on correlated research. In this case, even though the distribution of replies may reflect statistical significance, it is of no analytical or substantive significance whatsoever. On the other hand, assume that the question for which we are examining distribution is relevant to the hypothesis, but that the distribution is found to lack statistical significance. The fact of nonsignificance should not deter the researcher from examining the meaning behind this. If the question, for instance, is one which is normally found by others to significantly differentiate Democrats and Republicans, it would be incumbent upon the researcher to explore the reasons behind the present lack of significance. Another way of stating this is that the researcher is guided by a number of considerations, and that statistical significance is merely one of his guides, not a tyrant.

Underlying the use of inferential statistics are certain requirements. One such is that the sample must be drawn from the population in a random or known probability fashion; otherwise, the sample results cannot be generalized to the population with any assurance of the correctness of the generalization. There are two characteristics for a simple random sample. Each individual in the universe studied must have an equal and known probability of being included in the sample, and each must have an independent chance of being included in the sample.

RELIABILITY AND VALIDITY

Two other problems must be considered — validity and reliability. Reliability refers to the extent to which a measuring instrument produces consistent, precise, accurate results. For example, if a student were to take the same exam five times and his responses to a set of multiple choice questions on the exams were to vary greatly each time, the questions would be said to be unreliable as a measure of knowledge of the subject matter. Other synonyms for reliability of a measurement instrument include *dependability*, *predictability*, and *stability*.

Several different methods of evaluating reliability have been developed that focus on different aspects of reliability. The one we referred to in the preceding paragraph is *test-retest reliability*. Another method of evaluating is to develop two forms of the same test or measuring instrument and examine the extent to which scores on the equivalent forms are associated. Another method to measure reliability is to split the test in halves and correlate the responses on the two halves. In this method the internal consistency of the measuring instrument is examined.

Four kinds of validity can be distinguished; predictive, concurrent, content, and construct. *Content validity* is the representativeness or sampling accuracy of the measuring instrument. For example, do the statements in an attitude scale measuring economic conservatism adequately sample the concept's universe of content? Researchers generally agree that evaluation of content validity is largely judgmental; evaluation is based on the judgment of the researcher. Others may be requested to assist in the evaluation.

As an example of the evaluation of content validity, let us look at the most commonly used measure of the concept "sense of political efficacy." The researchers who first used this concept defined it as "the feeling that individual political action does have, or can have, an impact upon the political process, *i.e.*, that it is worth while to perform one's civic duties."[41] Political efficacy is measured by an attitude scale constructed from agreement or disagreement with the following statements:

1. "I don't think public officials care much what people like me think."
2. "Voting is the only way people like me can have any say about how the government runs things."
3. "People like me don't have any say about what the government does."
4. "Sometimes politics and government seems so complicated that a person like me can't really understand what's going on."[42]

The question is, do the four statements in the political efficacy scale adequately sample the content of the attitude indicated by the researchers' definition of political efficacy? For example, do individuals who block trains at embarkation terminals to prevent shipment of materials to a war feel politically inefficacious? If they thought their actions could

[41] Angus Campbell, Gerald Gurin and Warren E. Miller, *The Voter Decides* (Evanston, Illinois: Row, Peterson and Co., 1954), p. 187.
[42] Lester Milbraith, *Political Participation* (Chicago: Rand McNally, 1965), pp. 156-57.

not have an impact on the political process, would most of them still demonstrate? Such individuals could respond to all four statements in such a way as to indicate no political efficacy as measured by the scale, yet still feel highly efficacious as that term is defined by the researchers. In other words, the content validity of the scale is questionable; the statements do not adequately sample the wide range of political methods used in our political system to influence the decision-making input and to affect outputs of the political system. When students sack the ROTC building on campus or demonstrate against government policies in a peaceful fashion, do they feel that this can affect political processes? If they do, but do not respond with the efficacious answers to the above statements, should they be classified as having a low sense of political efficacy? Were the demonstrators in the Chicago streets at the 1968 Democratic National Convention totally devoid of a sense of political effectiveness, or did they believe that through their protests they could have an impact on political outcomes? The voting researchers' definition of political efficacy was more appropriate at the time of their first election studies, but in a time of political instability, of questioning of the established political processes and institutions, and of the use of confrontation politics, their measure of political efficacy may well be lacking in content validity.

Frequently use is made of outside criteria in evaluating research instruments; in this approach to validity one checks by comparing characteristics of the outcome to results available by other means. This is referred to as *concurrent validity*. *Predictive validity* refers to evaluating the measuring instrument on the basis of outcomes obtained after the measurement was made. For example, a university evaluates the probable academic success of potential students on the basis of College Board scores and high school grades. The measure has predictive validity if, after students have been admitted, it proves to be a good measure of their academic success.

The problem with which *construct validity* is concerned is measurement of the meanings of the concepts (constructs) which are involved in the hypothesis, law, or theory being considered. Construct validity is thus concerned with theory and theoretical concepts and empirical evaluation of hypothesized relationships. Kerlinger states the task succinctly: "One must try to validate the theory behind the test . . . there are three parts to construct validation: suggesting what constructs possible account for test performance, deriving hypotheses from the theory involving the construct, and testing the hypotheses empirically."[43]

[43] Kerlinger, *op. cit.*, p. 449.

Let us consider a problem of construct validity in political science. Members of the United States House of Representatives have before them a bill to change the system of aiding persons of low income. The bill would abolish existing aid programs and provide instead a supplement to a family's income, bringing their income up to a minimum level specified in the law, provided the head of household involved accepts work or training for work if he or she is physically able to do so. Let us focus on the problem of construct validity as it refers to the interpretation of the congressman's vote. What is the meaning of the vote in terms of what theory can explain it? A number of different meanings could be attributed to the vote. One could argue that the vote reflects the congressman's attitude toward social welfare. Therefore, his vote for the bill reflects his support for aid to more impoverished members of our society. However, it may be that the congressman views people on welfare as "do nothing loafers," and he supported the bill because the program would require able-bodied persons to work in order to receive income supplements. Hence, his vote in favor of the legislation is an anti-welfare-loafer vote. A third congressman did not have any clear understanding of the detailed and complex contents of the bill, so he voted for the bill because the committee chairman argued it was a good bill — and this particular congressman takes his voting cues from the relevant committee chairman. A fourth congressman supported the legislation because the president requested it, and as a member of the president's political party he is a strong supporter of the president out of party loyalty. A fifth congressman voted for the bill because an influential constituent asked him to support the legislation. A sixth congressman supported it because an interest group in his district urged his support of the bill. We have listed six different meanings for the pro-income supplement vote, reflecting attitudes toward six different objects and/or situations. The validity of using the roll call vote as a measure of attitudinal support for income supplements per se is thus very dubious, and the construct validity of the measure viewed in those terms is highly questionable.

The dependent variable (the variable to be explained) is the vote cast by each congressman. What theory and what concepts related to that theory can be used to analyze the congressman's vote? Congressmen have a number of voting decisions to make on very detailed and complex legislation. Since each can have knowledge in depth of only a few legislative proposals, each must seek voting cues from respected sources who would know more about a particular legislative proposal. Over a period of time, congressmen would develop a pattern of cue seeking and receiving. One can examine the general pattern of cue seeking and evaluate each congressman's vote on income supplements legislation to see if it follows or deviates from the congressman's general pattern of cue taking. In other words, the vote is explained in terms of decision-making theory. Other theoretical approaches can and have been used; for example, the vote, it can be argued, reflects the congressmen's attitudes toward the party's stand on issues, or their attitudes of presidential support or opposition, or their role orientations toward their constituencies. In each case, the vote is conceptualized in terms of a particular theory, and research proceeds in an attempt to validate the theory behind the concepts.

The choice of the data collection techniques to be employed in a study is in part a function of the approach used in analyzing a problem. If, for example, we wish to examine the relationship between the voting behavior of congressmen and their attitudes on issues, then we would use some variety of attitude measurement technique, since we cannot validly infer attitudes from the roll call votes themselves. We would want to interview them if we were interested in their motivations for becoming active in politics, their attitudes on specific issues, or their perceptions of the issues presented by a particular bill or case. If the problems of access prohibit the direct operational measurement of indicators of the concept, then other methods such as content analysis must be used. One might, in working with congressional behavior in some prior historical period, use content analysis of congressional debates in an attempt to gain some understanding of the attitudes of those participating in the debates. While this is less satisfactory than direct administration of attitude scales, of course, such direct observational methods as interviews cannot be used in researching many problems of interest to us. Thus, while the technique to be used in data collection is dictated in part by the concepts used in the analytic approach, limitations are placed on the research by the accessibility of the appropriate data.

In many research problems, data which can be used in political analysis already exist. Thus we do not need to interview Supreme Court judges or legislators to find out how they voted; we can turn to the printed opinions or the recorded roll calls for that information.

CONCLUSION

In reading empirically-based works, the student should address himself to a number of questions, including:

1. Is the hypothesis clearly stated? Are concepts isolated and defined in an operational manner?
2. Is the methodology explicitly stated? Is it appropriate to the ends of the research?
3. Does the research itself reflect an underlying theory and design? Or does the design and execution of the research possibly serve to buttress the author's value holdings?
4. Is the work consistent? Does it address itself to the problem stated, or does the author attempt to validate other unrelated hypotheses? Are the concepts consistently operationalized or do different and value-laden interpretations skew the final work in such a way that the author may appear to have validated his hypothesis?

While this list of questions is not exhaustive, it can serve as a reminder of the constant dangers to which empirical work is susceptible.

Part Two

The remainder of this book focuses on approaches to political analysis and examines a number of approaches to political theory. What do we mean by approach? One definition of an approach is that it

> consists of criteria of selection — criteria to be employed in selecting the problems or questions to consider and in selecting the data to bring to bear on it; it consists of standards governing the inclusion and exclusion of questions and data.[1]

Approaches can be contrasted to method and to technique. Method generally refers to theories of knowledge, and especially to the grounds for knowledge, including validity and limitations. Epistemology, as this subject is labeled, is a subject of much dispute in most disciplines, and we have indicated some aspects of the problem in the preceding chapter. Sometimes method is also used to refer to the means for the acquisition of data and its manipulation in some manner, such as through statistical analysis, for the purposes of drawing inferences usable

---

[1] Vernon Van Dyke, *Political Science: A Philosophical Analysis* (Stanford: Stanford University Press, 1960), p. 114.

in testing hypotheses. However, technique generally refers to a specific data gathering device, such as survey research or experiments, or to a statistical technique for data analysis, such as analysis of association between variables by a correlation measure. Empirical theory which focuses on the behavior of individuals can be labeled *micro-theory*. The four chapters which follow present four broad approaches to the development of micro-theories of politics. None of these approaches is new. While they are present in the writings of many classical political philosophers, their present use in political science has been expanded and enhanced by drawing on contemporary psychology, sociology, social psychology, and anthropology.

These units for the analysis of individual behavior, taken together in a systematic fashion, contribute to *macro-theory*, which focuses on the study of larger units. Thus, Chapters Seven through Ten consider, respectively, group theory, decision making, systems, and communications. Each of these approaches must take the findings of micro-theory into consideration if a valid empirical theory is to be developed, a theory which explains and also predicts behavior. The approaches are not to be taken as mutually exclusive. In considering groups, we must be aware that there are decisional processes inherent in groups. Similarly, these same processes are evident in the larger political system, or in communications theory, for that matter.

The task of operationalizing the variables upon which the varieties of empirical theory rest is difficult and demanding. Each of the macro-theories we consider suffers in this regard to some extent, but this criticism does not necessarily mean that they are invalid. One of the tasks of theory is to guide research, and in this area our nascent macro-theories have generally fulfilled their purpose. The development of a paradigm for political science is still necessary, as we shall see, but only by organizing our research around such broad categories as we now consider can we ultimately hope to have a valid empirical theory.

Personality

3

INTRODUCTION

Personality can be defined as "the relatively enduring qualities which are observed in the behavior of individuals and which are believed to play a major role in determining that behavior." Gordon Allport has defined personality as "the dynamics of organization within the individual of those psychological systems that determine his unique adjustments to his environment."[1] According to Henry A. Murray, "the term 'personality' has been reserved for the hypothetical structure of the mind, the consistent establishments and processes of which are manifested over and over again (together with some unique and novel elements) in the internal and external proceedings which constitute a person's life."[2] The functions of personality are "to exercise its processes, to express itself, to learn to generate and release insistent need-tensions, to form serial programs for the attainment of distant goals, and

[1] Gordon Allport, *Personality: A Psychological Interpretation* (New York: Holt, 1937), p. 48.
[2] Henry A. Murray and Clyde Kluckhohn, "Outline of a Conception of Personality," in *Personality in Nature, Society, and Culture*, C. Kluckhohn, H. Murray, and D. Schneider, eds. (New York: Knopf, 1953), p. 30.

finally, to lessen or resolve conflicts by forming schedules which more nearly permit the frictionless appeasement of its major needs."[3] Murray indicates that personality is located in the brain and the processes of the mind. Murray emphasized motivation, or the directing of human behavior, as the key element; a set of twenty needs which stimulate and guide activity was elaborated.[4]

Others have argued that a person's behavior is controlled by stable attributes or qualities (behavioral dispositions); it is these which constitute the individual's personality. Personality can be examined in terms of consistency, development of structure, potential for change, integration, and motivation and control.[5] The consistency of personality characteristics can be evaluated in terms of the style of acting, thinking, and perceiving which the individual follows. Some psychologists, such as Sigmund Freud, have emphasized the early establishment of an individual's personality structure, with this personality structure persisting over time.[6] Other psychologists admit of possibilities for change.[7] Personality is, in effect, a set of inferences we make, described in terms of concepts. Personality characteristics are inferred by a number of methods, such as observation of an individual's expressive movements, his own introspection about his behavior (as, for example, when talking with a psychiatrist), his response to structured questionnaire items, his goal-oriented behavior and inferences made from that, and perhaps from physiological indicators of emotional states.

Why study the relationship between political behavior and personality? It is generally agreed that behavior is a function of the environment or situation in which the individuals involved are located and the psychological predispositions which they bring to the situation. If we want to explain political behavior, we need to understand those aspects of personality that contribute to the psychological predispositions which precede that political behavior.

There are several approaches to the study of personality. One focuses on the traits that individuals may possess, such as sociability, dominance, tolerance, and self-control. As such, it emphasizes the individual's characteristic patterns of responses to certain types of situations

---

[3] *Ibid.*, p. 39.

[4] Henry A. Murray, *Explorations in Personality* (New York: Oxford University Press, 1938), pp. 152-226.

[5] Richard S. Lazarus, *Personality and Adjustment* (Englewood Cliffs, N.J.: Prentice-Hall, Inc., 1963), pp. 37-40.

[6] See, for example, Sigmund Freud, *The Interpretation of Dreams*, Trans. A. A. Brill (New York: Macmillan, 1933).

[7] See, for example, C. G. Jung, *Analytical Psychology* (New York: Pantheon Press, 1968).

or stimuli.[8] A related approach is the classification of types, with individuals who share a certain trait or set of traits being characterized as a particular personality type, such as authoritarian, dogmatic, introvert, inner-directed or other-directed, agitator or administrator, or advertiser, lawmaker, reluctant, or spectator.[9]

Another approach is based on stimulus-response learning theory. The processes by which the individual develops his characteristic patterns of response to various stimuli become the central object of study. In such an approach the focus is on the drive which initiates responses, with the responses satisfying the drive. The satisfaction results in reinforcement of the connection between stimulus and response. Learning the appropriate response is enhanced by establishing the association between cues to the appropriate response and the initial drive.[10] In political research we might ask, for example, how some persons learn to satisfy certain needs through political activity, and what drives can be satisfied through it.

A third approach is based on Gestalt psychology. It emphasizes the perception of phenomena as a whole and the perceiver's drive toward ordering the perceptual field in its simplest and most orderly fashion. Another approach which has been used to a limited extent in political science is that of psychoanalytic theory. The difficulties in using the propositions and operationalizing the concepts in that type of approach to personality are acknowledged by political scientists.[11]

The diversity of theoretical approaches to the study of personality can be accounted for by the inability of any one formulation to be highly successful in predicting behavior. Because of this, psychologists continue to try various approaches in an effort to develop predictive capabilities.

[8] Gordon W. Allport, *Personality: A Psychological Interpretation* (New York: Holt, 1937).

[9] David Riesman, Nathan Glazer, and Reuel Denney, *The Lonely Crowd* (Garden City, N.Y.: Doubleday and Company, 1953); Harold D. Lasswell, *Psychopathology and Politics* (New York: The Viking Press, 1960); James David Barber, *The Lawmakers* (New Haven: Yale University Press, 1965).

[10] See, for example, Neal E. Miller and John Dollard, *Social Learning and Imitation* (New Haven: Yale University Press, 1941).

[11] For Gestalt theory, see Wolfgang Kohler, *Gestalt Psychology* (New York: Liveright, 1929) and Kurt Koffka, *Principles of Gestalt Psychology* (New York: Harcourt, Brace, 1935). Gestalt psychology has influenced social psychologists such as Kurt Lewin and Leon Festinger, whose work in turn has influenced political scientists in their studies of political behavior. For various psychoanalytic theories, see such works as Erik Erikson, *Childhood and Society* (New York: W. W. Norton, 1950); *The Basic Writing of Sigmund Freud*, A. A. Brill (ed.), (New York: Random House, 1938); C. G. Jung, *The Integration of Personality* (New York: Farrar and Rinehart, 1939); Karen Horney, *The Neurotic Personality of Our Time* (New York: Norton, 1937).

How can we organize an analysis of the psychological studies of political behavior? Fred Greenstein has suggested that studies of the psychology of political behavior can be categorized as being one of three types: the study of individual actors; the development of typologies of political personalities; and the analysis of aggregative effects of citizens' personality characteristics on the political system.[12] A major area of aggregative effects analysis of political behavior has been the study of attitude and motivation in relation to their effects on participation, on ideology, and on the kinds of demands made on the political system. We consider attitudes in the next chapter.

AGGREGATIVE EFFECTS OF PSYCHOLOGICAL VARIABLES

Lazarus asserts that two constructs are present in most psychological theories; motivation and control.[13] The concept of motivation has been used extensively by political scientists, particularly in the analysis of individual behavior.

Some approaches to the study of motivation emphasize biological factors, with behavior viewed as a response to certain innate drives or instincts, such as hunger, sex, and thirst. The extreme alternative to this is represented by those approaches which focus on sociological derivations of motivation, with man's motives being determined by various social processes. Approaches which emphasize drives imply that men are pushed or driven to certain patterns of behavior, while those which emphasize goals, incentives, or rewards focus on the end to be attained.

Several definitions of the concept of motivation have been developed in psychology. In general they incorporate one or more of three separate elements: motivation is viewed as the process of energizing, regulating, and/or directing behavior. The construct of motivation was elaborated by psychologists in an attempt to account for human behavior where other constructs were deemed inadequate for explaining that behavior.

Aristotle and Thucydides incorporated theories of motivation into their political analyses, indicating that the drives which impel action are those of honor- or prestige-seeking, desire for profit or material gain, and

---

[12] Fred I. Greenstein, *Personality and Politics* (Chicago: Markham Publishing Company, 1969).

[13] Richard Lazarus, *op. cit.*

fear of disgrace or of loss of valued things.[14] Plato's thought contains a drive theory of motivation, in which man is viewed as being motivated to compete, which Plato views as a higher form of motivation. The problem of controlling these drives exists, and this draws on the rational part of man's being.[15]

Abraham Maslow has suggested a system of five basic needs which stimulate human behavior: physical (food, water, sex); security; affection, love, and belongingness; self-esteem; and self-actualization.[16] Let us consider the implications of this set of needs for political behavior. Thomas Hobbes argued in The Leviathan that the absence of security in the natural order of men's relations to one another leads them to form governments. Through regulation by government authority men can gain security. Governments which cannot guarantee the personal security of their citizens are more likely to face problems of lack of support, both for incumbents of political office and probably also for the regime or institutional structures and rules of political conflict.[17] Maslow perceives needs as being hierarchically organized, with the need for safety developing only after basic physical needs have been satisfied.[18] A starving man will take greater risks and will not be as concerned about his personal safety as a man who is adequately fed. Men who are insecure will not be concerned with the need for affection. Reports from the Soviet Union during the famines of 1918-1922 and the purges of the 1930's, and from Nazi Germany, provide support for these assertions; concentration camp internees focused on their own basic physical needs or needs for security, ignoring or denouncing others in order to obtain satisfaction of these basic needs.[19] The lack of satisfaction of physical and safety needs or even the threat of inability to satisfy these needs can contribute to riots and civil disorders. The Catholic versus Protestant

[14] Aristotle, The Politics of Aristotle, trans. Ernest Barker (London: Oxford University Press, 1958), Book V. Ch. II; Thucydides, The Complete Writings of Thucydides, trans. John H. Finley, Jr. (New York: The Modern Library, 1951).

[15] Plato, Timaeus, in The Dialogues of Plato, trans. B. Jowett (New York: Random House, 1937), Vol. II, 69 ff.

[16] Abraham Maslow, "A Theory of Human Motivation," Psychological Review, 50 (1943), pp. 370-96; Motivation and Personality (New York: Harper and Row, 1954).

[17] Thomas Hobbes, The Leviathan, ed. Michael Oakeshott (Oxford: Basil Blackwell, 1960).

[18] Maslow, Motivation and Personality, op. cit., pp. 80-92.

[19] Pitirim A. Sorokin, Man and Society in Calamity (New York: E. P. Dutton and Company, 1942); Eugenia S. Ginzburg, Into the Whirlwind (Harmondsworth, Middlesex, England: Penguin Books, Ltd., 1968); Bruno Bettelheim, "Individual and Mass Behavior in Extreme Situations," Journal of Abnormal and Social Psychology, 38(1943), pp. 417-52.

conflicts in Northern Ireland, urban riots in the United States in the 1960's, and the so-called draft riots in New York in the 1860's can be partially accounted for by this factor. Prior studies have suggested that unemployment results in desocialization, political apathy, and political alienation.[20] Lipset has argued that certain occupations which are more likely to experience extreme insecurity of income are more likely to have high rates of voting for left or radical left authoritarian political parties; such occupational groups include one-crop farmers, miners, fishermen, and lumbermen.[21]

Maslow argues that the need to be loved and to belong to the group is third in the hierarchy of needs. To what extent can this type of need be related to political behavior? Argument can be made from several perspectives that a relationship does exist. Several studies have indicated that persons who are relatively isolated from society are more likely to support radical political movements, either of the right or of the left. The politics of extremism has greater appeal to the socially isolated and those psychologically alienated from various social institutions.[22]

The fourth need suggested by Maslow is the need for self-esteem. Some writers such as Lasswell and Barber have indicated that this may be a significant motive for political activity, particularly among those who seek elective political office.[23] Davies suggests that the drive for a sense of equality is an aspect of the need for self-esteem or self-respect.[24] The political manifestations of such a need are evidenced in the women's suffrage movement in the developed democracies at the beginning of the twentieth century, the Catholics' demands for equal treatment in employment and civil rights in Northern Ireland in the 1960's, and the blacks' much more vigorous demand for equality of treatment and opportunity in the United States since the Second World War. Evidence has begun to accumulate that political instability and civil violence are associated with the unequal distribution of resources, opportunities, and values within political systems.[25]

[20] George C. Homans, The Human Group (New York: Harcourt, Brace, and World, 1950), pp. 334-51; Mira Komarovsky, The Unemployed Man and His Family (New York: Dryden Press, 1940), pp. 112-22; E. Wight Bakke, Citizens Without Work (New Haven: Yale University Press; 1940), pp. 46-70; Michael Aiken, Louis A. Ferman, and Harold L. Sheppard, Economic Failure, Alienation, and Extremism (Ann Arbor: University of Michigan Press, 1968).
[21] Seymour Martin Lipset, Political Man (Garden City, N.Y.: Doubleday and Company, Inc., 1960), p. 231.
[22] Ibid., p. 175.
[23] Harold D. Laswell, Politics: Who Gets What, When, How (New York: Meridian Press, 1958), p. 13; Barber, op. cit., pp. 217-25.
[24] James C. Davies, Human Nature in Politics (New York: John Wiley and Sons, 1963), pp. 45-63.
[25] See, for example, Hayward R. Alker, Jr., Mathematics and Politics (New York: The Macmillan Company, 1965), pp. 108-10.

While the need for self-esteem may be a motivating factor for political participation, it appears that the relationship may be curvilinear, with persons of very high and very low self-esteem being less likely to participate. Related to the concept of self-esteem are those of personal effectiveness and political effectiveness. The latter has been measured by a political efficacy scale.[26] Persons high in efficacy have been found to be more likely to vote and to take part in spectator activities (voting, talking to others in support of a candidate) than gladiator activities, such as attending rallies or working in a political campaign.[27] Political efficacy is highly associated with the individual's sense of personal effectiveness.[28] However, the association of political efficacy with personal effectiveness varies with education, being stronger among persons with less education.[29] Generally, however, the more highly educated tend to have a higher sense of political efficacy and a higher sense of personal effectiveness.[30]

The argument has been made that those who participate in politics are able to participate because a minimum level of need for belongingness has been met and because they seek to satisfy social needs.[31] Studies have indicated that political activists who indicate they were originally motivated for political activity for other than social reasons are likely to report current satisfactions as being of a social nature and a decrease in other types of rewards derived from their continued political activity.[32]

The fifth type of need specified by Maslow is the need for self-actualization; inherent satisfactions derived from development of one's capabilities and pursuit of interests. Government activities which are

[26] For a discussion of the political efficacy scale, see Angus Campbell, Gerald E. Gurin, and Warren E. Miller, The Voter Decides (Evanston, Illinois: Row, Peterson, and Company, 1954), pp. 187-94; Lester Milbrath, Political Participation (Chicago: Rand McNally, 1965), pp. 156-57. We have previously discussed the narrow scope of items contained in the political efficacy scale and the consequent problem of content validity, in terms of the definition of political efficacy ("the feeling that individual political action does have, or can have, an impact upon the political process, i.e., that it is worth while to perform one's civic duties," The Voter Decides, p. 187). The narrow operationalization of political efficacy has been found to be related to these particular forms of political participation, such as voting and political discussion. One must keep in mind, however, that a scale more broadly encompassing all facets of the given definition of political efficacy would probably also be highly related to other forms of political participation, such as protest marches, demonstrations, and other manifestations of confrontation politics.

[27] Milbrath, op. cit., pp. 56-57.

[28] Ibid.

[29] Ibid., p. 59.

[30] Ibid., p. 57.

[31] Ibid., p. 58.

[32] Samuel J. Eldersveld, Political Parties (Chicago: Rand McNally, 1964), p. 287; M. Margaret Conway and Frank B. Feigert, "Motivation, Incentive Systems, and the Political Party Organization," American Political Science Review, 62 (December, 1968), p. 1170.

perceived as inhibiting or preventing self-actualization would stimulate opposition to government policy. The pursuit of happiness was declared by the Declaration of Independence to be an inalienable right of men and a justification for a colonial revolution. Men who perceive their inalienable right to the pursuit of happiness to be hindered by the social system or the government are likely to oppose the policies, institutions, or processes perceived as limiting their self-actualization. Opposition to an unpopular war which drained $30 billion a year in resources from desired domestic programs and expended considerable human resources is one example of this phenomenon. Others include demands for community control of local schools, arguments for segregation or desegregation of schools, movements to preserve undeveloped land in national seashores or parks, and the development of local cultural centers and training programs in the arts. Davies argues that political elites are primarily motivated by the need for self-actualization.[33] Perhaps studies of recruitment of political leaders should include as a relevant variable the existence of alternative opportunities for self-actualization; politics may be perceived in certain environments or social situations as the most efficacious way to attain that self-actualization. An historical pattern in the United States has been for members of recently arrived immigrant groups to obtain upward mobility first through the political system.[34]

Maslow's motivational hierarchy is suggestive of possible explanations for certain aspects of political behavior. However, evidence for the validity of the hierarchy of needs is far from conclusive. Maslow's orientation has been toward the formulation of propositions, not the careful testing of those propositions through empirical research. The usual problems of the lack of careful operationalization of concepts are presented by his work, and insufficient experimental research has been completed by others to permit appropriate assessment of the worth of his theoretical propositions.

A major focus in motivation has been on participation in politics. Robert Lane has distinguished between the satisfaction of conscious and unconscious needs in politics. Conscious needs include economic gain, social adjustment, and the pursuit of meaning and understanding. Unconscious needs include release of psychic tensions, need for dominance and deference, and the need for self-esteem.[35]

[33] Davies, op. cit., p. 61.

[34] Two other avenues of upward mobility for a disadvantaged group in a society may be organized crime and professional sports.

[35] Robert E. Lane, Political Life (Glencoe, Illinois: The Free Press, 1959), pp. 101-31.

Graham Wallas asserted that all men have impulses; these being fear, the need for affection, and the desire to excel — all of which can be satisfied through political participation.[36] Lasswell also argued that men's political activities are aimed at attaining selected values, such as power, wealth, well-being, affection, and respect.[37]

It has been argued that individuals suffering from high levels of tension would withdraw from politics. However, tension release may be achieved through some form of activity, of which political activity is one alternative.[38] Similarily, aggression may be externalized by participation in a political movement, such as the Nazi movement in Germany in the late 1920's, the Students for a Democratic Society, the Ku Klux Klan, or in a radical political party, such as the Communist Party.

One evaluation of motivation utilized in political analysis was developed by David McClelland and his associates.[39] McClelland argued that three dominant needs are need for achievement, need for power, and need for affiliation. For example, timing of economic development of developed nations was found to be associated with an emphasis on need for achievement.[40] Others have studied the relationship between the distribution of these needs and patterns of political stability in nations.[41] Another use has been in studying the recruitment of politicians and their behavior while in office. Rufus Browning has suggested that individuals high in achievement and power needs and low in affiliation needs are more likely to become organizational activists. His data from interviews with political and non-political organizational elite indicated that half the political activists came from politically active families, while none of the non-political organizational elite did so. He suggests that family activity in politics is thus important in teaching individuals with certain needs that those needs can be satisfied through politics.[42]

Browning also indicates that differences in patterns of needs may be related to differences in patterns of behavior in political office. For

[36] Graham Wallas, *Human Nature in Politics* (Lincoln: University of Nebraska Press, 1962), pp. 53-61.

[37] Harold D. Lasswell, *Politics: Who Gets What, When, How, op. cit.*, pp. 1, 26-27.

[38] Davies, *op. cit.*, Ch. 3; John Dollard, Neal E. Miller, Leonard W. Doob, O. H. Mowrer, and Robert R. Sears, *Frustration and Aggression* (New Haven: Yale University Press, 1939), Ch. 7; Lane, *op. cit.*, pp. 115-24.

[39] See David C. McClelland, *The Achieving Society* (New York: The Free Press, 1961), pp. 36-62, for a discussion of the concepts and measurement procedures.

[40] *Ibid.*, pp. 89-97.

[41] Stanley A. Rudin, "The Personal Price of National Glory," *Trans-Action*, 2 (Sept.-Oct., 1965), pp. 4-9.

[42] Rufus Browning, "The Interaction of Personality and Political System in Decision to Run for Office: Some Data and a Simulation Technique," *Journal of Social Issues*, 24 (July, 1968), p. 98.

example, individuals high in affiliative needs tend to be recruited by others, having no great desire to hold office.[43] Additional support for this proposition is provided by Barber's study of motivation, recruitment, and performance by freshmen legislators in a session of the Connecticut legislature.[44]

Browning finds that political activists ranking high in need for power and low on other needs have little interest in influencing policy, focusing on control and maintenance of the organization. Individuals high in need for achievement and low in affiliation and power needs tend to focus on policy matters rather than organizational control, but are not likely to persist in efforts to influence policy. Those who are oriented toward policy influencing and who persist in this interest and activity were found to rank high in both need for power and need for achievement. These activists were also interested in organizational maintenance and control.[45]

The research by Browning is based on a limited amount of survey data, essentially on responses from two matched groups which consist of twenty-three political activists and eighteen non-politicians. While the research is stimulating in terms of the additional hypotheses it suggests, considerably more research would be required before an adequate test of the hypotheses had been conducted.

Research has indicated that need for achievement has several dimensions which are independent of each other. These are a sense of mastery over the environment, trust in people, independence of family ties, and a desire for occupational accomplishment.[46] A distinction must be made between high need achievement and high optimism. Those ranking high in optimism strive for excellence in all assigned tasks, while high-achievement-need types work hard only at those tasks which are perceived as a challenge. McClelland argues that this distinguishes managers from those who seek to build a financial empire.[47] Onc can hypothesize that this may distinguish between those who become active in appointive or party office and those who seek elective office.

High need for achievement appears to be promoted by a certain pattern of relationships with one's parents. This pattern consists of warmth and nurture from the parents accompanied by demands for

[43] *Ibid.*, p. 103.
[44] Barber, *op. cit.*, pp. 214-17.
[45] Browning, *op. cit.*, p. 103.
[46] See, for example, Bernard Berelson and Gary Steiner, *Human Behavior* (New York: Harcourt, Brace, and World, 1964), p. 260; Roger Brown, *Social Psychology* (New York: The Free Press, 1965), Ch. 9.
[47] McClelland, *op. cit.*, pp. 227-28.

excellence expressed in a non-authoritarian manner.[48] Merelman has suggested that the development of a political ideology is fostered by a similar pattern of cognitive development.[49]

Other researchers, working with the set of needs enunciated by McClelland and his associates, have raised the following questions: How do nations differ in their patterns of motivational drives? How has this varied over time? How, if at all, are variations in patterns of needs within nations related to political behavior within and between nations?[50] Achievement motivation as indicated in popular plays and ballads, and economic production in England over a 400-year period were highly related, production rising about fifty years after an increase in achievement motivation in these popular expressions. The ballads correlated with production twenty-five years later. McClelland interprets the ballads as reflective of working-class values and the plays as reflecting middle-class values. McClelland also studied the relationship between the types of motives and values emphasized in 1925 and production in 1950 in the nations located in temperate climates. The indicators of motives emphasized were the stories in children's schoolbooks. The predicted relationship between emphasis on achievement in 1925 and higher economic production in 1950 existed.[51]

What is the association between motivational patterns and variations in political behavior? Countries in which the need for power is emphasized and need for affiliation is much lower in importance tend toward dictatorship.[52] Rise in emphasis on need for power in the United States has been accompanied by an expansionist foreign policy. Does the combination of high need for power and high need for achievement in a society result in psychological stress which has unpleasant consequences? Rudin related the 1925 analysis of motivational patterns in the seventeen Westernized nations with deaths in 1950 from psychogenic illness. These illnesses are divided into two types, those related to inhibition and repression (ulcers and high blood pressure) and those due to aggressiveness and acting out of impulses (murder, suicide, and

[48] See the discussion of research on the subject in Edward Zigler and Irvin L. Childs, "Socialization," *Handbook of Social Psychology*, eds. Gardner Lindzey and Elliot Aronson (Reading, Mass.: Addison-Wesley Publishing Company, 1969), Vol. III, pp. 543-54.

[49] Richard Merelman, "The Development of Political Ideology: A Framework for the Analysis of Political Socialization," *American Political Science Review*, 63 (September, 1969), pp. 750-68.

[50] Rudin raises these questions and indicates the various approaches being used to provide answers. See Rudin, *op. cit.*

[51] McClelland, *op. cit.*, *passim.*

[52] See Rudin, *op. cit.*, p. 6.

alcoholism). High need for achievement prevelant in the culture in 1925 was found to be related to high incidence of deaths due to inhibition and repression causes while high need for power was related to a higher death rate from causes related to aggressiveness and acting out of impulses. The Anglo-Saxon countries tended to rank high in deaths due to inhibition, Germanic cultures scored high in deaths related to aggressiveness, and the United States on deaths associated with both types.[53]

Motivations within the Western developed nations may follow a particular pattern. Once a high need for achievement is present in a society, the desire to attain without having to suffer the inhibition, repression, and resulting frustration grows. Thus incentive is generated for power motivation, with accompanying manipulation and exploitation of others. The unpleasantness in such a manipulated society would result in an increasing need for affiliation, love, and belongingness. Rudin suggests that in the United States the needs for achievement and power were emphasized from 1840 to 1910. The need for affiliation began to be emphasized in the 1920's in the literature of the country, continuing through the 1930's. It has been argued that the New Deal's rhetoric and policies were an expression of this need for affiliation. The shift to a need for power is then suggested to have occurred, evidencing itself clearly by 1950.[54] An examination of the popular songs, movies, television entertainment, and literature of the late 1960's would probably indicate an emphasis on the need for affiliation and an accompanying reorientation away from an internationalist and expansionist foreign policy. Several questions remain unanswered. Why does achievement motivation come to be the dominant need in a society? Does the same cycle exist in societies at various stages of modernization and in various types of non-Western cultures? What causes a decrease in need for affiliation and the predominance of some other need, such as need for achievement or need for power? Does the introduction or increase in rate of use of electronic media of communications affect either the rate of change in the cycle of needs or induce a change in the pattern of needs?

Several criticisms have been made of McClelland's work using motivational theories. The definition of motive used by McClelland is "a redintegration by a cue of a change in an affective situation."[55] The

---

[53] *Ibid.*, pp. 6-8.
[54] *Ibid.*, p. 9.
[55] D. C. McClelland, J. W. Atkinson, R. A. Clark, and E. L. Lowell, *The Achievement Motive.* (New York: Appleton-Century, 1953), p. 28.

affect base of motive suggested by this definition has been criticized as lacking either a logical or an empirical basis. Criticisms have also been made of the methods used to develop indices of key concepts in the hypotheses. For example, a number of alternative measures of economic development are possible. Should it be gross national product, production of electrical power, production of coal, miles of railroad track, number of telephones, or what? Use of different indices of key variables may result in different conclusions. In addition, the original aim of the researchers was to develop a measure of need for achievement in any area of endeavor. However, the actual content of their measures places a heavy emphasis on business or economic achievement. Hence, its content validity as a general measure of achievement motivation is questionable. As the research was conducted, a reconceptualization of the basic concept of need achievement occurred.

McClelland and other researchers using his conceptualization of achievement motivation have generally focused on describing the patterns of motivation present in a society and correlating the described pattern of individual motivations with selected measures of economic development at a later point in time. Multiple problems of inference are involved. One essential assumption is that one can adequately measure the distribution of motivations historically present in a society through analysis of plays, ballads, stories, school text materials, and other such indicators. Can one infer the dominant motivational patterns of a society from that type of indicator? In other words, are the measures used by McClelland valid measures of motivation? For example, what kind of indicator would one use to study the current transmission of values in the United States? Could one infer the motivational patterns of a representative sample of either the general citizenry or the economic elite from an evaluation of popular records, best-selling novels, or the most frequently watched television programs? Assuming the sample of cultural indicators is valid and representative, is it the dominant motivation or the distribution of motivations among key groups and occupants of key positions in society which influences the rate of economic growth and the level of economic development? The selection of both the cultural forms to be studied for their transmission of values and the selection of the sample of items within the forms present two possibilities for an unrepresentative sample. The inferential leap from predominant themes in selected cultural artifacts to inferences about predominant motivations for society is a very large one, and highly subject to criticism.

Another problem in the research on achievement motivation, other types of needs, and their relationship to political behavior is in the use of the content analysis technique. Sufficient reliability in scoring must be developed so that several individuals could analyze the same material and assign it the same score. A scoring manual has been developed for use by investigators using achievement motivation content analysis techniques in an attempt to resolve this problem. Objectivity in analysis is judged to exist if a set of investigators apply a common set of evaluative standards with a high degree of uniformity.

The predictive validity of the measure of achievement motivation has been demonstrated through the measure's high — or at least statistically significant — correlation with a number of other measures of achievement, based on either different levels of accomplishment in normal activities or in tasks assigned in experimental situations.

However, McClelland is assuming that the general level of achievement motivation in a society is directly reflected at a later period of time in economic decision-making. A higher level of explanation might be achieved if it could be ascertained that those more exposed to certain kinds of training do acquire higher levels of achievement motivation (considerable research has focused on this), and do acquire the other characteristics orienting them toward entrepreneur activities (such as desire for personal responsibility, willingness to take risks, and deferred gratification). Those with higher levels of this set of characteristics — of which achievement motivation is just one — are more likely to be recruited into entrepreneur activities, with higher levels of economic development following from that. A society may be so structured that those ranking higher in achievement motivation are more likely to be recruited into some other societal roles in the dominant elite; the military, the church hierarchy, or the bureaucracy or official party. Therefore, further research is needed to examine the concomitant elements of the entrepreneur role and the extent to which individuals with both higher levels of achievement motivation and the full set of entrepreneurial characteristics are recruited into economic decision-making roles. In summary, McClelland and those who use his approach are still faced with both unresolved conceptual and operational indicator problems which must be resolved before valid inference from individual to societal level can be made.

Other approaches to aggregative effects analysis are found in the survey studies of national political behavior which have usually focused on explaining levels of participation, direction of the vote, party image or party identification differences, and variations in political ideology. For example, characteristics such as nostalgia, trust in others, strong-mindedness, and personal competence can be classified as personality variables.[56] Several studies have examined the relationship of sense of personal competence, sense of political competence, and political participation. Persons high in personal competence have been found to be more likely to have a higher sense of political efficacy, to perceive the government as responsive to the public's preferences and interests, and to indicate higher levels of trust in government than individuals low in personal competence.[57] In a study of five developed nations, the relationship between competence and efficacy varied among the countries. However, those high in political competence generally tended more to perceive both the bureaucracy and the police as more likely to treat them fairly and to be responsive to the individual.[58] Situational differences in the five nations studied can in part account for the variations found. Also related to the sense of personal competence and trust in others is political trust, with the more alienated ranking lower in competence and trust in others.[59]

Another aspect of personality which has been examined for its relationship to political attitudes is that of personal control. Some individuals may be overcontrolled (restrained in personal relationships), while others are unrestrained (undercontrolled). One study found overcontrolled blacks to be more politically conservative than undercontrolled blacks, and undercontrolled whites to be more liberal than overcontrolled whites. Both overcontrolled blacks and whites were lower in political efficacy than the undercontrolled. Among whites, style of personal control was related to civil rights attitudes, with undercontrolled more supportive of pro-civil rights positions. The study's authors concluded that the control dimension of personality was related to aspects of the political belief system, even when controlling for race and social status variables.[60] This one study is not sufficient to confirm propositions about the relationship between control and political attitudes, as it is based on a sample of 538 individuals in one southern city at one point in time, but it indicates the nature of the relationships which might exist and the promise of further research in this area. In addition, of course, the problem of the content validity of the political efficacy scale needs to be considered in any future research.

[56] John P. Robinson, Jerrold G. Rusk, and Kendra B. Head, Measures of Political Attitudes (Ann Arbor: Survey Research Center, Institute for Social Research, September, 1968), pp. 649-99.
[57] See Milbrath, op. cit., pp. 59-60, 80.
[58] Gabriel Almond and Sidney Verba, The Civic Culture (Princeton, N.J.: Princeton University Press, 1963), pp. 214-21.
[59] Milbrath, op. cit., p. 80; Almond and Verba, op. cit., p. 285.
[60] James W. Dyson and Douglas St. Angelo, "Personality and Political Orientation," Midwest Journal of Political Science, 12 (May, 1968), pp. 202-23.

TYPOLOGIES AND POLITICAL PERSONALITIES

A typological approach to personality and politics was advocated by
Harold Lasswell, who analyzed the developmental patterns of certain
political types in order to understand what experiences contributed to
the development of types and traits.[61] Typologies of political personality
types were not new or original with Lasswell. The terms "reformer,"
"martyr," "anarchist," and "liberal" imply styles of thought and action
related to personality differences.

Lasswell's developmental approach is expressed in a formula,
$p\}d\}r=P$, in which p stands for private motives of the individual as they
are structured by his relationship with the parental family, d represents
displacement of private motives onto public objects, r equals the rationalization of the displacement in terms of serving public interests, P
equals political man, and $\}$ equals transformed into.[62]

Lasswell characterized two types of political personality as agitator
and administrator. The agitator is characterized by the importance he
places on the emotional response of the public. Agitators tend to characterize all opponents as all bad, and are undisciplined and issue-principle
oriented.[63]

Administrators may be distinguished by their displacement of affective (liking or disliking) orientations on more immediate objects, rather
than on remote, abstract principles. However, according to Lasswell,
the developmental processes through which individuals come to exhibit
the administrator personality type may be quite different.[64]

[61] Harold D. Lasswell, *Psychopathology and Politics, op. cit.*
[62] *Ibid.,* pp. 74-75.
[63] *Ibid.,* p. 78.
[64] *Ibid.,* p. 151. More recently Lasswell has suggested a classification of what has
been labeled personality types. The nuclear type denotes a person who devotes his
total interest and energies to a particular value, such as gaining a particular elective
office. Co-relational types are delineated by the patterns of personal qualities which are
found associated with a particular role occupant or pattern of behavior; for example,
politicians may be more likely than bureaucrats to be aggressive, dominant, gregarious,
and willing to take risks. The developmental type indicates not only the pattern of
personal qualities associated with a role but accounts for how those patterns are
developed. Lasswell argues that politicians are primarily motivated to seek power, and
to seek that value through a specialized pattern of behavior. Also analyzed are the
mechanisms used in internal adaptation and resolution of conflict. Developmental
types can be established by analyzing the values, indulgences, and deprivations received
as a youth, the practices which express these, and the mechanisms utilized to adapt to
these. For a discussion of these types, see Harold Lasswell, "A Note on 'Types' of
Political Personality: Nuclear, Co-relational, and Developmental," *The Journal of
Social Issues,* 24 (July, 1968), pp. 81-91.

A more recent typology is Barber's classification of presidential-style types. By style is meant "a collection of habitual action patterns in meeting role demands. Viewed from outside, a man's style is the observed quality and character of his performance. Viewed from inside, it is his bundle of strategies for adapting, for protecting and enhancing self-esteem."[65] Two criteria are used to formulate the typology; activity-passivity in performing the presidential role, and positive-negative affect, or feeling, towards his activity.[66]

PRESIDENTIAL STYLE ORIENTATIONS

Activity-Passivity in Role Performance	Affect Toward His Activities	
	Positive	Negative
Active	productiveness	personal ambition
Passive	affection	minimal performance of duty

By examining the rhetorical patterns, type of presidential activity (business) focused on, and patterns of relations with others in terms of the active-passive, negative-positive dimensions, Barber argues that presidential style can be classified.[67] Presidential styles are viewed as deriving from a man's first political success, with use in a successful political act resulting in continued use in political activity. The initial situation in which the style is used is accompanied by development of new confidence, different patterns of adaptation to groups, and increased public acclaim and attention.[68] The condition surrounding this situation can be evaluated in terms of the future president's motives, the resources the man has, and the opportunities available to him.[69]

Another example of typological analysis is Barber's typology of freshman legislators based on their level of legislative activity and their willingness to serve for at least three or more additional sessions of the legislature. In the course of his analysis Barber makes use of psychological characteristics other than motivation to distinguish among legislators; among these are their self-perceptions and strategies of adjustment to others and to the situation, such as submission, aggression, displacement, and projection.[70]

[65] James David Barber, "Classifying and Predicting Presidential Styles: Two Weak Presidents," *Journal of Social Issues*, 24 (July, 1968), p. 52.
[66] *Ibid.*, pp. 52-53.
[67] *Ibid.*
[68] *Ibid.*, p. 61.
[69] *Ibid.*, p. 62.
[70] *Ibid.*, passim.

Barber's research has utilized the application of psychoanalytic theory, depth interviewing, and content analysis to aspects of political behavior. The limited number of cases on which his conclusions are based inhibit the acceptability of the findings; considerable additional testing of the hypotheses is therefore required before they can be accepted. Studying freshmen legislators in one legislative session or a selected set of elected leaders in one country is not an adequate base on which to test a theory.

One typological approach which has been much used in political analysis derives from the study of the authoritarian personality.[71] The genesis of the study was an attempt to isolate psychological correlates and antecedents of ethnic prejudice, stimulated by the rise of Hitler and the Nazi extermination of the Jews. The study argues that extensive co-variation (joint variation of two or more variables) exists between anti-Semitic attitudes, other ethnic prejudices, political conservatism, and selected psychological needs and characteristics. Authoritarianism has been explained as the result of childhood experience within the family, particularly of rigid discipline, resulting in status anxieties. Repression of these anxieties is accompanied by aggression against figures of authority which is displaced on social out groups, such as racial and ethnic minorities.[72]

The authors of *The Authoritarian Personality* examined nine aspects in F (fascism) Scale. The authoritarian personality was viewed as having the following characteristics: conformist and conventional in values; submissive to authority; concerned with power, toughness, and identification with a strong leader; generalized hostility; projective of unconscious emotional impulses; tending to condemn and punish individuals who violate or reject conventional values; rigid in his belief system; anti-subjective and unimaginative; and having an exaggerated concern with sex and being punitive toward those who violate or advocate violating sexual norms.[73]

A number of studies have examined political correlates of the F Scale. Party identification is not related to F Scale score; however, authoritarianism was positively associated with preferences for more conservative candidates and a conservative ideology. Differences in authoritarianism were related to variations in motivation for voting but not to

[71] T. W. Adorno, Else Frenkel-Brunswik, Daniel J. Levinson, and R. Nevitt Sanford, *The Authoritarian Personality* (New York: Science Editions, 1964), Parts I and II.

[72] *Ibid.*, Ch. 10.

[73] Forms 40 and 45 of the F Scale contain the items designed to measure the presence of these characteristics. *Ibid.*, pp. 255-57.

differences in rate of voting. Non-authoritarians in one study rated higher in political efficacy than those ranking high in authoritarianism. The within-party differences were significant, with non-authoritarian Republicans being considerably more supportive of federal government programs in the social welfare area.[74]

Campbell, Converse, Miller, and Stokes, using a conservatism scale and short versions of the F Scale, concluded that authoritarianism was not related to attitudes on specific issues. They also found a negative correlation between original and reversed items on the F Scale. The results of their research lead them to discontinue use of the authoritarian personality scale in their later studies of political behavior.[75] The evidence indicates that the emphasis by the authors of The Authoritarian Personality on ethnic prejudice and political and economic conservatism as component parts of the authoritarian's belief structure is unwarranted.

The Authoritarian Personality has been extensively criticized from both a conceptual and a methodological perspective. The F Scale has been alleged to measure potential fascism, not authoritarianism.[76] The samples used to develop and to validate the scales were criticized as unrepresentative. Controls over relevant variables, such as the level of education or the sophistication of the individual, were not exercised. Also criticized were the statistical analyses made of the data and the failure to test alternative hypotheses.[77] Questions have been raised as to whether inferences can be made about psychological characteristics from attitude questions; one is forcing a response to an item which might not be one that the individual would normally give. Secondly, one cannot easily ascertain the significance to the individual of the content of the statement or of the response.[78] The role of the other situational characteristics which impede or promote the expression of prejudice has generally been ignored. Findings that less educated, less intelligent, and lower socio-economic status individuals are much more likely to score high in authoritarianism has resulted in the suggestion that the scale reflects sophistication rather than authoritarianism. A counter-argument is that all these items correlate with authoritarianism because less educated,

[74] Robert E. Lane, "Political Personality and Electoral Choice," in Politics and Social Life, Nelson Polsby, Robert Dentler, and Paul A. Smith, eds. (Boston: Houghton Mifflin Company, 1963), pp. 231-43.

[75] Angus Campbell, Philip Converse, Warren Miller, and Donald Stokes, The American Voter (New York: John Wiley and Sons, Inc., 1960), pp. 512-15.

[76] John P. Kirscht and Ronald C. Dillehay, Dimensions of Authoritarianism (Lexington: University of Kentucky Press, 1967), pp. 57-69.

[77] Ibid., p. 7-29; R. Christie and M. Jahoda, Studies in the Scope and Method of the Authoritarian Personality (Glencoe, Illinois: The Free Press, 1954).

[78] Solomon E. Asch, Social Psychology, (New York: Prentice-Hall, Inc., 1952), pp. 536-38.

lower socio-economic status parents with such characteristics tend to be more authoritarian, with the resulting personality and attitudinal consequences for their children.[79]

The lack of consistent relationship between scores on the authoritarian personality scale and specific beliefs and attitudes has been analyzed by Milton Rokeach, who argues that the authoritarian is distinctive in how he holds beliefs and not in the specific content of those beliefs.[80] The social situation or references such as peer group opinions can act as a constraint on whether or not the authoritarian personality expresses his views in the predicted style.

Rokeach has devised a measure of this general authoritarian style which he labels *dogmatism*. The distinguishing characteristics of this style include intolerance of ambiguity, rigidity, and inflexibility. The basic distinction is in terms of whether an individual's belief system is open or closed. The belief system consists of all beliefs, hypotheses and explanations that the individual accepts as true. The converse, his disbelief system, consists of all beliefs, hypotheses, and explanations he accepts as false.[81] Three dimensions are present in the belief system: a belief-disbelief dimension; the central-peripheral dimension; and the time perspective dimension. The central-peripheral dimension has three components: the central region which encompasses basic beliefs about the nature of the physical world, the self, and others; an intermediate region which contains beliefs about authority and persons exercising authority over him; and a peripheral region, representing beliefs about the rest of his world. The time perspective refers to beliefs about the past, present, and future. This dimension is characterized as varying from narrow to broad, with a narrow time perspective representing a focus on one time period and a broad perspective incorporating all three. The belief-disbelief dimension refers to two interdependent parts, with varying degrees of similarity possible between beliefs that are accepted and beliefs that are rejected (disbeliefs).[82]

One can evaluate belief-disbelief systems in terms of the degree of isolation among different beliefs. Indicators of this are the "coexistence of logically contradictory beliefs" in a person's belief or disbelief system, the judgment of objectively relevant facts as irrelevant, and the extent to which differences are emphasized and similarities are minimized in comparing belief-disbelief systems. This can be judged by the degree

[79] Kirscht and Dillehay, *op. cit.*, pp. 37-39; Greenstein, *op. cit.*, pp. 108-10.
[80] Milton Rokeach, *The Open and the Closed Mind* (New York: Basic Books, Inc., 1960).
[81] *Ibid.*, p. 33.
[82] *Ibid.*, p. 34.

of knowledge an individual possesses about his beliefs and disbeliefs, and the degree of similarity about disbeliefs.[83] For example, what amount of knowledge underlies an individual's beliefs and disbeliefs about the Soviet Union and communist China? Secondly, does he believe that communism in the Soviet Union is the same in ideology and practice as in communist China? A third measure of the belief-disbelief system is the degree of comprehensiveness of the system. Thus we would evaluate the number of disbelief systems within a person's total belief-disbelief system.

The open-versus-closed-minded distinction is based on more than the degree to which an individual relies on authority in restructuring his belief system. Yielding to others and resistance to acculturation (acceptance of the predominant culture) as well as reliance on authority all have a common cognitive basis, according to Rokeach. That basis is the extent to which an individual distinguishes between the substance of the communication and the character of or information about the source.[84]

Critics have argued that the data do not support the assertion that there is a left wing authoritarianism. Certainly the survey studies of samples of the American voting age population do not provide this kind of evidence. Rokeach administered his dogmatism scale and the F Scale to samples of English Communists and adherents of other English political parties. The Communists ranked lowest on the F Scale and higher on the dogmatism scale, but on the latter the differences were not large enough to be considered statistically significant. The problem may be that the dogmatism scale (designed to measure the openness or closedness of a belief system) and the opinionation scale (designed to measure the extent to which people are rejected or accepted because of the beliefs they hold, the leftness or rightness of opinionation, and liberalism-conservatism) do not measure that which they purport to measure.[85]

It can be argued that the key to the character of an authoritarian is that he has a closed belief system, changing his beliefs only when authorities to whom he is highly responsive advocate policies or perceptions at variance with his own beliefs. Non-authoritarians would require a different kind of stimulus before they would change their beliefs; the stimulus would be an awareness of the logical inconsistency between their preferred values and professed beliefs.[86]

[83] *Ibid.*, pp. 36-39.
[84] *Ibid.*, p. 60.
[85] *Ibid.*, pp. 80-87; 114.
[86] Roger Brown, *op. cit.*, pp. 541-43.

THE ANALYSIS OF INDIVIDUAL POLITICAL ACTORS

The analysis of individual political actors, focusing on the psychological antecedents or correlates of each individual's response to a political problem, has been limited. The focus is usually on a major political figure who, through his personal judgments and actions, had a significant impact on the course of history. The premier example is the analysis of Woodrow Wilson. Two students have suggested that Wilson's relations with his father caused him to develop such unsatisfied needs and patterns of perceptions that in certain kinds of situations he tended to make inappropriate decisions. Wilson was dominated, ridiculed, and humiliated by his father as a child, resulting in a low sense of self-esteem. As president of the United States, Wilson refused to compromise on particularly important issues, such as the 14 Points and the accompanying agreements at the Peace Conference in 1919 and the ratification of the League of Nations charter in the United States Senate.[87] Alexander and Juliette George argue that Wilson's inability to compromise when in the position of power wielder on issues central to his interests was a consequence of standard defense mechanisms, especially repression and reaction formation.[88]

Defense mechanisms are means of adapting to extreme tension or stress, distorting or denying reality in some unconscious manner. A number of defense mechanisms have been enumerated by psychologists. These include repression (refusing to perceive reality), fantasy (gratification through imaginary accomplishment), projection (attributing the source of anxiety to the external world rather than one's own acts, impulses, or mental states), identification (compensating for one's feelings of inadequacy through associating one's self with an individual or institution regarded as superior), displacement (displacing feelings of hostility on out groups or individuals regarded as unworthy or inferior), reaction formation (replacing an anxiety-producing feeling with its opposite, such as replacing fear or hate with love), regression (withdrawing to an earlier and less mature level of development), emotional insulation (passivity), rationalization (convincing one's self that one's

[87] Sigmund Freud and William C. Bullitt, *Thomas Woodrow Wilson, Twenty-Eighth President of the United States: A Psychological Study* (Boston: Houghton Mifflin, 1967); Alexander L. George and Juliette L. George, *Woodrow Wilson and Colonel House: A Personality Study* (New York: Dover Publications, Inc., 1964).
[88] George and George, *op. cit.*, pp. 11-12.

behavior is rational and therefore acceptable), and compensation (emphasizing admirable traits or over-gratification in one area to compensate for other deficiencies or deprivations).[89]

A limited number of studies have used this approach. In addition to Woodrow Wilson, other subjects have been James Forrestal, the first secretary of defense of the United States, who ended his career by committing suicide, and Anton Cermak, a Great Depression-era mayor and political boss of Chicago who died a month after being shot in an assassination attempt aimed at Franklin Delano Roosevelt. Cermak was the first and last foreign-born person elected mayor of Chicago, and some would argue he was the strongest political boss in the history of Chicago.[90]

Some of these studies have been heavily criticized because of inadequacies in conceptualization, operationalization of concepts, and the presentation of evidence in support of propositions. For example, the study of Woodrow Wilson completed by Sigmund Freud and William C. Bullit in 1938 and not published until after the death of the second Mrs. Wilson, sought to examine the psychological basis for his actions. Bullit and Freud, who strenuously disagreed with some of Wilson's policies, have been accused of injecting their personal antipathies toward Wilson into the analysis. The authors do admit that they had only limited access to facts, and a problem is presented by the use of limited historical material to evaluate the personality of Wilson and the causes of that personality structure. Furthermore, before one can accept the validity of the analysis, one must accept the theoretical structure created by Freud and used in this analysis. Because of the biases brought to the analysis by the authors, the use of Freudian psychoanalytic theory, and the problems of drawing inferences from the paucity of data available to them, the study has been heavily criticized.

More material was available to the Georges for their research than was available to Freud and Bullit. While the latter had access to the published volumes of Wilson's works and papers edited by R. S. Baker as well as his official biography of Wilson, the Georges also had access to unpublished materials in the Baker collection. In addition, the objectivity necessary for valid research missing from the Freud and Bullit study was present in the study by George and George.

[89] See Lazarus, op. cit., pp. 20-23 for a discussion of these processes.

[90] Arnold A. Rogow, James Forrestal: A Study of Personality, Politics, and Policy (New York: The Macmillan Company, 1963); Alex Gottfried, "The Uses of Socio-Psychological Categories in a Study of Political Personality," in Political Behavior, eds. Heinz Eulau, Samuel J. Eldersveld, and Morris Janowitz (Glencoe: The Free Press, 1956), pp. 125-32.

The study of the first secretary of defense, James Forrestal, who committed suicide shortly after his resignation from office in 1949, exemplifies the difficulties presented by the psychoanalytic approach. The precise statement of explanatory propositions, careful definition of terms, and exhaustive search for evidence to test those propositions is difficult to achieve, and a deficiency of explicit propositions and the presentation of data appropriate for testing those propositions is evident in the study of Forrestal. Transference and projection of Forrestal's own personality needs onto policy objects and recommendations is alleged, but both the presence of the needs and the tie between personality needs and policy recommendations is not sufficiently established. In addition, it would be necessary to show that those policy recommendations would not have been made if the personality needs had not been present, or in other words, that there was not an objective basis for his policy recommendations.

Criticism of many such studies stems from their reliance on Freudian psychoanalytic theory, which overemphasizes the impact of early childhood socialization on later personality and behavior. The impact of agents of socialization other than the family and the influence on personality needs and political orientations of post-childhood experiences is inadequately considered.

We can ask, then, of what utility are such studies for political science? They can add to the description of historical events, but do they contribute to the expressed aim of political science, the development of explanatory theories? The analysis of single cases cannot "prove" a theory; it can be argued that an accumulation of single case studies can lend support to a theory. The weight of evidence in such a theory is based on the attempt to explain behavior of a political actor which deviates from what would normally be expected from him or one in that role and in that situation. The first problem, then, is to establish what normal behavior would be. Statistical variance and the significance of that variance are difficult if not impossible to establish in single-case analysis.

SUMMARY AND CONCLUSION

An argument for the study of psychological variables is their proximity or immediate antecedent relationship to the political behavior we wish to study. If, for example, we are interested in voting behavior in the next presidential election, the psychological state of the individual and the immediate situation in which the vote is cast are most proximate to the event of voting. This justification has been used by Campbell, Converse, Miller, and Stokes for a social-psychological analysis of voting behavior in which major explanatory variables are perceptions and attitudes, rather than the social and economic characteristics of the voters as used by prior studies of voting behavior.[91] M. Brewster Smith has suggested that social variables constitute the environment and antecedents for the development or acquisition of psychological predispositions; immediate situation and psychological variables are more proximate to behavior. Smith classifies personality processes and dispositions functionally, labeling the dispositions as attitudes. Attitudes are viewed as performing object appraisal, mediation of self-other relations, and externalization and ego-defensive functions. As such the first two function in evaluating the relevance and consequences of political situations and actors' activities for the individual and govern his relations with political actors.[92] The externalization and ego-defense functions have been emphasized in Lasswell's political-man formulation, the studies of individual political actors such as Woodrow Wilson, "Boss", Cermak, and James Forrestal, and the analysis of authoritarianism and of dogmatism.

However, a number of problems exist in the use of psychological variables to account for variations in political behavior among individuals and between nations. Some of these are methodological; for example, can one adequately assess the nature of psychological variables, such as alienation, trust in others, authoritarianism, dogmatism, or dominance through use of scales imbedded in a questionnaire format? Psychological analysis of both single individuals and of psychological types examines first the behavior patterns of these types and then seeks to identify the psychological factors underlying the behavioral patterns. The third aspect of this approach is to trace the development of the psychological characteristics in childhood and later experiences. Certainly the validity of inferences about the nature of childhood experiences and implications for personality of such experiences is difficult to establish.

The nature of the situation may place constraints on how and the extent to which personality may influence political behavior. Certain situations permit personality to be more of a determining factor. Such situations would include those in which one's reference groups are in conflict, or appropriate behavior is unclear or undefined, or those in which current expectations about appropriate behavior appear to conflict with expectations that applied in the past.

One can also ask if constraints arising from the expectations of others about how an occupant of a particular political position ought to behave might limit the range of behaviors which are considered appro-

[91] Campbell, Converse, Miller, and Stokes, op. cit., pp. 24-37.
[92] M. Brewster Smith, "A Map for the Analysis of Personality and Politics," The Journal of Social Issues, 24 (July, 1968), pp. 15-28.

priate for any political actor. Proponents of this argument assert that personality differences would have little influence. Several responses can be made to this argument. One is that even if the range of alternatives is limited, the difference should be significant, as, for example, in variations in presidential style. Secondly, the limitations applying to the behavior of an occupant of a political position might be rather minimal.

Another argument is that personality types are randomly distributed in various political roles. However, some researchers have presented preliminary evidence which tends to refute this assertion. Browning's study of the recruitment of political and non-political organization leaders, as well as research by McConaughy[93] on the characteristics of legislators, indicates that in some psychological characteristics political activists differ from control groups.

Several general criticisms can be made of research on the relationship between psychological characteristics of individuals and their political behavior. A basic problem is the all too frequent unrepresentativeness of the samples on which the hypotheses are tested. Researchers tend to develop research measures and test hypotheses on captive populations of college students who certainly are not representative in many ways of the general population. This has negative implications for both the content validity and the construct validity of their research. Research instruments which may be appropriate for measuring the presence or absence of a particular variable among college students could be inappropriate for the general population. College students differ from the adult non-college population not only in age and educational attainment but also perhaps in their value systems, range of experiences, and many attitudes.

Where results are compared with established norms for a particular research instrument, the norms may have been established through research on sets of individuals who are not representative of the adult population. Establishment of norms through testing measures on activist members of middle class organizations is still a more than occasional occurrence.

When one develops a research instrument through evaluation of results from non-representative samples of the population he wishes to study, or through its use with other populations, the content validity becomes suspect. Use of measures lacking in content validity then contributes to the absence of construct validity.

[93] John B. McConaughy, "Certain Personality Factors of State Legislators in South Carolina," *American Political Science Review*, 44 (December, 1950), pp. 897-903.

Attitudes, Beliefs, Opinions, and Values

4

INTRODUCTION

Does the public approve of the president's domestic policies? Does the public think he has been doing a good job as president? What is the attitude of white blue-collar workers toward a guaranteed annual wage, mandatory health insurance, equal opportunity employment laws, or increasing property taxes to improve the public schools? Do Americans value peace, freedom, equality, or prosperity more highly? Do the beliefs about politics of midwestern Republicans differ significantly from those of midwestern Democrats; does this vary with the level of education or size of residential town? These types of questions are asked by political scientists, politicians, and the interested public. The subjects they cover can be labeled political attitudes, values, beliefs, and opinions. We shall examine in this chapter the study of the relationships among values, beliefs, attitudes, opinions, and political behavior. First we must define these concepts.

DEFINITION OF THE CONCEPTS

Beliefs represent an individual's description of his environment. They have been characterized in a number of ways; one distinction is in belief in something and beliefs about something.[1] An example of the first type is a belief in God; this type is not a matter of fact but an act of faith and as such cannot be tested empirically. The second type — a belief about something — can be tested empirically. Examples include the belief that government is no more corrupt than any other form of social decision-making process or that competition among conflicting interests is a satisfactory method of maintaining a distribution of power in a society.

Attitude theories generally agree that an attitude is a predisposition, but of what kind is a subject of considerable debate. Is it a predisposition to respond, to evaluate, to experience, to be motivated, or to act? One definition of attitude is that presented by Rokeach, who defines attitude as a relatively enduring organization of interrelated beliefs that describe, evaluate, and advocate action with respect to an object or situation, with each belief having cognitive, affective, and behavioral components. Each belief is a predisposition which, when suitably activated, results in some preferential response.[2] The key to distinguishing this definition from others is determining what is meant by *advocate*; the term has a rational or argumentative connotation. Is that equivalent to motive? Rokeach argues that considering an attitude a predisposition to respond is a more useful construction. Thus, a number of different types of responses is possible. Is the response based on cognition or evaluation or both? That is also debated among psychologists. Rokeach avoids taking a stand on that issue, limiting his definition merely to a predisposition to make a preferential response. The preferential response may not only be to the situation or object, but also to others who share one's preferential response, and to the maintenance of the attitude itself.

An alternative approach is that of Newcomb, Turner, and Con-

[1] Lewis A. Froman, Jr., *People and Politics* (Englewood Cliffs, N.J.: Prentice-Hall, Inc. 1962), p. 19. Milton Rokeach develops a different categorization of types of beliefs, suggesting that beliefs are of three types: descriptive (I believe it is raining); evaluative (I believe Chrysler Corporation makes very dependable cars); or exhortative (I believe the New York Mets should win the pennant). Regardless of their type, all beliefs are predispositions to act. See M. Rokeach, *Beliefs, Attitudes, and Values* (San Francisco: Jossey-Bass, Inc., Publishers, 1968), pp. 115-16.

[2] Rokeach, op. cit., p. 112.

verse, who state that "from a cognitive point of view, an attitude represents an organization of valenced cognitions. From a motivational point of view, an attitude represents a state of readiness for motive arousal. An individual's attitude toward something is his predisposition to be motivated in relation to it."[3] They distinguish attitude from motive in several different ways. A motive is seen as characterized by a drive state which appears, disappears, and reappears, while an attitude does not have a drive state. An attitude refers to the likelihood that a drive state can be aroused. It is also argued that attitudes involve less specific objects than motives. When an object or state has been associated with reduction of a drive, behavior tends to be directed toward that object when the motive is aroused again. Thus the conception of attitude they emphasize is that of "a state of readiness for motive arousal."[4] Within this framework, an attitude is distinguished from other types of motives by the presence of a cognitive as well as an affective and conative component. Attitudes differ from cognitions or beliefs in that they have an affective or valence component.

The relationship between motive and attitude is also confronted by Rokeach, who raises the question, "Does an attitude possess drive producing properties or do motives come from sources other than the attitude itself?"[5] He concludes that empirical research has not been conducted to provide an answer to this question.

A third definition of attitude is that presented by Froman, who defines an attitude as a predisposition to evaluate some object or aspect of the environment favorably or unfavorably.[6] This disposition of approval or disapproval has three components, affective, cognitive, and conative.[7] The affective component consists of feelings of like and dislike which can vary in direction (positive or negative) and in intensity (strong or weak). The cognitive component describes the perception of the attitude's object, such as the nature of civil rights (housing jobs, schools, etc.). The conative component refers to the behavioral tendencies toward the object. Examples of an attitude object include a presidential candidate, a protest organization, protest organizations or demonstra-

[3] Theodore M. Newcomb, Ralph H. Turner, and Philip Converse, *Social Psychology* (New York: Holt, Rinehart, and Winston, Inc., 1965), p. 40.

[4] *Ibid.*

[5] Rokeach, *op. cit.*, p. 129.

[6] Froman, *op. cit.*, p. 20. Gordon Allport has stated that an attitude has "at least five aspects: (1) it is a mental and neural state, (2) of readiness to respond, (3) organized, (4) through experience (5) exerting a directive and/or dynamic influence on behavior." Quoted in William McGuire, "The Nature of Attitudes and Attitude Change," in *Handbook of Social Psychology*, ed. by Gardner Lindzey and Eliot Aronson (Reading, Mass.: Addison-Wesley Publishing Company, 1968), Vol. III, p. 142.

[7] McGuire, *op. cit.*, pp. 155-57.

tions in general, a bill to reduce federal income tax rates, integration of schools, blacks, whites, your mother, or the president of the United States.

Social psychologists do not agree in their definitions of the term *opinion*. Opinion can be defined as a verbal expression of an attitude,[8] and public opinion would then be the verbal expression of attitudes on public issues and events. It must be emphasized that attitudes can be expressed in a variety of behavioral forms, such as facial expressions, gestures, or actions; an opinion (verbal statement) is just one of many ways.

Attitudes are functional to the individual; one or several functions may be performed for the individual by holding certain attitudes.[9] First, attitudes perform a cognitive function, enabling the individual to organize his environment; thus the individual develops a pattern of response to a set of similar stimuli. Attitudes also serve an ego-defensive function, protecting the individual from threatening stimuli. Dislike of the police and labeling them "pigs" serves to protect one psychologically from the threat an individual perceives the police to present to him. Attitudes are also value-expressive, enabling the individual to indicate to others the nature of his character. Finally attitudes serve a utilitarian function, enabling one to obtain those things he values. Thus a politician's holding a certain set of attitudes and acting on that basis is utilitarian if it enables him to be elected to the office he desires.

Values are defined by Lewis Froman as statements of "goods," of things which are thought to be desirable.[10] Milton Rokeach has divided values into instrumental and terminal types; instrumental values being idealized ways of behaving, such as imaginative, intellectual, loving, and courageous, and terminal values being idealized end states, such as freedom, happiness, equality, and peace.[11] In contrast Froman divides values into three types; wants, oughts, and means-ends.[12] An example of a "want" is contained in the statement, "I want a new Thunderbird." An "ought" is represented by the statement, "Nations should resolve their differences through negotiation rather than through armed conflict." A means-ends form of values is illustrated by the statement, "To

---

[8] Carl I. Hovland, I. L. Janis, and Harold H. Kelley, *Communication and Persuasion* (New Haven: Yale University Press, 1953). Rokeach defines it as a verbal expression of an attitude, belief, or value. Rokeach, *op. cit.*, p. 125. For a discussion of a variety of approaches, see McGuire, *op. cit.*, p. 152. It may be, as McGuire argues, that empirically such a distinction cannot be made.

[9] Daniel Katz, "The Functional Approach to the Study of Attitudes," *Public Opinion Quarterly*, 24 (Summer, 1960), pp. 163-204.

[10] Froman, *op. cit.*, p. 19.

[11] Rokeach, *op. cit.*, p. 124.

[12] Froman, *op. cit.*, p. 19.

obtain an effective national transportation system the federal government should establish a unified transportation trust fund to finance
metropolitan subway systems, interstate highways, high-speed inter-city
passenger train service, and airport and air control facilities." The last
value statement thus specifies a means to achieve a given end state.

Several questions have concerned behavioral scientists who have
focused on the study of opinions, beliefs, values, and attitudes. How do
they develop? (One approach to this question is indicated in the chapter on political socialization.) How do attitudes, beliefs, opinions, and
values change? Who (what kinds of people) hold what values, opinions, beliefs, and attitudes? What are the consequences of their pattern
and distribution in different societies, both for variations in the political
behavior of citizens within a nation and for the different patterns of
behavior among nations? By the nature of what is studied and the method
used in studying it, we are usually focusing on verbal expressions and
inferring from them the nature of the underlying beliefs, values, and
attitudes from which the verbal expressions spring.

However, other methods can be and have been used to assess the
nature of attitudes, beliefs, and values. These include an examination
of forms of behavior rewarded or punished by various agents in the social
and political system. Thus, social scientists study the values instilled in
children by parents in a particular country, such as Germany or Burma,
by observing what kinds of behaviors are punished or rewarded,[13] or the
values and actions promoted by the political system by observing the
kinds of relationships to the local government encouraged or discouraged
through treatment accorded individual citizens by the local bureaucracy
or the police.[14]

One emphasis in political research has been on public opinion. A
number of different definitions of public opinion has been presented.
We shall define it quite simply as views on political or politically relevant issues held by persons with an interest in those issues. Public
opinion is frequently described in terms of its patterns of distribution
among different ethnic and religious groups, residents of various geographical regions and social classes, the degree of conflict and consensus
on various issues and the change over time in these, the variations
between mass and elite opinion, the intensity of opinion on issues
and the saliency of the issues to the public, and the formation of opin-

[13] Lucian Pye, Politics, Personality, and Nation Building (New Haven: Yale
University Press, 1962), pp. 177-86.
[14] See Gabriel Almond and Sidney Verba, The Civic Culture (Princeton: Princeton University Press, 1963), pp. 106-14.

ion through various socialization experiences.[15] The links between public opinion and public policy are also of central concern to political science.

DIMENSIONS OF ATTITUDES AND ATTITUDE OBJECTS

Among the basic properties of an attitude toward an object are the direction of the attitude and the intensity of feeling.[16] Terms used to describe the direction include such comparisons as good-bad, agree-disagree, like-dislike, and fair-unfair. In studying attitudes and opinions, we are concerned not only with their direction and intensity but also their stability over time and the extremity of the opinion or attitude in comparison to the mode or mean in a population group.[17] Attitudes and opinions also have a quality of latency, becoming active after perception or recall of the appropriate stimulus, which may not occur even if the stimulus is presented to the individual.[18] Rokeach has suggested that we can also describe the organization of attitudes in terms of several other structural dimensions.[19] Among these are the differential (the extent to which various parts are articulated), the time perspective (past, present, or future orientation), and the range of phenomena represented by an attitude structure. Rokeach points out another aspect of attitude organization; the values which form the frame of reference for an attitude.[20] The consistency of opinions may be minimal, as different objects come into focus. For example, an individual may express support for equal employment and desegregation of schools but be opposed to fair housing laws.[21]

The informational concept associated with a set of beliefs, attitudes and opinions can be examined. To find strong opinions associated with a lack of knowledge about the issues involved is not unusual. Fre-

[15] See, for example, V. O. Key, Jr., *Public Opinion and American Democracy* (New York: Alfred A. Knopf, 1963); Harwood Childs, *Public Opinion* (Princeton: D. Van Nostrand, Inc., 1965); Bernard Hennessy, *Public Opinion* (Belmont: Wadsworth Publishing Company, 1965).

[16] Newcomb, Turner, and Converse, *op. cit.*, pp. 48-50.

[17] V. O. Key, Jr., *op. cit.*, Ch. 3 and 10.

[18] Newcomb, Turner, and Converse, *op. cit.*, pp. 58-63; Key, *op. cit.*, Ch. 11.

[19] Rokeach, *op. cit.*, pp. 116-18.

[20] Milton Rokeach, "The Role of Values in Public Opinion Research," *Public Opinion Quarterly*, 32 (Winter, 1968-69), pp. 547-59.

[21] For a discussion of this see Philip Converse, "Constraint and Variety in Belief Systems," in *Ideology and Discontent*, David Apter, ed. (New York: Free Press, 1964), pp. 207-08; Newcomb, Turner and Converse, *op. cit.*, pp. 149-52.

quently researchers find that the individual holding an opinion is unaware of its implications. Another aspect which can be studied is the degree of integration or isolation of attitudes or of opinions. An individual who operates at the level of ideology has well-integrated political attitudes, with each related to the others and internally consistent.[22]

In order to understand the nature of attitudes it is also useful to characterize certain aspects of the perceived objects which are the focus of the attitude. Among the characteristics of attitude objects on which researchers have focused are their dimensionality, inclusiveness, centrality to the individual, and social character.[23] Some objects involve a greater number and variety of elements than others; for example, studies have found that voting choice in France involves two dimensions: a clerical-anticlerical dimension and left-right dimension.[24] Only recently researchers have developed methods for more adequately treating multi-dimensional attitude objects.[25] The number of properties of an object, perceived as clusters, is known as inclusiveness. Thus, one can have a generalized attitude toward the federal government and distinct attitudes toward particular aspects such as the president, the Congress, a particular Supreme Court decision, and draft, defense, and welfare policies. The attitude toward the federal government would be much more inclusive than the attitude toward a particular Supreme Court decision. "Centrality of an attitude object" means the importance of the object to the individual or its persistence in his realm of awareness. Comparing a 20-year-old eligible for military service and a 65-year-old congressman, attitude toward military policies would probably be more central to the 20-year-old than to the congressman. An object need not be inclusive and central to an individual, it can be inclusive but remote; for example, the average citizen's attitudes on foreign aid policy, communism, or exploration of outer space.

There need not and usually is not a one-to-one correspondence between an attitude and related behavior. A number of attitudes may be related to a particular behavior. For example, a citizen may vote for a particular presidential candidate whose issue stands he prefers although he personally dislikes the candidate and also dislikes his political party. In this case, three attitudes are involved, focusing on three different objects, all of which are related to voting choice. The three kinds of atti-

[22] Converse, op. cit., pp. 208-09.
[23] Newcomb, Turner, and Converse, op. cit., pp. 50-66.
[24] Philip Converse, "The Problem of Party Distance in Models of Voting Change," in The Electoral Process, M. Kent Jennings and L. Harmon Ziegler, eds. (Englewood Cliffs, N.J.: Prentice-Hall, Inc., 1966), pp. 175-207.
[25] Clyde Coombs, A Theory of Data (New York: John Wiley and Sons, Inc., 1964), pp. 140-80.

tudes are: the evaluation of the candidates, the political parties, and the issues. The positive and strong intensity of affective orientation on the issue component outweighs the negative and the weak orientation on the other two components.

Other factors may also result in a tenuous link between an object and behavior. These factors include the situation in which the behavior occurs, motivation, and attitudes toward that situational context.[26] One study examined the acceptability of non-whites in public accommodations by writing letters to hotels and motels to inquire if non-whites were permitted to register; in this situation (written exchange of communications) more motels indicated that they would not register minority group members than was actually the case when non-whites tried to register in person. The face-to-face situation resulted in different behavior.[27] In addition, an attitude may remain latent until aroused by a particular motive, drive, or need.

SALIENCY AND PERCEPTION

The policy implications of values, beliefs, attitudes, and opinions has been a subject of much interest but limited research. Generally it is agreed that the policy implications are in part a consequence of the salience of the value, belief, attitude, or opinion to the individual.[28] Salience means "the importance or significance of the object." The connection with policy is also a function of the means elected for its expression and the perception of the public's concern with the issue by the policy-makers. This aspect has been labeled the "latency of opinion." Obviously, on any issue there is an attentive public, concerned about the problem, and an inattentive public.[29] However, politicians may be aware of the direction and intensity of attitudes held by an inattentive segment of the public which could be motivated to action by a pronouncement of public policy to which they would be opposed. Thus, if more stringent air safety rules for private planes are being considered, policy-makers are aware that owners of small private airplanes

[26] Rokeach has emphasized the need for evaluating attitude toward the situation as well as attitude toward the object. See *Beliefs, Attitudes, and Values, op. cit.,* pp. 126-28.

[27] B. Kutner, C. Wilkins, and P. R. Yarrow, "Verbal Attitudes and Overt Behavior Involving Racial Prejudice," *Journal of Abnormal and Social Psychology,* 47 (1952), pp. 649-52.

[28] Key, *op. cit.,* Ch. II.

[29] Key, *op. cit.,* p. 265.

may be angered by such a policy pronouncement and the policy-makers' actions may be inhibited without any activity by those who would oppose such a policy.

David Truman, in his discussion of policy-making, presented an analysis of the influence of interest groups in American politics.[30] Individuals who share a common attitude which may be activated by an event are referred to as a *potential interest group*. Latent attitudes mobilized by government actions and non-actions, resulting in political activity, were manifested in the 1963 March on Washington for civil rights, political protest demonstrations during the 1968 nominating conventions, electoral campaigns which developed various organizations to oppose the Viet Nam War, and defeat of open housing referenda in local elections. Mobilization of a latent attitude by a stimulus is not a simple response mechanism. Perceptual screens, imperfections of communications, and inadequate information impede the process. Studies of selective perception have resulted in a number of propositions about the process.

Generally individuals perceive only a small and non-random sample of the stimuli presented to them. Those actually perceived are a function of the nature of the stimulus previously learned, as it relates to the individual's development of a set of expectations about possible stimuli and the motives governing the individual at the time the stimulus is presented. Studies indicate that the intensity with which the stimulus is presented has a major influence on its perception or non-perception.[31] A newspaper account of a student riot presented on a paper's obituary page will not gain much attention; however, if the story becomes the page one headline feature and is the first story covered on the evening's national television networks' news programs, the stimulus is presented with much greater intensity. Likewise, if a political convention delegate reads about a riot in the paper, the stimulus is probably received with minimal intensity. However, if he is tear-gassed, clubbed, or shoved through a plate glass window, the stimulus is presented with a stronger intensity. People also tend to perceive those things they need or want; the greater the motivation, the greater the tendency to ignore nonrewarding cues. Hence, politicians under pressure to conclude a war with victory or an honorable peace, and generals under pressure from politicians to bring about such a conclusion, tend to perceive those stimuli which indicate the desired outcome will occur and not to per-

[30] David B. Truman, *The Governmental Process* (New York: Alfred A. Knopf, 1951).
[31] Bernard Berelson and Gary Steiner, *Human Behavior* (New York: Harcourt, Brace, and World, 1964), pp. 100-21.

ceive contradictory or unfavorable events. To the thirsty man in the desert, the mirage of an oasis appears. On the other hand, threatening stimuli such as hovering vultures tend not to be perceived. Experimental studies of perception indicate that when stimuli can be organized in several different ways, the best organization occurs in terms of continuity, simplicity, closure, and symmetry.[32] Both selection and organization of stimuli are affected by our expectations and motivations; i.e., we tend to perceive that which we expect, need, and desire. This can account, in part, for a politician predicting a sure victory in an up-coming election when he is about to experience an overwhelming defeat. In politics and policy-making, as elsewhere, the more ambiguous the stimulus and/or the stronger the motivation, the more the interpretation of the stimulus will be in the desired manner.

DETERMINANTS OF ATTITUDES

A number of determinants have been suggested by researchers in social psychology and political science. These have included changes in physiological conditions such as occur with maturation and aging; experiences within a particular institution, examples of which are child-rearing practices, socialization activities within an economic institution (corporation) or social organization (college fraternity), or brainwashing (communist prisoner-of-war treatment); non-verbal communication, such as facial expression or gestures; and verbal communications. Most studies of attitude change have focused on the effects of verbal communications.[33]

Formation of beliefs, attitudes, and values begins at an early age, with parents having the major influence in their formation. In later years education, personal experiences, peer-group's influence, and, perhaps, rebellion against parents and their attitudes, beliefs, and values, result in a deviation from earlier learned patterns.[34] However, children who rebel against their parents are more likely to carry that rebellion into politics if their parents are very interested in or active in politics.[35] This

---

[32] *Ibid.*, p. 108.

[33] See McGuire, *op. cit.*, for a review of types of determinants of attitudes and research on their effects.

[34] See Ch. 5, "Political Socialization," for a discussion of their influences.

[35] Eleanor Maccoby, Richard E. Matthews, and Anton S. Morton, "Youth and Political Change," in *Introductory Readings in Political Behavior*, ed. S. Sidney Ulmer (Chicago: Rand McNally and Company, 1961), pp. 75-85.

occurs infrequently in the United States because of the low salience of politics to most Americans. Research results indicate that individuals with more education differ in certain basic values and attitudes from those with less education, but we are not sure whether this is a consequence of education or of differences in family background and personal experiences. In other words, the selection process involved in who advances to higher levels of education may be the primary factor.[36] The suggestion that education results in a change or modification in earlier learned attitudes, beliefs, and values is based on several arguments. One is that education provides the informational base which can cause doubt of earlier learned patterns and can indicate the variety of alternatives available. Awareness of the range of alternatives presumably results in increased tolerance of alternative values and attitudes held by others.

ATTITUDE CHANGE

Considerable research on politically relevant attitudes has focused on the relationship between verbal communication and attitude change. One can structure analysis of the process in a number of ways. Harold Lasswell argued that we should focus on who says what to whom with what effect.[37] McGuire suggests that the independent variable of communication can be analyzed in terms of its source, message, channel, receiver, and destination. Source means "the characteristics of the perceived originator of the message." Message variables are the structure and content of what is communicated. Channel refers to the media by which the message is transmitted. Receiver variables refer to the personal characteristics of the individual for whom the message is intended. Destination factors include factors related to the message target, such as long-term versus short-term change or change in overt action as contrasted with change in attitude.[38]

The dependent variable of attitude change can be analyzed as a series of five elements: attention to the communication; comprehension of the message; yielding to the suggestion for change contained in the

[36] Kenneth P. Langton and M. Kent Jennings, "Political Socialization and the High School Civics Curriculum in the United States," American Political Science Review, 62 (September, 1968), p. 866.

[37] Harold Lasswell, Politics: Who Gets What, When, How (New York: Meridian Books, Inc., 1958), p. 26.

[38] McGuire, op. cit., p. 172.

message; retention of the attitude change; and action based on the changed attitude.[39]

Research has been directed toward examining the effect of the communication at each step of the five stage process contained within the dependent variable of attitude change. Experimental studies usually focus on the degree of resultant yielding to accept a new attitude (the third stage). Much of our interest in political research is the final step of the attitude change process — the action which results from the communications persuasion effort. Thus, a political campaign director is concerned with the effectiveness of his candidate's television presentations in building support. Other political concern might be with enticing voters to adopt a new party affiliation (stage three) or the action consequences of adopting a new party identification (stage five).

Undoubtedly there is considerable interaction among the five components of the independent variable; for example, the impact of source credibility is probably affected by the structure of the message. One cannot adequately assess the impact of one aspect of the independent variable without taking into account the other four elements.[40] It may be that not all the suggested five stages of the attitude change (dependent variable) are always present in an attitude change situation. For example, if post-hypnotic suggestion is effective, no conscious yielding by the subject to the suggestion of the hypnotist would have occurred.[41]

Research on the influence of peer groups on political attitudes indicates that the prevailing norms have considerable influence on basic values and attitudes. Changes in attitudes among adults can also be accounted for in part by peer group influence; the upward social mobiles may change to conform to the values and attitudes of the new peer group. Thus, the young lawyer of working class origin may become an active supporter of the Republican Party after joining a Wall Street law firm. Geographical mobility may have the same effect, with a Yankee Republican who moves to the deep South becoming a Democrat to conform to his new peer group's political preferences. Conformity to the new peer group's political views is more likely to occur when politics is

[39] *Ibid.*, p. 173. See also Milton J. Rosenberg, Carl I. Hovland, William J. McGuire, Robert P. Abelson, and Jack W. Brehm, *Attitude Organization and Change* (New Haven: Yale University Press, 1960); Muzafer Sherif and Carl I. Hovland, *Social Judgment* (New Haven: Yale University Press, 1961); and Carl I. Hovland, Irving L. Janis, and Harold H. Kelley, *Communication and Persuasion* (New Haven: Yale University Press, 1953).

[40] McGuire, *op. cit.*, p. 174.

[41] For a discussion of this and other possible instances of attitude change where all five elements of attitude change may not be present, see McGuire, *op. cit.*, pp. 174-75.

important to the group and when acceptance by the new peer group is important to the individual.[42]

A number of researchers have examined the influence of social groups on the creation, retention, and alteration of beliefs and values. An individual is more likely to work for group goals and conform to group norms when he accepts and clearly understands the group goal and perceives the group contributing to attaining his own goals. Conformity is more likely among individuals with average rather than high or low acceptance in the group. Conformity will also be greater to the extent that cooperation is necessary for the attainment of group goals, if the group perceives itself as threatened by attack from outsiders, and if group membership is highly attractive to the individual member. The higher the status of the group and the fewer the attractive alternative groups, the more attractive group membership is likely to become to the individual. Pressure to conform is usually greater in a small group than in a larger one. Frequency of contact and degree of mutual liking also affect the degree of conformity to group norms. Research has also indicated that members are more likely to conform to group norms if they participate in the making of group decisions.[43]

Stimuli are more likely to be accepted or to be attended to if they come from trusted sources (friends as compared to strangers, radio and television rather than newspapers). If stimuli appear reasoned and objective rather than emotional and subjective, they are more likely to produce change; individuals tend not to perceive stimuli which are heavily fear-arousing, so that a message is more likely to be perceived if it is moderately threatening.[44]

Certain personality types are more receptive to particular kinds of messages than other personality types. The authoritarian personality is characterized by submissiveness to authority, rigidity of opinions, concern with toughness and power, generalized hostility, conformity to con-

[42] For a more extensive discussion of these findings, see Sidney Verba, *Small Groups and Political Behavior* (Princeton: Princeton University Press, 1961), pp. 22-45; A. Paul Hare, *Handbook of Small Group Research* (New York: Free Press, 1962); Clovis R. Shepherd, *Small Groups* (San Francisco: Chandler Publishing Company, 1964); Charles A. Kiesler and Sara B. Kiesler, *Conformity* (Reading, Mass.: Addison-Wesley Publishing Company, 1969); Robert E. Lane and David O. Sears, *Public Opinion* (Englewood Cliffs, N.J.: Prentice-Hall, Inc., 1964), pp. 34-42; Hovland, Janis, and Kelley, *Communication and Persuasion, op. cit.*

[43] *Ibid.*

[44] Bernard Hennessy, "Public Opinion and Opinion Change," in *Political Science Annual,* Vol. 1, ed. James A. Robinson (Indianapolis: Bobbs-Merrill Company, Inc., 1966), pp. 274-75. McGuire, *op. cit.,* pp. 203-05, summarizes research which indicates the degree of relationship between fear arousal and attitude change may be curvilinear. Intervening variables may be the individual's level of anxiety (need or motive) and the complexity of the message.

ventional values, and projection of unconscious emotional impulses.[45] Authoritarians are likely to change their attitudes and opinions when someone accepted as authoritative endorses the position that would represent a change. Some individuals are highly susceptible to opinion change, others are resistant to change. Those susceptible to change tend to agree with whatever suggestion or statement is made to them; those resistant to change give a negative response to whatever suggestion is made to them. The argument has been made that this "response set" is related to personality characteristics.[46]

These generalizations can be used to account for variations in holding values, attitudes, and beliefs. For example, if we were to interview northern Republican migrants to southern cities or to interview central city Democrats who have moved to suburbia and to attempt to explain their change in party affiliation or lack of change, these generalizations would be useful. They are concerned with the processes by which changes in attitudes, values, and beliefs are brought about. Much research on attitude change has been conducted, and several alternative approaches to understanding attitude change have resulted.

Several different theories of attitude change have been developed by psychologists. Frequently cited in political science is cognitive dissonance theory developed by Leon Festinger, which predicts that inconsistency between cognitive elements will not be tolerated by the individual if the inconsistency is above a certain magnitude.[47] Festinger defines cognition as "any knowledge, opinion, or belief about the environment, about oneself, or about one's behavior."[48] Dissonance is a relationship with two elements being in dissonance with each other if, "considering these two alone, the obverse of one element would follow from the other."[49] As an example, if one believes smoking cigarettes causes lung cancer and one smokes cigarettes, the two elements are dissonant. Cognitive dissonance can have a number of sources, such as exposure to new information, realization of logical inconsistency, cultural values, conflicting past experiences, the withdrawal of previously existing social support, or

---

[45] T. W. Adorno, Else Frenkel-Brunswik, Daniel J. Levinson, and R. Nevitt Sanford, The Authoritarian Personality (New York: Science Editions, 1964), Part I, p. 228.

[46] See McGuire, op. cit., pp. 241-43, for a review of research findings.

[47] Leon Festinger, A Theory of Cognitive Dissonance (Stanford: Stanford University Press, 1957).

[48] Ibid., p. 3.

[49] Ibid., p. 13.

change in another contingent opinion.[50] The pressure to reduce dissonance would be a function of the magnitude of the dissonance. Festinger suggests that dissonance can be reduced by changing behavior, by changing the situation to which a cognitive element belongs (which may contradict reality), or by adding new cognitive elements.[51] To return to our example of the smoker who views smoking as contributing to lung cancer, he can reduce his dissonance by giving up smoking cigarettes, or he can start using a filter in the belief that this adequately reduces the inhalation of cancer-causing agents, or he can read and believe articles which claim that scientific research has not "proven" that smoking cigarettes causes cancer.

Reduction of dissonance may be inhibited by the resistance to change of behavioral or environmental cognitive elements. Festinger also suggests that the maximum dissonance which can exist is equal to the resistance to change of the least resistant element.[52] If two cognitive elements are highly resistant to change, a high level of dissonance would be created. Thus, if one intensely dislikes a particular political candidate but has a strong attachment to the candidate's party and has always supported the nominees of that party, a high degree of dissonance is created.

Festinger's work has stimulated considerable further research which has utilized his approach to attitude change, and he and others have conducted a number of studies which have contributed to the elaboration and refinement of his theory.[53] The propositions contained in his work are presented in such a format that they can be tested using a variety of types of subject matter. For example, one variable considered in the theory of cognitive dissonance is the role of social support in the retention or change in cognitive elements. The magnitude of dissonance created by an individual's expressing an opinion contrary to one's own is related to both the number of other cognitive elements which are consonant with one's own and the number of individuals with whom one knows opinions are shared. The more of either, the less the magnitude of dissonance. Other relevant variables include one's assessment of both the relevance and the attractiveness of the individual or group expressing a contrary opinion and the degree of dissonance between the

[50] *Ibid.*, pp. 12 15.
[51] *Ibid.*, pp. 18-24.
[52] *Ibid.*, pp. 28-29.
[53] See Leon Festinger, *Conflict, Decision, and Dissonance* (Stanford: Stanford University Press, 1964); J. W. Brehm and A. R. Cohen, *Explorations in Cognitive Dissonance* (New York: John Wiley and Sons, Inc., 1962).

total clusters of cognitive elements of which the two dissonant elements are a part.[54]

Reduction in dissonance resulting from social disagreement can be brought about by changing one's own opinion, influencing those expressing the contrary opinion to change or at least to reduce the magnitude of the disagreement, or to discount in some way the person or group expressing the dissonant opinion. One can attribute the other's conflicting opinion to motives, experiences, or other characteristics different from one's own and hence allowable.

The propositions about dissonance and change in cognitive elements as a consequence of social support variables provide a theoretical base which can be used in examining many aspects of political behavior. For example, one can test hypotheses about change in vote intention as a consequence of changes in perceptions of social support for the candidates, or one could study voting behavior in the legislature as a function of consonance between significant cue givers and other legislators on policy issues or party affiliation. Thus, one advantage of Festinger's theory of cognitive dissonance is that it is formulated in such a way that it lends itself easily to empirical research focusing on a number of different substantive questions. The concepts can easily be operationalized, and data can be collected for the testing of hypotheses using both experimental and survey research methods.

Other approaches to creating theories of attitude change have been developed in psychology. One is the functional approach, in which one studies the functions performed by the attitudes and opinions for the individual; attitudes change because the needs of the individual change.[55]

One example of the functional approach to the study of attitudes is

---

[54] For a recent assessment of varieties of cognitive consistency theory, see *Theories of Cognitive Consistency: A Sourcebook*, Robert P. Abelson, Elliot Aronson, William J. McGuire, Theodore M. Newcomb, Milton J. Rosenberg, Percy H. Tannenbaum, eds. (Chicago: Rand McNally and Company, 1968). For other presentations of several varieties of attitude and attitude change theory, see Milton J. Rosenberg, Carl I. Hovland, William J. McGuire, Robert P. Abelson, and Jack W. Brehm, *Attitude Organization and Change* (New Haven: Yale University Press, 1960); Muzafer Sherif and Carl I. Hovland, *Social Judgment* (New Haven: Yale University Press, 1961); Charles E. Osgood and Percy Tannenbaum, "The Principle of Congruity in the Prediction of Attitude Change," *Psychological Review*, 62 (1955), pp. 42-55; Fritz Heider, "Attitude and Cognitive Organization," *Journal of Psychology* 21 (1946), pp. 107-12; Dorwin Cartwright and Frank Harary, "Structural Balance: A Generalization of Heider's Theory," *Psychological Review*, 63 (1956), pp. 277-93; Chester A. Insko, *Theories of Attitude Change* (New York: Appleton-Century-Crofts, 1967); and Roger Brown, *Social Psychology* (New York: The Free Press, 1965), Ch. 11.

[55] M. Brewster Smith, Jerome Bruner, and Robert W. White, *Opinions and Personality* (New York: John Wiley and Sons, Science Editions, 1964), p. 56.

provided by *Opinions and Personality*, an assessment of the psychological functions for the individuals sampled of their attitudes toward the Soviet Union. The researchers defined an attitude as "a predisposition to experience, to be motivated by, and to act toward, a class of objects in a predictable manner."[56] The characteristics of an object include differentiation, saliency, time perspective, informational support, and object value; with saliency being defined as "the extent to which a particular object or class of objects is central to the everyday concerns of a person."[57] The researchers declined to make a distinction between attitudes and opinions, as both refer to the kind of predisposition with which they were concerned.[58]

Smith, Bruner, and White were concerned in *Opinions and Personality* with the adjustive functions served by an individual's holding a certain opinion toward the Soviet Union, with the possible functions of holding an opinion being object appraisal, social adjustment, and externalization. By object appraisal is meant assistance in evaluating or assessing objects (or situations) with reference to their relationship to one's own interests. A second function is that of facilitating (or disrupting) one's relations with others. The third function is that of externalization; this occurs when analogies between external events and inner, personal problems are perceived, and the attitude established is a reflection of the method which the individual has adopted for dealing with his inner difficulty. This works as a tension-reduction mechanism for the individual.[59]

To evaluate the functions of attitudes, the researchers did an in-depth study of opinions toward Russia held by ten men. From these case studies they drew a number of conclusions about the functions of attitudes or opinions. They found that the attitudes of the ten men had different contents, were differently structured, and had differing valences. The orientations toward the Soviet Union could be characterized as approach, avoidance, or hostility. In the political realm, such a wide range of opinion must be expressed through a narrow range of policy alternatives. A vast complex of varying opinions held by many different individuals may result in a common pattern of support for a particular policy. One might conclude that both pollsters and politicians would be well advised not to infer too much about the underlying bases for responses to very simply structured policy opinion questions in the popular polls.

[56] *Ibid.*, p. 35.
[57] *Ibid.*, p. 33.
[58] *Ibid.*, pp. 39-43.
[59] *Ibid.*, pp. 253-79.

The ways in which attitudes toward the Soviet Union contributed to object appraisal, externalization, and social adjustment functions for the ten subjects were noted by the researchers. Thus, they found that the functions of attitudes or opinions for each individual were a result of the role played by the attitude in mediating personal requirements. The requirement which predominates determines whether the individual might be considered to be reacting rationally or emotionally. In addition, the method by which change in attitudes could be effected would be a result of which requirement predominates and what function is being served by an attitude.[60]

While their sample was much too small to test adequately the propositions suggested, the research did generate a number of additional hypotheses and thereby contribute to the development of a functional approach to the study of attitudes and attitude change.

Other alternative approaches for studying attitude change are to study it as a consequence of learning processes[61] or as a consequence of perceptual processes. In the learning theory approach, one studies the relationship between the independent variable and aspects of learning; a relationship between the independent variable and attitude change is predicted. Thus, presentation of persuasive materials about a candidate is predicted to have an effect on his attitude toward the candidate. Unfortunately, these psychological theories of attitude change have yet to be fully developed; certain inconsistencies between aspects of the theories and research results remain to be resolved. In addition, political scientists have all too frequently not designed their research to focus on change in attitudes, beliefs, and opinions; research also tends to be inadequately anchored in psychological theories of attitude-opinion-belief formation, activation, stability, and change.

THE STUDY OF VALUES

Most of the research and theorizing on the subjects of values, beliefs, attitudes, and opinions has focused on attitudes and opinions. Several reasons can be given for this; undoubtedly one is attentive public concern — catered to by mass media — with public opinion on political and social issues. Certainly it is easier to measure opinion than it is to measure attitudes, beliefs, and values. Considerable research has been conducted by social psychologists on attitude formation and change; the

[60] Ibid.
[61] See Hovland, Janis and Kelley, op. cit.

methods and theories developed by the psychologists have been borrowed for application in studying problems of interest to political scientists, such as factors related to legislative, judicial, and mass public voting behavior. The failure to focus on the study of value holdings and their role in political behavior may also be a consequence of the scientific orientation of the discipline. The rejection of the idea of the superiority of particular values being scientifically provable may also be carried over to the rejection of the study of the influence of differences in value patterns on political behavior. However, Milton Rokeach has suggested that greater understanding of political behavior can be achieved by determining the value systems which are associated with different patterns of behavior. Rokeach defines an attitude as "an enduring organization of several beliefs focused on a specific object or situation, predisposing one to respond in some preferential manner,"[62] while "values, on the other hand, transcend specific objects and specific situations: values have to do with *modes of conduct and end-states of exist*ence. More formally, to say that a person has a value is to say that he has an enduring belief that a particular mode of conduct or that a particular end-state of existence is personally and socially preferable to alternative modes of conduct or end-states of existence."[63] As such, a value provides a standard of motives, wants, actions, and attitudes which can be used to justify and rationalize one's life patterns. Values are organized into value systems, which are hierarchical rank orderings of importance.[64] Rokeach in his own research has found that individuals with different value systems have different attitude structures and behave different politically. Individuals with different value systems were found to differ in attitudes toward civil rights, in liberalism-conservatism, and in candidate preference.[65]

For example, in a 1968 sample survey of the United States voting population, the mean ranking of the terminal value of *peace* was seventh for liberals, eleventh for middle-of-the-roaders, and fifteenth for conservatives. (Terminal values were defined as end-states of existence.)[66] The terminal value of *equality* was ranked among the eighteen terminal values as follows by supporters of different presidential candidates in 1968:[67]

[62] Rokeach, "The Role of Values in Public Opinion Research," *op. cit.*, p. 550.
[63] *Ibid.*
[64] *Ibid.*, p. 551.
[65] *Ibid.*, pp. 556-60, "Voters and Value Systems," Washington *Post*, August 11, 1968, p. B1.
[66] Rokeach, "The Role of Values in Public Opinion Research," *op. cit.*, p. 556.
[67] Rokeach, "Voters and Value Systems," *op. cit.*

	Equality
R. Kennedy	4
McCarthy	6
Johnson	4
Rockefeller	9
Nixon	12
Reagan	10
Wallace	14

Based on his analysis of a sample of the 1968 national electorate, Rokeach concluded that the overall terminal value structure of Wallace supporters was closest to those of Nixon and Reagan supporters, Rockefeller adherents were closer to Senator Eugene McCarthy's in terminal value systems, and Johnson supporters were closest to Robert Kennedy's in terminal value structure. However, for both terminal and instrumental values, differences were not extreme. In contrast, a study of differences in the value systems of supporters of different parties or candidates in Italy, France, or Germany might produce quite dissimilar patterns of value hierarchies between adherents of different parties in each country.

SUMMARY AND CRITIQUE

What arguments can be made for focusing on the study of values instead of on attitudes, beliefs, and opinions? The best argument, of course, would be that we can better explain the behavior of individuals if we know their value systems. However, that assertion only can be made after adequate research, and very little research has been done on the relationships between individual value systems and individual political behavior. Rokeach gives the following argument for focusing on the study of values rather than the study of attitudes: first, value is a more dynamic concept as it includes the study of motivation; secondly, values are determinants of attitudes as well as of behavior. Assuming an individual has fewer values than attitudes, it is more economical in terms of research time and effort to study values. In addition, value is also a relevant concept in a greater number of academic disciplines. Therefore a greater number of perspectives and greater inter-disciplinary efforts can be brought to bear on the research.[68]

The wide use in research of conceptual frameworks involving beliefs, attitudes, and/or values in political analysis indicates the utility which this theoretical approach has in political analysis. A number of problems of interest to political scientists can be researched using this analytical approach; studies of voting behavior,[69] political culture,[70] political recruitment,[71] comparative political elites,[72] and political and economic development[73] have made use of one or more of the concepts. The elaborate body of research and generalizations which exists in psychology and social psychology also enhances the attractiveness of a value-belief-attitude approach to the study of political behavior.

An additional advantage of a value-belief-attitude approach is that it can easily be used in combination with learning theory, communications theory, or decision-making approaches to study very complex research problems. For example, one can examine the calculus of legislative decision-making through a study of the attitudes, beliefs, and values which the freshmen legislators bring to the legislature, their acquisition of new or modification of existing values, beliefs, and attitudes, and their learning to respond to certain types of cues in decision-making.

However, studies of the influence of attitudes, beliefs, and values in political behavior have been hampered and the development of useful theory impeded by a number of methodological problems. The multiplicity of definitions of essential concepts, differences in manipulation of independent variables, alternative methods of initial measurement of variables and of assessment of the effects of manipulation, and variations in assumptions underlying the research efforts have inhibited the development of a consistent, cumulative body of knowledge. For example, suppose we wished to find out the effects of exposure to a can-

[68] Rokeach, Beliefs, Attitudes, and Values, op. cit., pp. 157-58.

[69] Angus Campbell, Philip Converse, Warren Miller, and Donald Stokes, The American Voter (New York: John Wiley and Sons, 1960); Donald R. Matthews and James W. Prothro, Negroes and the New Southern Politics (New York: Harcourt, Brace, and World, 1966).

[70] Almond and Verba, op. cit.

[71] David C. Schwartz, "Toward a Theory of Political Recruitment," Western Political Quarterly, 22 (September, 1969), pp. 552-71.

[72] Karl Deutsch, Lewis J. Edinger, Roy C. Macridis, and Richard L. Merritt, France, Germany, and the Western Alliance: A Study of Elite Attitudes on European Integration (New York: Charles Scribner's Sons, 1967).

[73] Samuel Huntington, Political Order in Changing Societies (New Haven: Yale University Press, 1968); Daniel Lerner, The Passing of Traditional Society (New York: The Free Press, 1958).

didate's campaign efforts in which the same message is presented in two different ways. In one method of presentation, the candidate makes the statement directly into the television camera, with the visual image of the candidate the only image on the screen. The alternative method is a presentation of scenes of the candidate at work, with his family, and campaigning, while a narrator presents the spoken message. The desired effects are an attitude change bringing about support for the candidate among those who did not previously support him and a reinforcement of support among those who did. The task in such a situation would include a measurement of the change which has occurred. How can the change be measured? A number of methods have been used to measure attitude change in various studies; these include the percentage of subjects showing any change, those showing positive change, those indicating a specified amount of change, indicators among subjects of net change, and the ratio of change occurring for all subjects. In addition, while attitudes are sometimes defined as having both affective and cognitive components, measurement usually focuses on only one. If we can discuss several different dimensions of attitude structures and if these have implications for behavior, then our measurement ought to take into account these different dimensions.

The impact of values, beliefs, and attitudes — and change in these — upon political behavior can be studied and understood better when an appropriate theory or theories are developed. These would provide us with a common definition of the key concepts and with criteria for operationalizing them; researchers would be more likely to use a standard method of measuring change and variables which might affect change and to have appropriate criteria for evaluating the effects of independent variables.

Political Socialization

5

INTRODUCTION

How do individuals learn the attitudes, beliefs, and values they hold about political objects? How do they learn different political roles, whether the role be that of voter, revolutionary activist, interest group member, campaign worker, or legislator? In summary, by what processes do individuals learn patterns of political behavior? We can ask additional questions, such as; is there a particular sequence to the learning of patterns of political behavior which occurs in all countries or in all parts of the society of a particular country? Are there, for instance, urban-rural, north-south, or black-white differences in the processes of learning and the patterns learned in the United States? If differences do exist, what factors can account for these differences?

Although interest in the socialization of citizens to politics is as old as the writings of Aristotle and Plato, it has been a subject of renewed interest in the past decades, and particularly in the past ten years.[1] In part this interest may have been stimulated by recognition of new nations' need to instill in their citizens support for the political community (nation), the regime (the political institutions and rules of the game), and the occupants of political roles. Nations which have undergone a sharp change in the nature of the regime, such as the countries in eastern Europe, or frequent changes in regime structure, such as France, have also been faced with this problem of educating citizens, both young and old, to acceptance of the regime and its political leaders. The riots, protests, and demonstrations directed against aspects of the American political system in recent years have also stimulated interest in the processes and consequences of political socialization.

DEFINITIONS OF POLITICAL SOCIALIZATION

A number of alternative definitions of political socialization have been used by political researchers. It has been defined as the learning of politically relevant social patterns which correspond to the individual's social positions, as these are mediated through various social agents or roles.[2] Others have given it a broader definition.[3] Fred Greenstein defines political socialization as

> . . . all political learning, formal and informal, deliberate and unplanned, at every stage of the life cycle, including not only explicitly political learning but also nominally non-political

[1] Other academic disciplines have been concerned with the study of socialization and have contributed to the study of political socialization. Cultural anthropologists and sociologists have studied the socialization of both children and adults to appropriate role behavior in different societies and the development of various personality characteristics. Several approaches to psychiatry focus on the effects of primarily childhood socializing experiences on the personality of the adult. The authors of a comparative study of political culture in five nations acknowledge the influence on their work of the psycho-cultural approach to studying political phenomena. See Gabriel Almond and Sidney Verba, *The Civic Culture* (Boston: Little, Brown and Company, 1965), p. 11.

[2] Herbert Hyman, *Political Socialization* (New York: The Free Press, 1959), p. 25.

[3] According to Robert LeVine, "political socialization is the acquisition by an individual of behavioral dispositions relevant to political groups, political systems, and political processes. Examples of the kinds of behavior dispositions included are: attitudes concerning the allocation of authority, the legitimacy of a regime, and political participation; patterns of decision-making and deference; images of leaders and foreign nations; group loyalties, antagonisms, and stereotypes." Robert LeVine, "Political Socialization and Cultural Change," in *Old Societies and New States*, Clifford Geetz ed. (New York: The Free Press, 1963), pp. 280-81, footnote 1.

learning that affects political behavior, such as learning of politically relevant social attitudes and the acquisition of politically relevant personality characteristics.[4]

Other definitions shift from a focus on the individual to a focus on the system as actor on the individual or to an emphasis on the context of the socialization process as either perpetuating or creating the learned patterns which are considered appropriate. An example of this approach is provided by Gabriel Almond's discussion of political socialization. Almond raised the question,

> What do we mean by the function of political socialization? We mean that all political systems tend to perpetuate their cultures and sub-cultures through time, and that they do this mainly by means of the socialization influences of the primary and secondary structures through which the young of the society pass in the process of maturation . . . Political socialization is the process of induction into the political culture. Its end product is a set of attitudes, cognitions, value standards, and feelings—toward the political system, its various roles, and role incumbents. It also includes knowledge of values affecting, and feelings toward the inputs of demands and claims into the system, and its authoritative outputs.[5]

Definitions of political socialization have been criticized for tending to emphasize only learning which is supportive of the existing political culture and political system. To avoid this problem, perhaps political socialization would be better defined as "developmental processes through which persons acquire political orientations and patterns of behavior."[6]

The different definitions of political socialization indicate some of the variations in focus which the study of political socialization has taken. One emphasis has been on the character of a country's political culture and its persistence or change over time.[7] An alternative is the

[4] Fred I. Greenstein, "Political Socialization," in *International Encyclopedia of the Social Sciences*, Vol. 14 (New York: Crowell-Collier and Macmillan, 1968), p. 551.

[5] Gabriel A. Almond, "A Functional Approach to Comparative Politics," in *The Politics of Developing Areas*, G. Almond and J. S. Coleman, eds. (Princeton: Princeton University Press, 1960), pp. 27-28.

[6] David Easton and Jack Dennis, *Children in the Political System* (New York: McGraw-Hill Book Company, 1969), p. 7.

[7] Almond and Verba, *op. cit.*; Lucian Pye, *Politics, Personality and Nation-Building* (New Haven: Yale University Press, 1962); Henry W. Ehrmann, *France* (Boston: Little, Brown and Company, 1968); Lewis J. Edinger, *Germany* (Boston: Little, Brown, and Company, 1968); Easton and Dennis, *op. cit.*

origins and development of individual political orientations.[8] Thus political socialization has been used in the analysis of different political systems and the analysis of the political behavior of individuals.

MODELS OF LEARNING

Several different explanations for learning have been developed by learning theorists in psychology. However, these can be divided into two different schools, cognitive theories and connectionist theories. Connectionist theories view learning as the process of associating stimuli with the appropriate responses. Connectionist theories differ in the names given the connection, the importance of variations in individual characteristics in learning, and the emphasis given to rewards and reinforcement in the learning process. Cognitive theorists emphasize the cognitions (beliefs, perceptions, or attitudes) held by the individual and the influences of these cognitions on the individual's interactions with his environment. Learning, then, to cognitive theorists, is the study of the acquisition and modification of these cognitions. Within each of these two approaches a number of variations in theoretical formulations have developed.[9]

Most research on political socialization has been descriptive, oriented toward measuring the type and degree of political orientations held. Critics suggest more emphasis should be placed on how the orientations are learned. Several models of learning could be used in accounting for the way individuals acquire their orientations to politics.

The accumulation model assumes that acquisition of political knowledge proceeds by additions of units of knowledge without a consistent logical connection between information and attitudes, with no particular sequence in the learning process, and with no assumptions about the limitations on learning inherent in the properties of children at a particular age level.[10] An alternative model presents the proposition that a child's capacity to develop certain kinds of political orientations

[8] Hyman, op. cit.; Lewis A. Froman, Jr., "Personality and Political Socialization," *Journal of Politics*, 23 (May, 1961); Fred I. Greenstein, *Children and Politics* (New Haven: Yale University Press, 1965); Robert D. Hess and Judith V. Torney, *The Development of Political Attitudes in Children* (Chicago: Aldine Publishing Company, 1967).

[9] For a discussion of various theories of learning, see Winfred F. Hill, *Learning: A Survey of Psychological Interpretations* (San Francisco: Chandler Publishing Company, 1963).

[10] Hess and Torney, op. cit., p. 19.

is limited by his stages of cognitive development.[11] Piaget's research on concept formation in children lends support to the latter model.[12]

A distinction can be made between direct and indirect political socialization.[13] Indirect socialization means the learning of non-political but politically relevant aspects of behavior; this includes personality characteristics and orientations toward various roles and role relationships, such as orientations toward figures of authority. In contrast, direct learning experiences are explicitly political in content.

One form of indirect learning is that of interpersonal transfer, in which explicit predispositions, such as orientations to authority, are developed. The underlying assumption is that patterns learned in other social roles are transferred to political roles. Hence, orientations developed in the family, the school, and work experience are transferred to the individual's role expectations for authority figures in the political system. A second form of indirect learning is that of apprenticeship, in which skills and values necessary for performance of political roles are developed. In this fashion children's organizations such as the Boy Scouts, 4-H clubs, church groups, and the extra-curricular activities in the schools serve as agents of political socialization. The individual learns to accept the rules of the organization and to participate. A third and related type of indirect political socialization is the extension of general social values onto the political system. The beliefs and values of the general culture have their extensions or manifestations in the political system; for example, a low sense of personal effectiveness has been found to be related to a low sense of political effectiveness. The processes of indirect political socialization are continuous throughout the life cycle, changing and occurring with variations in the individual's circumstances. Parenthetically, a feedback process probably exists whereby the existence of democracy in one social system may result in increased demands for democracy in another, such as the work group or school or family. An example is the demand by students for more participation in university and college decision-making. Awareness of this feedback process may have been present in Soviet Russia's fears of democratic processes in the economy and society as proposed by Czech liberals in the late 1960s. The existence of democracy in those spheres probably would have stimulated demands for greater participation in the Communist party's and government's decision-making activities.

[11] *Ibid.*, pp. 21-22.

[12] Jean Piaget's research is discussed in Henry W. Maier, *Three Theories of Child Development* (New York: Harper and Row, 1968), revised edition.

[13] For a more extensive discussion of direct and indirect socialization, see Hess and Torney, *op. cit.*, pp. 19-22; Richard Dawson and Kenneth Prewitt, *Political Socialization* (Boston: Little, Brown and Company, 1968), Ch.5.

A number of direct modes of political socialization exist.[14] Imitation of the political orientations and behavior of others is one major direct socialization process. The acquisition of political party identification by young children, copying that of their parents, can be explained in these terms; the adoption by a wife of her husband's political attitudes, including party identification, is also explainable through this type of learning process. A second type of direct learning is anticipatory socialization; in such a process individuals adopt the political orientations, role expectations, and role behaviors appropriate to a future role which they wish to acquire in the political arena, whether it be as partisan voter, party official, or candidate for elective office. Thus, in high school and college, adherents of political parties who aspire to political roles develop orientations and behaviors appropriate to the desired future role through their participation in the Young Democrats, Young Republicans, or other political clubs. A third type of direct socialization is provided by the activities of the educational system and other agencies such as the family, church, or social groups which work directly to create political attitudes and patterns of behavior. The high school civics curriculum, with such courses as Problems of Democracy, American Government, and American History, represents a deliberate attempt at political socialization. Such courses usually aim at developing support for the political community and the regime. In some nations, such as communist China, support for incumbent political leaders is also a major objective of the educational system's efforts. Rituals such as saluting the flag, singing the national anthem, or studying major historical events or the sayings and speeches of political leaders are used to create the desired political orientations through the educational system. Expressions by teachers of their own attitudes may also have a direct but perhaps unintended effect on their students' political orientations. A fourth type of direct political education occurs through the impact of direct political experiences on the individual. A political campaign, an incident with a representative of the regime such as a policeman, legislator, welfare worker, housing inspector, zoning official, or highway worker, or an appearance in court may have an effect on the individual's political orientations toward the regime, role incumbents, or even the political community. Direct political experiences shape one's expectations, orientations, and future behavior in political roles. Admittedly, it is easier to study political orientations of individuals and the activities of socializing agents than it is to study the actual process of learning those political orientations.[15]

[14] Dawson and Prewitt, *op. cit.*, pp. 73-80.
[15] *Ibid.*, p. 80.

As an example of political learning we can examine the process by which a regime acts to foster support for itself from the public through the creation of a sense of regime legitimacy; the process has been analyzed by Richard Merelman. Legitimacy means that the government is viewed as having the moral right to exercise authority over the individual; obedience is given not because of penalties such as imprisonment which will be imposed if one does not obey but because one believes he has an obligation to accede to the rules and regulations enacted and enforced by the government.[16] Merelman suggests that the development of legitimacy for a regime is a six-stage stimulus-response learning process, the first stage being that of unconditioned reinforcement. The regime provides the stimulus for the populace in the form of material inducements such as food, security, and shelter, or the provision of situations in which these can be acquired. The population responds through learning how to acquire these inducements and this serves as a reinforcement. The second stage is that of classical conditioning, in which the regime associates itself with the stimulus which provokes the behavior in the first stage, the association occurring through institutions or processes being paired with the unconditioned stimulus of material inducements. The government thus becomes the cue for the stimulus and the reward. In the third stage, that of intermittent reinforcement, the government needs to provide the reward only intermittently, which reduces the cost of providing the reward. In the fourth stage, a new behavior pattern is demanded of the population by the regime; the response demanded is given because the government assures the citizens that if they respond, the regime will produce the institutional processes which symbolize unconditional reinforcement. This stage of secondary reinforcement is followed by the stage of cognitive dissonance; having submitted to the demand for the new behavior pattern, the population shifts the positive affect toward the regime into a conferring of legitimacy on the regime. This is done to reduce the cognitive dissonance (the discrepancy between attitudes or attitudes and cognitions) between gaining primarily symbolic rewards and having to learn new behavior patterns. The last stage in this learning of legitimacy process is the development and use of condensation symbols, in which the symbols of legitimacy become substitute gratifications.

Condensation symbols may include the nation's flag, Constitution, national heroes, and slogans such as "the American way of life" and

[16] Legitimacy, according to Merelman, is "the quality of 'oughtness' that is perceived by the public to inhere in a political regime. That government is legitimate which is viewed as morally proper for a society." Richard Merelman, "Learning and Legitimacy," *American Political Science Review*, 60 (September, 1966), p. 548.

"the law of the land." A number of problems exist in the use of such symbols; the regime must attempt to minimize the discontinuity between symbols and policy, to restrain the application of the symbol to the appropriate politics so as to maintain the symbol's credibility, and to generate new legitimacy symbols, as symbols over time tend to be broadly applied and to lose their effectiveness. For example, President Lyndon Johnson's justification of the United States' increased participation in the Viet Nam war utilized such symbols as "our national interest" and "protecting the right of a people to determine through democratic processes their own form of government." New symbols must be generated over time; one source of new symbols is campaign rhetoric, as for example the slogans "New Deal," "New Frontier," and "The Great Society."

Symbols can be used to increase the rate of learning, with the symbols conveying either a negative or positive sanction. According to Merelman, the three different ways of using symbols are in opposition, avoidance, or pure reward.[17] For example, in opposition, if an individual opposes the war in Viet Nam, he is accused of acting against the national interest. The avoidance use of a symbol would entail being told that all who support the war are acting in the national interest. Merelman asserts that national policy is usually formulated and presented to the public in terms of avoidance and escape use of symbols. It should be pointed out that this multi-stage process is not sequential, as an individual comes to accept certain sixth-stage condensation symbols, while he simultaneously is in another stage relative to another problem of government policy and legitimacy.

DISCONTINUITIES IN POLITICAL SOCIALIZATION

Problems exist in political socialization in that individuals may be incorrectly socialized, for the institutions and political cultures to which they are socialized may change over time, creating an incongruence between learned orientations and the actual political system. During the time lags between early learning of political orientations and the actual time of entry into participation in the political system, political arrangements may change, with the structure of institutions altering or with a shift in their roles occurring.[18] A second source of discontinuity is the presenta-

---

[17] *Ibid.*, p. 555.

[18] A key focus in the five-nation study conducted by Almond and Verba was the degree of consistency between the orientations of the citizens and the political institutions of the society. Almond and Verba, *op. cit.*, Ch. 1.

tion of different stimuli by various socializing experiences; indeed the agents may present conflicting stimuli. For example, the family may support the Democratic party and its candidates, while one's friends are all Republicans. An additional potential source of discontinuity is the variance between the personal socializing experiences and the more impersonal situations in which political behavior may occur.[19] Another source of discontinuity which has not been adequately explored is that created by the presentation of an idealized version of the political system to children in the classroom and the home, with later personal experiences and observations of mass media content presenting a picture of the processes and outputs of the political system at variance with the previously learned ideal. This discrepancy may serve as a stimulus for political alienation or radical political activity by the disillusioned.

The nature of the political system itself may contribute to discontinuities in political socialization. Robert Levine has suggested that congruence between types of authority systems varies inversely with the degree of social stratification, specialization, and stability of the political community's political structures, and the presence of secondary structures such as schools and organized peer groups for political socialization. As one might anticipate, greater discrepancies in political socialization are likely to occur when a number of different socializing agents are present in the system.[20] In a developed country such as the United States, individuals are exposed not only to the family and the educational system but also to many other agents such as several types of mass media and a plethora of agents within each type of mass media, many social groups, and a variety of clubs, interest groups, organizations, religious institutions, and government agencies which act or attempt to act as socializing agents.

AGENTS OF POLITICAL SOCIALIZATION

Which agent or agents are the most important in creating and transmitting political orientations? What kinds of political behavior are learned from each type of agent? Unfortunately, the findings of various studies do not present a consistent pattern. In part this may be a func-

[19] Dawson and Prewitt emphasize this as a source of discontinuity; *op. cit.*, pp. 87-88.
[20] Robert LeVine, "The Role of the Family in Authority Systems; A Cross Cultural Application of Stimulus Generalization Theory," *Behavioral Science*, 5 (October, 1960), p. 295.

tion of inappropriate research designs or of differences between different cultures or between different sub-cultures within a society. The role of the family in political socialization may vary with the social class of the family; recent research indicates that children from working class families who receive little exposure to political interest and information from the family are more likely to perceive the school as a primary source of political information.[21] The relative influence of the family may also vary with the pattern of paternal authority, with children from homes with disrupted family patterns, such as the absence of a father figure or presence of a matriarchical dominance pattern, having different attitudes than children from homes with a more normal family pattern.[22] A study by Robert Hess and Judith Torney indicates that children's levels of interest in politics may also be related to family structure, with children who perceive their fathers as more powerful having more interest in politics.[23] The testing of these hypotheses has been limited and the evidence is not conclusive. Rather than the presence of a particular pattern of parental authority, the style in which authority is exercised may influence children's orientations toward authority. Dean Jaros tested the relationship between degree of parental punitiveness (as perceived by the child), children's levels of anxiety and authoritarianism, and their perceptions of presidential benevolence and strength. He found children's anxiety levels to be related to their level of authoritarianism, and levels of authoritarianism to be related to their perceptions of presidential strength. However, no relationship existed between the degree of authoritarianism and perceptions of presidential benevolence.[24]

Kenneth Langton found male children from maternal families (father absent) tended to hold more authoritarian attitudes and to have lower levels of political interest than males from families with both parents present. Both boys and girls from maternal families had lower levels of political efficacy.[25]

These effects of lower interest and high authoritarianism were also found in both working- and middle-class nuclear families where the mother was dominant. Langton's study also examined the relative influence of the father and mother in the transmission of political party identification and issue positions; the results lead him to reject the hypothesis of father dominance in the transmission of values.[26]

[21] Hess and Torney, op. cit., pp. 100-01.

[22] Dawson and Prewitt, op. cit., pp. 120-21.

[23] Hess and Torney, op. cit., p. 101.

[24] Dean Jaros, "Children's Orientations Toward the President," Journal of Politics, 29 (May, 1967), pp. 383-84.

[25] Kenneth P. Langton, Political Socialization (New York: Oxford University Press, 1969), p. 166.

[26] Ibid., p. 169.

Langton found that among the sample of high school students surveyed in Jamaica, West Indies, increased deviation from parental party identification accompanied the more autocratic parental authority patterns, except among the most autocratically-run families. Children from the most autocratic families equalled the least autocratic families in low deviation from the parental norm on party identification.[27]

Children acquire from the parents certain basic orientations, with the most basic being a sense of belonging to a political community.[28] These basic interpretative orientations are largely affective (emotional); through elementary school years and adolescence the child builds on this affective base a set of cognitive (knowledge-based) orientations. The school and peer groups, by the processes previously discussed, become important in conveying these cognitive orientations. Later, direct political experiences, the mass media, and secondary groups act as socializing agent of some importance in establishing orientations toward political role incumbents and public policy concerns and may work to alter earlier-learned affective and cognitive orientations. The earliest agents have direct authority over the child, with those operating in later periods tending to be either equals or removed from direct personal contact with the individual. It is interesting to note that children generally view civil authorities as projecting a benevolent image, presumably because that is the way they view parental authority.[29] Also, lower class children tend to have a more trusting orientation toward political figures and lower levels of political cynicism. In adults, this pattern is reversed, with citizens of higher social status having more benevolent, trusting orientation toward the government.[30] Some research has suggested, however, that children in an economically deprived community are less trusting of government than those from more affluent sub-cultures.[31]

In examining the correlation of selected attitudes between parents and a national sample of high school seniors, one study found the transmission of political values from parent to child to vary extensively with the nature of the political values involved.[32] The values studied included party identification, political cynicism, political cosmopolitanism, opinions on four political issues, and evaluations of Catholics, blacks, and

[27] Ibid., pp. 26-28, 164-65.
[28] Dawson and Prewitt, op. cit., p. 108.
[29] Greenstein, Children and Politics, op. cit., pp. 37-52.
[30] Lester Milbrath, Political Participation (Chicago: Rand McNally, and Company, 1965), p. 80.
[31] Dean Jaros, Herbert Hirsch, and Frederick J. Fleron, Jr. "The Malevolent Leader: Political Socialization in an American Sub-Culture," American Political Science Review, 62 (June, 1968), pp. 564-75.
[32] M. Kent Jennings and Richard Niemi, "The Transmission of Political Values from Parent to Child," American Political Science Review, 62 (March, 1968), pp. 169-84.

Jews. Except at the extremes of the political cynicism scale and generally for party identification, a high degree of correspondence was not present between parental and high school senior value holdings.

Family influence on voter preference and partisan identification increases when family members agree on a party choice, political interest is high among family members, and the same family party identification has persisted over time. This is reinforced if family members are in frequent contact, they like each other, and they have a similar life style. Affiliation with peer groups such as friends or co-workers who have a different party preference will weaken an individual's attachment to his parental family party preference. If children from a lower social status family rebel against parental over-control, one form the rebellion may take is the rejection of parental party identification. A similar pattern was not found among young voters from upper socio-economic status backgrounds.[33]

While some researchers have concluded that the family is the more important socializing agent,[34] others believe that in other than the development of partisan attachments the school is the more important agent of political socialization.[35] A study of elementary and junior high school students found that children from lower status groups and those of lower intelligence, regardless of social status background, themselves perceive teachers as more effective in their political socialization.[36]

The influence of the school in political socialization may operate in three ways: 1) the classroom, including formal curriculum, the rituals presented in the classroom, and the values and attitudes transmitted unconsciously by the teacher; 2) the informal characteristics of the school such as its social climate, youth organizations of both a political and a non-political nature, and opportunities for participation in various types of extracurricular activities; 3) the effects of being educated on interest in, information about, and participation in political affairs.[37]

Noting the distinction between civic education, which seeks to inform children about the nature of political institutions, processes, and "rules of the game," and political indoctrination, which attempts to instill in the individual a set of preferences for an ideology, party, or

[33] Herbert McClosky and Harold E. Dahlgren, "Primary Group Influence on Party Loyalty," in S. Sidney Ulmer, ed., Introductory Readings in Political Behavior (Chicago: Rand McNally and Company, 1961), pp. 221-37; Eleanor Maccoby, Richard E. Matthews, and Anton S. Morton, "Youth and Political Change," in Ulmer, op. cit., pp. 82-84.

[34] Greenstein, Children and Politics, op. cit., pp. 44-46, 72-74.

[35] Hess and Torney, op. cit., p. 101.

[36] Ibid., pp. 100-01.

[37] Dawson and Prewitt, op. cit., p. 146.

regime, research indicates that civic education efforts of the schools may have a greater impact on children from lower social status backgrounds.[38] However, a study of a French village indicates that where formal curriculum materials are highly incongruent with orientations presented by family and others in informal socializing experiences, the formal socialization effort is discounted and ineffective.[39] A national study of American high school seniors concluded that generally the high school civics curriculum had little impact on seniors' levels of political knowledge and sophistication, political interest, spectator politicalization, political efficacy, political cynicism, and civic tolerance,[40] suggesting that for most students the civics curriculum merely reinforces socialization stemming from other socializing agents. In a comparison between black and white students, blacks tended to score lower on the scales of political knowledge, political efficacy, political cynicism, civic tolerance, political discussion, and media usage; in addition the number and type of civic education courses taken had a greater impact on black students than on whites.[41] The research attributes this to a lesser degree of information redundancy resulting from the curriculum exposure among black students than among whites.[42]

Other socializing stimuli are presented by rituals observed in the schools, such as the salute to the flag, singing of the national anthem, celebration of national historical events, and displays of historical portraits or events on classroom walls. In addition the teacher, by her expressions of opinions and displays of interest in political events, may have an unconscious impact on the political orientations of students. However, a study of American elementary and junior high school students evaluated the degree of congruence between children's and teacher's views, concluding that congruence was highest in those areas representing generally accepted orientations.[43] Almond and Verba in their study of a sample of adult citizens in five nations indicated that the more democratic the classroom environment, as demonstrated by reported participation in classroom discussion, the higher the sense of personal political competence. The school environment and extra-curricular activities also serve to instill certain values, such as participation, com-

[38] Ibid., pp. 147-55.

[39] Laurence Wylie, Village in the Vaucluse (New York: Harper and Row, 1964), pp. 207-09.

[40] Kenneth P. Langton and M. Kent Jennings, "Political Socialization and the High School Civics Curriculum in the United States," American Political Science Review, 62 (September, 1968), pp. 857-59.

[41] Ibid., pp. 859-65.

[42] Ibid., p. 866.

[43] Hess and Torney, op. cit., pp. 114-15.

petitiveness, achievement motivation, and observing the rules of the game.[44] The more educated may differ from the less educated in the following ways:

1. The more educated are more aware of the impact of government on the individual;
2. The more educated are more likely to follow politics in the mass media and to consume communications about election campaigns;
3. The more educated have a greater store of political information;
4. The more educated have political opinions on a greater range of subjects;
5. The more educated are more likely to take part in discussions of political subjects;
6. The more educated person feels free to discuss more political subjects with a wider range of individuals than the less educated;
7. The more educated are more likely to consider themselves capable of influencing the government;
8. The more educated are more likely to be members of organizations; and,
9. The more educated are more likely to express a sense of personal competence and of trustfulness of others.[45]

However, others have argued that the more highly educated possess greater competence even before acquiring a college education, and also tend to come from families with a higher social status background, having higher income, educational, and occupational levels. As a consequence, conclusions about the influence of education may represent a confusion of selection processes with the political socialization consequences of education.[46]

Another possible influence on socialization to politics is the individual's peer groups. A study of Jamaican children indicated that those whose best friends came from heterogeneous social class backgrounds, if they themselves were of working class social status, tended to be resocialized in the direction of higher social class norms. Those whose peer groups were heterogeneous also tended to be more ambivalent and less supportive of the political system.[47] A study of the party identifica-

[44] Almond and Verba, op. cit., pp. 284-94.
[45] Ibid., pp. 317-18.
[46] Langton and Jennings, op. cit., p. 866.
[47] Kenneth P. Langton, "Peer Group and School and the Political Socialization Process," American Political Science Review, 61 (September, 1967), pp. 751-58.

tion of American high school students found that those in a high school with a predominance of party identification contrary to that of their family were more likely to deviate from family party identification than were students in high schools where students had similar partisan attachments. The relevance of the environmental climate may vary with the youth's level of political interest and with his degree of psychological dependence on the family.[48]

Although several studies have examined the influence of family, peer groups, and the school in the socialization of children, the relative influence of each as compared to the other has generally not been studied. One exception is the study by Langton and Karns of the relative role of family, peer group, and school politicization on Jamaican high school students' levels of political efficacy. Using sophisticated causal modeling techniques which assumed that each of the three contributed additively to the development of high school students' political efficacy, Langton found the family to be four times more influential than the school or peer groups along the entire range of levels of political efficacy. However, when controls for social class were applied, among upper class children peer group politicization was more influential.[49] Among the children studied, a higher level of school politicization tended to be effective in moving students from a low to a medium level of political efficacy, but not in moving students from a medium to a high level of political efficacy.[50]

Little research has examined directly the relationship between children's consumption of the various mass media of communications and their political orientations. Herbert Hyman has suggested that the importance for the media for socialization varies between undeveloped, transitional, and modern societies, with exposure to media being general and diffuse in traditional societies and being more specialized and selective in developed nations.[51] What is absorbed from the mass media is a function of the individual's existing predispositions, which acts as a perceptual screen on what he receives from the mass media. Studies have indicated that receiving political information from the mass media is also a two-stage process in which a limited number of individuals, labeled "opinion leaders," receive information and political orientations through radio, television, and newspapers, and then transmit them to

[48] Martin L. Levin, "Social Climate and Political Socialization," *Public Opinion Quarterly*, 35 (Winter, 1961), pp. 596-606.

[49] Langton, Political Socialization, *op. cit.*, pp. 154-58.

[50] *Ibid.*, pp. 140-60.

[51] Herbert Hyman, "Mass Communications and Political Socialization: The Role of Patterns of Communications," in *Communications and Political Development*, ed. Lucian Pye (Princeton: Princeton University Press, 1963).

others in their immediate environment. Comparison of the consumption of mass media by a sample of American high school seniors and their parents indicates that consumption by seniors is lower than that of the parents; it has been suggested that consumption by the seniors will increase to approximate the level of their parents in the future.[52] Considerable variation in the pattern of mass media usage with regard to politics and public affairs also existed, with seniors most closely approaching parents in radio usage and least in the consumption of television programs related to public affairs. However, the analysis does not assess the direct socializing effects of the mass media. Another evaluation of mass media effects, citing a number of studies, indicates that the mass media have primarily a reinforcing effect and do not create patterns of belief or thought or act to convert.[53] However, one must point out that the child may absorb from television some role expectations about political and governmental roles, as for example through watching shows dealing with the FBI, policemen, inter-planetary space travelers, or spy organizations, as well as from from observing participation by situation comedy characters in more normal political events on occasional programs. During election campaigns, they are also exposed to commercials urging support and participation on behalf of a particular candidate or party and also to a variety of comedy efforts on the same subjects.

PATTERNS OF CHILDREN'S POLITICAL ORIENTATIONS

The young child's image of government is largely personal and charismatic, focusing on a few role incumbents such as the president or mayor. Political socialization begins at about age three, orientations at that age being primarily to the broad political community and of an emotional nature. Subsequently, prominent public figures or symbols, such as the president, policemen, and the flag, are cognized. Over time, orientations become both more impersonal and more abstract, with the child focusing on the processes such as voting and law making.[54] As the

[52] M. Kent Jennings and Richard Niemi, "Patterns of Political Learning," *Harvard Educational Review*, 38 (Summer, 1968), pp. 448-49.

[53] Joseph T. Klapper, *The Effects of Mass Communications* (New York: The Free Press, 1960).

[54] See, for example, Greenstein, *Children and Politics*, op. cit.; Hess and Torney, op. cit.; David Easton and Jack Dennis, "The Child's Image of Government," in *Political Socialization*, Roberta Sigel, ed., *The Annals of the American Academy of Political and Social Science*, 361 (September, 1965), pp. 40-57. Roberta Sigel has suggested that the conclusion may be in part a function of inappropriate research

child becomes older, he becomes more aware of the group and institutional character of government and of government as processes as well as institutional structures. His own role in government as a participant also evolves in the cognitions of the child. A distinction between president as law-executor and Congress as law-enactor evolves, and the differentiation of various roles between private enterprise and public service also develops by the eighth grade.[55] Children in the United States tend to approve of the scope of government to a greater degree than do adults and do not believe that the government exercises undue or excessive power over citizens.[56]

The key orientations for political participation as a voter — party identification, issue orientation, and candidate orientation — do not develop simultaneously, with party and candidate awareness preceding issue concerns. In part this may hold true in the United States because parties are a stable organizing mechanism, persisting over time. In a country such as France which has experienced unstable party systems, children are oriented to politics through more stable social units, such as social class or religious affiliation.

Children first tend to view the rules of society as unchanging, but as they grow older the changeability of rules, and the possibility that breaking the rules may not bring punishment, becomes more evident. Early socialization processes result in the development of orientations of loyalty and of obedience to rules, with the stress on participation developing later.[57] Once again, we must remember that within any political system, political subcultures at variance with the total society's predominant pattern may exist. This variance places stress on the system and may result in system instability. If political socialization to the predominant cultural norms is effective, the stress on the system is considerably reduced. While several writers have suggested that sub-cultural differences exist in political socialization, few studies have examined these differences.[58] They may be based on regional, religious, ethnic, class, or

---

instruments. See Roberta Sigel, "Political Socialization: Some Reactions on Current Approaches and Conceptualizations," paper prepared for delivery at the 1966 Annual Meeting of the American Political Science Association, New York, Sept. 6-10, 1966.

[55] David Easton and Robert Hess, "The Child's Political World," *Midwest Journal of Political Science*, 6 (August, 1962), pp. 229-46. It should be noted that most studies have not examined the same children over time, but rather have assumed that differences among children of different ages studied at one time represent development differences rather than generational differences.

[56] David Easton and Jack Dennis, "The Child's Image of Government," in *Political Socialization*, Roberta Sigel, ed., *The Annals of the American Academy of Political and Social Science*, 361 (September, 1965), pp. 52-53.

[57] Hess and Torney, *op. cit.*, pp. 91-92.

[58] Jaros, *op. cit.*; Jaros, Hirsch, and Fleron, *op. cit.*

racial differences. The assumption underlying this view is that members of different social groupings are exposed to different experiences, both political and non-political but politically relevant, which have an impact on their orientations to politics.

ADULT SOCIALIZATION

While we have discussed extensively the learning of political orientations during childhood, it must be emphasized that political socialization occurs throughout one's life, not only because political institutions and the behavior patterns expected of the subject and citizen roles in the political system may change, but also for several other reasons. As we have indicated, children are usually socialized to hold certain values such as to support the system and the regime, to accept the regime as legitimate, and to obey the rules and laws of the system. They are also taught certain orientations which relate to the citizen role, such as to participate through voting. However, they cannot act on some of these orientations until reaching adulthood. Similarly, some relationships with the political system are not likely to be experienced until reaching the adult stage of one's life cycle; these include paying taxes, serving on a jury, dealing with government bureaucrats, or attempting to obtain a change in a rule or law. Certain political roles are open only to persons who meet special qualifications, including having attained a minimum age. To serve as a candidate for elected office, a party official, or a member of an appointive board or commission, the adult learns the role expectations and acquires the skills necessary to meet them. Few studies have been conducted of the processes of socialization to specialized political roles, although studies have been made of the orientations and expectations of those who are in a particular role.[59] A variety of factors could influence recruitment to specialized political roles; research has focused on having certain social background characteristics such as education, a particular occupation, or social class standing, the holding of requisite skills which provide competence for performance of a particular role, or being motivated by particular drives or needs or having certain other personality characteristics.[60] It has also been argued that those who

[59] See Chapter 7 for a discussion of role orientations held by those occupying specialized political roles.

[60] For a discussion of these various factors as a basis for political recruitment, see Lewis Bowman and G. R. Boynton, "Recruitment Patterns Among Local Party Officials: A Model and Some Preliminary Findings in Selected Locales," *American Political*

are recruited to activist roles are those who have been highly exposed to political activity. This exposure may occur through membership in a highly politically active family, involvement in school politics or a reform movement, or by being in an occupation which impinges in some fashion on the activities of government, such as the practice of law.[61] Evidence exists to indicate that for some political activists these socializing experiences have not been present.[62]

Of course, certain forms of participation, such as taking part in demonstrations, riots, and various forms of civil disobedience, are open to those who are excluded by various qualifications from what have been regarded as the more normal methods of expressing one's views and policy preferences in a democracy. However, even these forms of participation must be learned, whether through peer group agents, the mass media, or formal instructional methods.

One author has suggested five changes which generally occur as a consequence of adult socialization; these changes would also occur in political orientations. They include a shift in focus from learning values to performance of specific types of behavior, an emphasis on synthesizing what has been learned more than on acquiring additional orientations, and modification in orientations away from idealized expectations about the role incumbents, regime, and the political community. Increased awareness of conflicting demands present in political roles necessitates enhancing abilities to cope with these conflicts. One also continues learning how to apply learned orientations generally or specifically.[63] In addition, adults who are either geographically or socially mobile may be subject to agents who seek to impart new or different orientations, and changing roles as a consequence of maturation may also result in changed political orientations and behavior.

Science Review, 60 (September, 1966), pp. 667-76; Dwaine Marvick and Charles R. Nixon, "Recruitment Contrasts in Rival Campaign Groups," in Political Decision-Makers: Recruitment and Performance, Dwaine Marvick, ed. (New York: The Free Press of Glencoe, 1961), pp. 138-92; Rufus Browning, "The Interaction of Personality and Political System in Decisions to Run for Office; Some Data and a Simulation Technique," Journal of Social Issues, 24 (July, 1968), pp. 93-110; Herbert Jacob, "Initial Recruitment of Elected Officials in the U.S.: A Model," Journal of Politics, 24 (November, 1962), pp. 703-17.

[61] Kenneth Prewitt, "Political Socialization and Leadership Selection," in Political Socialization, Roberta Sigel, ed., op. cit., pp. 96-111.

[62] See Bowman and Boynton, op. cit.; Marvick and Nixon, op. cit.

[63] Orville G. Brim, Jr. "Adult Socialization," in International Encyclopedia of the Social Sciences, Vol. 14 (New York: Crowell Collier and Macmillan, 1968), pp. 559-60.

CRITIQUE OF THEORY AND METHOD

We must now consider two issues. What approach should future efforts to develop a theory of political socialization take? Secondly, what methodological criticisms can be made of past research, and what alternative methods are available to improve our knowledge of political socialization? A central issue in any discussion of political socialization is whether we should attempt to explain individual political behavior or focus on the implications of political socialization for the political system. Probably political socialization should be studied both from the perspective of understanding individual behavior and of understanding consequences for the political system.

If political socialization theory is to be approached from the perspective of implications for individual behavior, several sociological and social psychological theories could be utilized as a basis for analysis. Aspects of learning, attitude change, personality, motivation, small group, and role theories could provide a basis for improved understanding of political socialization. These approaches, it must be emphasized, examine how political socialization occurs among individuals, focusing on the processes by which they learn and the stages of learning specific types of content.

An alternative approach is to focus on the relevance to the political system of political socialization. Easton and Dennis have argued that logically this should be the first concern of those who study political socialization.[64] In examining the system relevance, three alternative theoretical approaches are feasible — allocative, system stability, and systems persistence. By allocative theory is meant a focus on development of political value structures and how values are allocated among members of a political community. The inadequacy of this approach to socialization is in part a consequence of the incompleteness of an allocative theory of politics. This approach can be attacked for its focus on identifying the antecedents of existing adult behavior patterns and attitudes, ignoring potentiality for change.[65] An alternative approach is that of system stability, or structural-functionalism, which is implicit in much of the comparative studies of political socialization. A key assumption in this approach is that a system attempts to maintain stability, or to state it very simply, maintain a particular state of being over

[64] Easton and Dennis, *Children in the Political System, op. cit.*, pp. 18-19.
[65] *Ibid.*, pp. 21-24.

time. A constant state does not imply peace or order; for example, system stability to China's Mao apparently meant permanent revolutionary fervor. The focus on stability or system maintenance may inhibit an adequate examination of the change-producing consequences of certain types of political socialization. Easton and Dennis advocate a systems persistence theory as the theoretical approach which should be used in the study of political socialization.[66] Two criteria exist for systems persistence: the system's members must be able to allocate values on a regular basis; and members of the system must accept the allocative pattern as authoritative. Using a systems persistence theory approach does not bias against the study of change in system patterns and emphasizes what Easton and Dennis believe should be the focus in socialization studies — the system-relevant consequences.

Even those who advocate a focus on explanation of the acquisition and development of individual political orientations are not satisfied with the knowledge we currently have of political socialization. Roberta Sigel has suggested that political scientists have studied neither learning processes nor the development of political orientations in individuals in their studies of political socialization.[67] Generally instead of studying development, they have examined the attitudes, values, and beliefs of children of different ages and assumed that any systematic differences among children of different ages can be attributed to development. This is faulty reasoning, as the older children may have been exposed to different political stimuli than the younger children or some extraneous factor may be at work. For example, because of different content in the mass media and in parental and school discussions to which they have been exposed and perhaps even through observation of the activities (such as strikes) of their teachers, younger children may be more likely than older persons to believe that political protest strikes, demonstrations, and civil disobedience are appropriate methods of expression of political views and of obtaining changes in both system structure and policy outputs. The only way we can validly generalize about the development of political orientations is to study the same individuals over time.

Generally the published studies of political socialization focus on what individuals have learned, not the processes by which individuals learn political orientations. Sigel points out that studying how children learn can have two connotations, one being the relevant political, social, and physical conditions under which people learn, the other being the

[66] Ibid., Ch. 3.

[67] Roberta Sigel, "Political Socialization: Some Reactions on Current Approaches and Conceptualizations," op. cit.

psychological principles which explain how individuals learn.[68] Acquiring knowledge of both is necessary and not impossible, but political scientists have been quite slow in beginning the task. For example, we would anticipate that different stimuli are presented at home or in the outside environment to children in different social groups or from diverse sub-cultures, their responses are not similarly rewarded or re-inforced by the various socializing agents to which they are exposed, and we might therefore reasonably anticipate that they would learn dissimilar patterns of orientations.

Studies of the same individuals over time are required if we are to understand how learning takes place both in the sense of understanding the social and psychological conditions under which it occurs and the psychological principles by which people learn. The interview method may be inadequate for longitudinal studies. The use of observation and in-depth interviews would eliminate certain other problems, such as "test" anxiety created by the structured questionnaire, inability to get at the reasons given by individuals for their answers, the significance of their answers, or their conceptualization of the subject being considered. In addition to the use of observation and in-depth interviews, Sigel suggests consideration be given to projective techniques, Guttman scaling of attitude questions, and small group experiments.[69]

Other criticisms can be made of the methods and theory used in socialization studies. Sigel has argued that the absence of theory resulting from these studies is due to researchers' failures to examine the goals and values held by socializing agents and the values of persons being socialized.[70] Little research has examined the relationship between general cultural values and political values, exceptions being Lucian Pye's study of Burma and the five-nation study by Almond and Verba which have examined the relationship between cultural values and political socialization.[71] Another weakness of research which impedes the development of theory is the relative absence of an examination of adult socialization experiences. It can be argued that manifest and later socialization experiences are more significant than latent and earlier experiences in influencing adult political behavior.[72] Researchers have emphasized the importance of childhood experiences in their studies; this may be a consequence of United States experiences. With a high degree of political stability present, orientations established early may persist into and through

---

[68] *Ibid.*, pp. 7-10.
[69] *Ibid.*, p. 12.
[70] *Ibid.*, pp. 7-10.
[71] Almond and Verba, *op. cit.*; Lucian Pye, *op. cit.*
[72] Almond and Verba, *op. cit.*, p. 33.

adulthood to a greater degree in the United States than in other countries. Elite socialization, generational change, subcultural differences, and discontinuities in socializing experiences have also been inadequately studied; only through the study of variations in stimuli and response associated with different social groups and their environments can an adequate theory of political socialization be developed.

The data base on which studies of political socialization have been based is not above criticism. The studies are few in number, and most have focused on one culture at one point in time, and usually in one small geographic area, such as a city or county, or a few selected cities. Because of both the limits of the universe from which the sample for a study is usually drawn, and, in some cases, the methods used for drawing the sample, generalization from the studies to a broad population is not possible. Many more studies are needed which test explicit hypotheses based on theory appropriate to the research problem and using correct methods to provide us with explanations of the learning and development over time of political orientations.

In order to develop adequate theories, the testing of hypotheses must contribute to an accumulation of knowledge; this is possible only if concepts are carefully defined and measured in a comparable fashion. Special problems in concept definition and measurement are present in political socialization studies of children, and particularly in studies of pre-high school children.

In order for research results to be useful and comparable with results of other studies, a concept must be defined in a manner useable in a number of studies and measured in a fashion which produces reliable and valid results. However, children's attitudes, beliefs, and values are developing, hence reliability in the test-retest sense is somewhat impeded. For example, a test-retest coefficient of .50 would not be unusual for an attitude scale administered to sixth grade students, while the same scale might have a test-retest reliability coefficient of .85 when administered to high school seniors. Young children's cognitive structures are more likely to be either latent or developing. The processes of political socialization have not yet resulted in the firm establishment of the attitude structures in which we are interested and which we find in older children and adults. If this problem exists, can one then even generalize about children's attitudes? The answer is yes, if the researcher makes clear the reliability, both in terms of stability over time and homogeneity of items, of the research instruments he is using.

A second problem is that of validity. We will focus on the problem of content validity, for without content validity, construct validity is not possible. First, if one wants to study variations in attitudes, beliefs, and values of children of different ages at one point in time, how can one ask a question in such a way that the younger ones can understand it and it is not infantile to the older children? The same problem is presented if one wants to study the same set of children over time; a questionnaire item which is appropriate when the children are younger may appear too simple when the children have developed more sophisticated cognitive structures. An additional problem is presented by the general use of structured, fixed-response questionnaires in the study of socialization. The researcher assumes that he knows the significance to the child of the child's response and the context in which the response is made. However, only by careful pre-testing of a questionnaire on a sample of children similar to those in the study can such be safely assumed; that pre-test should involve probing, open-ended follow-up questions, orally presented, which permit the researcher to evaluate the context and significance of the response to fixed alternative questions. Because of the contextual and significance problems, one can argue that socialization studies should use open-ended questions, or obtain data through presenting problems or situations to be analyzed, or use only experimental methods. Most researchers have preferred to sacrifice the type of knowledge which can be obtained through these data gathering formats for the larger samples and greater number of variables which are possible with fixed alternative questions and paper-and-pencil questionnaires on which children can easily indicate their preferred response.

Another problem found in other areas of inquiry is also present in political socialization studies; that problem is one of comparability of measures. While the objects of attention have been the same in several of the socialization studies, the operational definitions of the concepts, measurement techniques, and data collection methods have not been the same. For example, several researchers have studied the perceived benevolence of the president. In a paper and pencil questionnaire Greenstein asked children in the fourth through the eighth grades, "What kinds of things do you think the president does?" The proportion of responses to this open-ended question which were coded as benevolent declined from twenty-six per cent for fourth graders to four per cent for eighth-grade children. Greenstein inferred that questions more specifically structured would find considerably higher benevolence ratings for the presidential role.[73]

Easton and Dennis used a different method of testing for children's image of the president. Each child was asked to respond to a number of statements about the president, each of which was stated with six

[73] Greenstein, *Children and Politics*, op. cit., p. 40.

wordings going from positive to negative. For example, the child was asked to think of the president as he really is, then check one of the following:

1. Would always want to help me if I needed it.
2. Would almost always want to help me if I needed it.
3. Would usually want to help me if I needed it.
4. Would sometimes want to help me if I needed it.
5. Would seldom want to help me if I needed it.
6. Would not usually want to help me if I needed it.

The proportion picking alternative one declined from sixty-seven per cent in grades two to twenty-seven per cent in the eighth grade.[74] A second item which the researchers designed to evaluate perceived benevolence asked "Which do you think is most true? (Choose one)"

1. When you write to the president, he cares a *lot* what you think.
2. If you write to the president, he cares *some* what you think.
3. If you write to the president, he cares a *little* what you think.

The proportion in each grade selecting the first alternative declined from seventy-five per cent in the second grade to forty-three per cent in the eighth grade.[75]

The concept of presidential benevolence has been evaluated in still another way by Dean Jaros. Jaros designed a seventeen-item scale to measure presidential benevolence, with alternatives ranging from "agree very much" to "disagree very much." The scale was administered to a sample of Detroit area school children. Representative statements in the scale include "the president helps poor people," "the president helps us all to stay healthy," "the president does a great deal to help me," and "the president protects from war." The attitude scale was converted to an index ranging from 0 to 100. The mean score on the scale for the sample of 746 Detroit school children was 72.5[76]

While all three measuring instruments are indices of presidential benevolence, are they comparable? Obviously, they do not constitute the same operational definition of the concept "presidential benevolence." However, research results from their use evidence the same direction of the relationship, even if the magnitude of the relationship is not similar. Replicative studies using the same measurement procedures

[74] Easton and Dennis, *Children in the Political System*, Table 8-4c, p. 179.
[75] *Ibid.*, p. 184; Table 8-5c, p. 185.
[76] Dean Jaros, "Measuring Children's Orientations Toward the President," University of Kentucky, Lexington, Ky., mimeo., no date.; Dean Jaros, "Children's Orientations Toward the President," *op. cit.*, p. 379.

would be more persuasive in establishing the nature and magnitude of the relationship.

A second example of the problem of concept definition and the comparability of measures can be drawn from the study of peer groups as agents of socialization. Differing conclusions about their effects as agents of socialization may be a consequence both of methods used to measure their effects and of the political orientations on which the peer groups were hypothesized to have some consequence. Levin, in a study of high school students in Illinois, measured the effects of the social climate of the high school community on the students' deviations from parental party identification. An index of deviation was calculated by dividing the proportion of Republican-identifying students whose parents were Democratic by the sum of that figure and the proportion of Democratic students who were children of Republican identifiers. The association between the index of deviation and the high school community climate was then evaluated.[77]

To establish peer group associations among Jamaican students, Langton asked the students if their best friends were from the same social class or a different social class. On the basis of their responses, students were categorized as belonging to either homogeneous or heterogeneous peer groups. Variations in support for democratic values, attitude toward voting, support for civil liberties, and level of politicization were examined. Students from working class families generally scored lower on these measures, but those whose peer groups were heterogeneous tended to hold political orientations more in keeping with middle class norms. Langton concluded that working class students in heterogeneous peer groups were being re-socialized toward middle class norms, except for level of politicization.[78]

Another approach to the definition and measurement of peer groups influence is that used by Sebert in the analysis of peer groups influence on high school seniors' political orientations. Five political orientation variables were considered, these being party identification, presidential candidate performance in the 1964 election, political efficacy, political cynicism, and support for the vote for 18-year-olds. Peer group patterns were established by the high school seniors' indicating the names of the five members of the senior class with whom the student "went around most often." The basic assumption is that the significant peer group is composed of members of the same class in the same school. Three different definitions of friendship or peer

[77] Levin, op. cit., p. 599.
[78] Langton, Political Socialization, op. cit., p. 126-32.

group were used, these being the five students named by each student, the set consisting of individuals who named a specific senior as a friend, and the set of reciprocated friends (those who named a student and who had also been chosen by him).[79] Only moderate levels of association existed between high school seniors and their friends on the five different political dimensions. The level of association was lower for more basic orientations, such as party identification and level of political cynicism, than for current concerns, such as the most recent presidential election. For the sub-sample for which data were available, seniors' political orientations were closer to their parents for party identification and presidential vote preference, but more strongly associated for efficacy levels and preference for the 18-year-old vote.[80]

The methods used by Sebert permitted considerable refinement in the analysis, allowing evaluation of the independent, individual effects of such factors as student's participation in extra-curricular activities, sex differences, and social class background of the student. However, as Sebert indicates, research should also examine the cumulative effects of independent variables, patterns of orientations where paternal-friend conflict exists, and further research utilizing Levin's key variable of school atmosphere.[81]

We have considered only three studies which have examined peer group influence on student's political orientations. The orientations which have been examined have varied as have the methods used to assess peer group influence. The direction of the findings is again the same, but comparison of the findings and accumulation of a systematic body of knowledge are made difficult by the variations in definition and measurement.

How is the problem resolved? Through continued research, reliable and valid measures of concepts are developed. Over time, measures found to be reliable and valid are used by other researchers. Thus a concept, such as presidential benevolence, comes to have an accepted operational definition and is similarly measured by researchers using the concept. While the discussion has referred to the definition and measurement of two specific concepts, perceived presidential benevolence and peer group influence, it is only illustrative; the problem is far from unique in socialization studies or even in political science.

[79] Suzanne K. Sebert, "Friend and Peer Influences on the Politics of the High School Senior," paper prepared for delivery at the American Political Science Association meeting, Sept. 2-6, 1969, New York, p. 2.

[80] Ibid., passim.

[81] Ibid., p. 15.

Role

6

DEFINITIONS OF THE ROLE CONCEPT

As the concept of role developed in the disciplines of sociology, psychology, and anthropology, its use in these disciplines has resulted in several different meanings being assigned to it. One analysis has categorized these definitions into three different types.

One uses *role* to mean a normative cultural pattern. Certain rights and duties are associated with each status in society. Role thus refers to the *"attitudes, values, and behavior ascribed by the society to any and all persons occupying this status."*[1] Note that this construction places an emphasis on the society's definition of what is appropriate to each status, and is dependent on an appropriate and operational definition of status.

[1] Statuses are polar positions in patterns of reciprocal behavior: statuses have associated with them rights and duties, putting into effect the rights and duties associated with particular positions having a particular status. Ralph Linton, *Cultural Background of Personality* (New York: Appleton-Century, 1936), p. 77, quoted in Neal Gross, Ward S. Mason, and Alexander W. McEachern, *Explorations in Role Analysis: Studies of the School Superintendency* (New York: John Wiley and Sons, Inc., 1958), p. 12.

A second definition of role uses it to mean an *individual's definition of his situation* with reference to his and others' societal positions. Role in this use is the individual's orientation toward the situation with reference to his and others' social positions. His expectations become stimuli for others with whom he interacts, presenting cues to them as to how they should respond to him.[2]

A third use of the term applies to *the behavior of an individual* occupying a social position. Rather than referring to either cultural definitions of what should be or what an individual defines as model behavior or perceives others as defining as model behavior, role in this view is the actual behavior exhibited in a social situation.[3]

Thus three alternatives of the concept of role are present in the literature. The first is a normative application, referring to what the individual ought to do as defined by society or the social system; the second refers to the individual's orientations to the situation; while the third use applies the term to the actual behavior of the individual. Common among all the definitions, however, is the view that *an individual behaves with some reference and deference to the expectations which others have about how he should behave.*[4] The concept of role expectation can be viewed as having several different dimensions; these include generality or specificity (rigidity of definition of appropriate behavior), scope or extensiveness (the area of a person's life which is covered by the role), the applicability of sanctions to secure conformity to the role expectations, and the relationship to other informal or formal role systems.[5] Several variables can affect the performance of a particular role. These include the nature of role expectations held by others, the location of the role in a network of roles, and the demands made for a specific role enactment. Others are the degree of possession of the skills which are necessary for effective role enactment, the degree of

[2] Cotrell's use of the role concept is an example of this type; the term means an internally consistent set of conditioned responses by one member of a situation which represents the stimulus pattern for a similarly consistent set of conditioned responses of the other in that situation. See the discussion in Gross, Mason, and McEachern, *op. cit.*, p. 13.

[3] Biddle and Thomas have identified the three main variations in meaning given the term "role" by social scientists somewhat differently. The three definitions are (1) "a set of standards, descriptions, norms, or concepts held (by anyone) for the behaviors of a person or position"; (2) "a position"; and (3) "a behavioral repertoire characteristic of a person or position," Bruce J. Biddle and Edwin J. Thomas, eds., *Role Theory: Concepts and Research* (New York: John Wiley and Sons, Inc., 1966), pp. 11-12.

[4] Gross, Mason, and McEachern, *op. cit.*, p. 17.

[5] Theodore Sarbin and Vernon L. Allen, "Role Theory," in Gardner Lindzey and Elliot Aronson, eds., *The Handbook of Social Psychology*, Vol. 1 (2nd Edition, Reading, Mass.: Addison-Wesley Publishing Co., 1968), pp. 499-502.

congruence between the individual's perception of his identity and the requirement of the role, and the characteristics and impact of the audience.[6]

Other definitions of role are possible, and various aspects of the concept can be used in research. Theodore Sarbin has suggested that role is "a metaphor intended to denote that conduct adheres to certain parts (or positions) rather than to the players who read or recite them."[7] The focus of study can be on how people enact a particular role. Accordingly, the following questions could aid in guiding one's analysis of political behavior. Has the individual selected the correct political role? Does the behavior conform to the normative expectations considered appropriate by the observers of the performance? Does the role enactment lead one to conclude that the occupant is legitimately occupying the position?

To translate these questions to the political arena, we can consider the following problem. What style and politics should the president of the United States select as appropriate? This is, in part, a function of the dominant role expectations in the society or among that part of it which provides his majority support. Where resources are not unlimited, is he to be the defender of the free world or the leader in solving problems at home? The normative expectations applicable to a president may change, and one who survives politically to run for reelection will adjust his performance to meet these changing expectations. A president who cannot perform or conform to the expectations of his constituencies is denied approval, and either defeated or chooses not to run for re-election. For example, President Lyndon Johnson found that his popular support declined as the Viet Nam war continued and the role expectations of certain segments of the electorate about presidential behavior were not met.

Talcott Parsons has suggested that five dichotomous choices, termed *pattern variables*, are available to the individual in mediating his role orientations. These choices define how one relates to the other individual or individuals in the situations. One choice is that of *ascription* versus *achievement*; one can evaluate and respond to others in the situation on the basis of presumed or ascribed qualities of the role occupant or one can respond on the basis of the other's actual achievements. The second choice is between *affectivity* and *affective neutrality*; should one's personal emotions and feelings influence his orientation or should one control or ignore one's emotions? The third choice is between

[6] *Ibid.*, pp. 503-14.
[7] *Ibid.*, pp. 489; 514-34.

universalism or *particularism*; should general standards apply, or some specific to the situation or the individual? The fourth choice is between *selfish interests* and *selflessness*. The final choice is between viewing the other in the situation in terms of *specific* or *diffuse* properties. The contention of Parsons is that these five choices are always present and they are always dichotomous, either-or choices.[8]

The role expectations applicable to a particular position dictate what the pattern variable choices should be. For example, in the government administration or any other complex organization, the role expectations applied generally indicate the following pattern variable choices by bureaucrats would be appropriate: achievement, affective neutrality, universalism, selflessness, and specificity. However, when dealing with a functionary — be he government, university, or corporate — individuals would prefer to receive favorable treatment provided on the basis of special considerations such as the particular characteristics of one's problem or friendship with the official. In such a case the pattern variable choices made by the bureaucrat would be ascription, affectivity, particularism, selfishness, and diffuseness. Pattern variables have been used in analysis of such political phenomena as the role expectations applied to and the actual role behavior of public officials, the role strains on American public officials, and the differences in the dominant patterns of role expectations present in several types of political systems.[9]

ROLE SYSTEMS

Any set of related roles we can call a role system. This network of relationships may be focused on one role; when we examine the role set, we find one role at the core which is the focal point of the relationships within the set. In any social system the set of role expectations tends to persist over time. The rights of the occupant of a position and the

[8] Parsons has defined a social system as a system of interaction of a plurality of actors, in which the action is oriented by rules which are complexes of complementary expectations concerning roles and sanctions. Role expectations are defined by patterns of evaluation. Talcott Parsons and Edward Shils, eds., *Toward a General Theory of Action* (Cambridge, Mass.: Harvard University Press, 1962), pp. 23-24. Parsons indicates that the pattern variable choices of affectivity-affective neutrality, selflessness-selfishness, and universalism-particularism are modes of orientation while ascription-achievement and specificity-diffuseness constitute evaluations of the object modalities and the scope of significance. Parsons: *op. cit.*, pp. 88-91.

[9] William Mitchell, "Occupational Role Strains: The American Elective Public Official," *Administrative Science Quarterly*, 3 (September, 1958), pp. 210-28.

obligations or duties he has toward others in the role system acquire some relatively stable definition. Events, the acquisition of new roles, or the increased importance of some roles as contrasted to others may result in a re-definition or a conflict over the definition of part or all of the set of role relationships.

A change in one relationship in the set has implications for others. For example, if a legislator is appointed to a very important committee, such as the Appropriations Committee of the House of Representatives, certain relationships in his role set may become more important than previously, others will decline in importance, and the nature of the mutual expectations existent in the role set may also change. The representative may find that other representatives are more deferential to him. The government agencies dependent on his committee for funds become solicitous of his advice and respond more quickly to his requests for information or for assistance for resolving problems for his constituents. Lobbyists representing groups which would benefit from increased appropriations or funding of new government programs besiege him with information, advice, and assistance.

However, even if consensus generally exists on the expectations appropriate to a set of role relationships, variation in performance may and probably will occur. Because of the selectivity of perceptual processes, an individual may not correctly perceive the expectations others have for a particular role, and therefore he may perform it differently than others. The attitudes of individuals who occupy a similar role, such as teachers, may also vary which could result in variations in motivation; these variations in motivation may be related to variations in role performance. The role expectations applied to the party precinct leaders in a community may be the same throughout the community, but because of the variations in motivations, the role incumbents may vary considerably in actual performance.

One well developed elaboration of the concept of role indicates that in each social system an individual occupies a particular position; his position is his location in the system of social relationships. Determinants of his social position are such factors as the individual's age, sex, family membership, occupation, and social group memberships. Positions must be viewed in a relational context; one cannot describe a position until all positions related to it are described. The position studied is called *focal position*; the position related to it is called *counter position*. For example, if we study the American presidency, the presidency is the focal position studied, while counter positions include congressman, senator, party leader, interest group leader, executive department bureaucrat, and White House staff member. All positions must also be considered in the context of the situation, which is defined by the specific scope of the social system we are studying.[10] Thus, the role expectations applicable to the president probably vary with such situation characteristics as whether he is considering a domestic or a foreign policy question, whether his party controls the Congress, whether a presidential contest will be held in the near future, and the president's current standing with the public and with his party leaders.

For instance, when we are talking about presidents of institutions of higher education, situation specification refers to whether the schools in question are junior colleges or liberal arts colleges or branches of the state university, their relative tranquility, relationships with the community, and other such characteristics. The term role then applies to the expectations applied to an incumbent of a particular position, with the expectation indicating how the incumbent of that position should behave. As such, it is a normative, "ought" standard and not a prediction of how he will behave.

ROLE CONFLICT

Any incumbent of a particular position is subject to a number of sets of expectations as to how he should behave; these sets may not be consistent with one another. This conception of incompatible role expectation is called role conflict; there are two types of role conflict.[11] One occurs when occupants of different counter positions have inconsistent or conflicting expectations about how an occupant of a particular position will behave. The president of the United States may be expected to encourage the conservation of natural resources by leaders of various conservation interest groups, to maximize revenues available to the United States by the leaders of the Treasury, the Bureau of the Budget, and congressional finance committee members, and to promote the domestic economy by the leaders of business and industry. If the issue in question is the granting of permission to drill for off-shore oil, these three sets of expectations may result in the president receiving conflicting demands to grant or not to grant such permission. This type of conflict is intra-role conflict.

A second type of role conflict is that which arises when an indi-

[10] Gross, Mason, and McEachern, op. cit., pp. 48-69.
[11] Neal Gross, A. W. McEachern and Ward Mason, "Role Conflict and Its Resolution," in Eleanor Maccoby, ed., Readings in Social Psychology (3rd edition, New York: Holt, Rinehart, and Winston, 1958), pp. 447-59.

vidual occupies two or more roles, and the expectations applied to him as the occupant of various roles are sometimes conflicting. Thus a congressman is expected to remain in the House to complete voting on a particular bill's proposed amendments while his family expects him to attend junior's performance in the senior play or his district political party organization expects him to fly in to address an important fund-raising dinner. We can also illustrate this by focusing on the president of the United States. As the leader of his political party he is expected to be a partisan advocate of his party's views and a vociferous supporter of its candidates for various public offices, speaking out to present the party's issue stands and campaigning for party candidates for office. On the other hand, in the role of the leading representative of the United States in the making of foreign policy and the conduct of world affairs, he is expected to be non-partisan and a leader of all the country's citizens. This conflict arising from divergent expectations perceived by him in two different roles is called *inter-role conflict*. Note that in the case of both inter-role conflict and intra-role conflict, conflict occurs only when the role or roles incumbent perceives the expectations of being conflicting.

To illustrate further the notion of role and the idea of role conflict, we can examine the role of our United States senators. Donald Matthews in his *U.S. Senators and Their World*[12] discussed the role expectations applied to senators during the late 1950s. These expectations included serving an apprenticeship when one first entered the Senate. This role expectation applied to "freshmen" included presiding over the Senate when it conducted routine business so as to free the vice-president and other more senior senators for more important work. A freshman senator was not expected to participate in debate, as he was deemed too ignorant of the legislative history of the issue and its details to make an intelligent contribution to the debate. The freshman senator was also expected to limit his discussion in committee sessions. Generally, each senator was expected by others to do his legislative homework for the committees of which he was a member and to specialize in one or a limited set of problems so that he could contribute expert advice to his colleagues. Each senator was also to limit his participation in debate, generally discussing extensively only those issues on which he was an expert. Several of these expectations can be summarized under the rubric, "Be a work horse, not a show horse." Another expectation applied by senators to each other was to be courteous to one's fellow

---

[12] Donald Matthews, *U.S. Senators and Their World* (Chapel Hill, N.C.: University of North Carolina Press, 1960), Ch. 5.

senators; this encompassed refraining from being personal in conflict over policy and conducting debate in a friendly form of discourse with flattery and praise lavished on one's opponents. Thus, if one were to disagree strongly with another senator in floor debate, he might address his opponent as "My distinguished and esteemed colleague" before proceeding to shred the colleague's arguments. Another Senate role expectation found by Matthews was that of reciprocity; each is expected to help out his colleagues whenever he can. Hence roll call votes are scheduled so that members who may be going out of Washington on a certain date can be sure that the vote on the issues they are concerned about will not be held while they are out of town.

All of these were expectations held by senators about the behavior of other senators. Two kinds of role conflict are possible. The first, intra-role conflict, occurs when occupants of other focal positions have different expectations about the behavior of an individual senator. Illustrating this are the expectations held by the constituents of a large state about their freshman senator's behavior. He is expected to be active on issues of concern to them without serving an apprenticeship. Party leaders in his state also expect him to take a part in many politically oriented activities which would require frequent absences from the Senate and probably impair his conformance to Senate norms. Senators from large states, in order to enhance their re-nomination and re-election probabilities, frequently must conform more to non-Senate expectations than those of their fellow senators, which might have the consequence of significantly reducing their effectiveness as senators. Other senators cannot conform to the Senate norms because of inter-role conflict. A senator with ambitions to be president of the United States may assume the role of presidential candidate; the expectations appropriate to that role frequently conflict with those directed toward him by other senators in his role as a senator. As a presidential candidate he is expected to speak on a number of important issues, not just the few on which he is considered an expert by his fellow senators. As a "show horse" he must play to the grandstand of extensive mass media coverage of his opinions and activities, and make frequent trips out of Washington with consequent neglect of routine Senate committee work.

In both the inter-role and intra-role conflict situations, the senator must make a choice as to which set of perceived role expectations he will conform. Several factors may influence that choice. One influence is the perceived legitimacy of the expectations; in other words, do those making demands on him have the right to make such demands? He may also evaluate in terms of how well others are conforming to his expectations of them. A third factor, and perhaps the most important, is the sanctions which can be applied to him if he fails to conform to one counter position's role expectations of him. If a man's ambitions are primarily centered on being elected president of the United States, that he may not attain a particular Senate committee assignment perhaps is of considerably less importance to him than the earning of public acclaim and delegate votes through frequent contacts with party activists throughout the country or the gaining of public support through extensive television coverage of his statements on a wide range of public issues.[13]

Frequently an occupant of a position attempts to meet expectations which are beyond his capabilities, resulting in role strain. William Mitchell has pointed out that the sources of strain are likely to be presented to all incumbents of a particular political role, but perception of the sources of strain and reaction to them may vary with the individual role occupant. Of course, role occupants may try to restructure their environments in order to alter the expectations emanating from others, thereby minimizing the sources of role strain. According to Mitchell, those sources of political strain are: "(1) insecurity of tenure; (2) conflict among public roles; (3) conflict of private and public roles; (4) ambiguities in political situations; (5) diffused responsibility and limited control of situations; (6) time and pressure of demands; (7) and status insecurity."[14] For example, elected officials face the possibility of defeat if they seek re-election. Politicians may seek to reduce this by such devices as gerrymandering electoral districts or eliminating party rivals by securing appointive jobs for them. The frustration induced by role strains may be expressed and attempts made at eliminating their sources by such punitive activities as investigations, harrassing hearings, or unfriendly treatment of perceived sources of strain. Efforts may also be directed to obtaining compensations, such as high salaries and fringe benefits, lucrative pensions easily attained, or the development of access to financial rewards directly or indirectly arising from the official's role occupancy, such as can be attained through association with a law firm, or a corporate directorship, or stock purchases based on a favorable price or an inside tip about future profits.[15]

[13] *Ibid.*
[14] Mitchell, *op. cit.,* p. 212.
[15] *Ibid.*

ROLE SOCIALIZATION AND RESOCIALIZATION

A role is a learned set of expectations; in the socialization process, learning the expectations others hold about a particular position can occur in several ways. One of these is explicit education through formal training procedures; for example, courses in American history and United States government perform this function in our schools. Another method important in learning political roles is imitation; in this fashion one may acquire such aspects of political roles as party identification, or in the case of the legislator, an appropriate set of orientations toward his district, an interest group, or his fellow members, or even a desire to become a candidate for elected public office. One may identify with a position one wants to assume and acquire the orientations appropriate to that role before one actually achieves it.

Other methods of socialization to political roles is serving an apprenticeship; and serving as an officer in a business association or a service club. One gains experience in bargaining, coalition formation, decision-making, and dealing with the public in this way and also acquires training in skills and learns orientations appropriate to such a political role as city councilman. Still other methods of socialization to political roles exist, and are discussed in the preceding chapter dealing with socialization.

After one assumes a particular role, he is engaged in a process of further interaction during which change may occur in the expectations applied to that role. This development of new expectations, and even the learning of new roles appropriate to newly-assumed positions, is sometimes referred to as resocialization. We should not assume, however, that this is an easy process for those individuals who are to experience it. For example, as the situational setting changes the role occupant may find it difficult to adapt to new role expectations which develop. Thus a librarian who has learned to view her task as protecting the library's collection may be unable to adapt when her supervisors shift from expecting her to maintain the collection in pristine condition and imposing silence in the library to the promotion of interest in reading among disadvantaged children through giving away books and promoting the use of the library as a community center. The librarian is suffering from trained incapacity, an inability to accept resocialization.

Resocialization may be experienced by any occupant of a political position, whether in an executive, legislative, or judicial role. Using role theory and examining factors contributing to resocialization, one can evaluate the impact of selected experiences on the attitudes, values, and behavior of occupants of particular situations. Chadwick Alger examined the influence of assignment to a tour of duty at the United Nations on representatives from various countries.[16] He suggests that the role expectations applied to these individuals by those with whom they come in contact, such as mass media reporters, delegates from other countries, and members of the permanent United Nations secretariat, serve to alter in a number of ways the role expectations perceived by the national delegates and also their role behavior. For example, a French specialist in health care, interacting with delegates from more than one hundred countries in a special committee organizing a world wide attack on malaria, acquires new perspectives as a result of his experiences, modifying his existing role orientation.

The health care expert operates in an atmosphere which emphasizes expertise and attack on an international problem, working in an international rather than a national system, and this, rather than a particular national focus, probably will be emphasized in the role expectations held by his fellow experts. This type of modification of perceived role expectations is implied by Alger to occur among representatives of the specialized political committees of the United Nations General Assembly. Role conflict may arise. For example, those persons occupying positions counter to the French expert's may request or expect behavior at odds with the expectations of his superiors and co-workers in the French government.

Resocialization occurs when one acquires a new status for which no appropriate role model previously existed. This is a common occurrence in a developing nation, as both the political system and the economy evolve into more complex institutional arrangements. It is also common in a developed country such as the United States. For instance, the creation of quasi-governmental community action programs financed and sponsored by the Office of Economic Opportunity created new roles for both indigenous community leaders and for the paid organizers of the community action programs, setting into motion the process of resocialization. The attack on community action programs by local politicians, who tended frequently to perceive these programs as a threat to their control of local politics, is symptomatic of conflicting expectations about what the community organizers should do as perceived by the local community, the organizers, and the local politicians.

[16] Chadwick Alger, "Non-Resolution Consequences of the United Nations and Their Effect on International Conflict," *The Journal of Conflict Resolution*, 5 (June, 1951), pp. 128-45.

POWER AS A ROLE RELATIONSHIP

Some treatments of the concept of power are stated in terms of role expectations; this is not a new approach to the study of power. In a "how to succeed" handbook for autocratic rulers written by a sixteenth century Florentine politician-bureaucrat for a Renaissance prince, the role expectations and the choice of role behaviors to be followed by the prince in order to survive as a ruler are examined. For example, Machiavelli pointed out that princes should make appointments on a merit basis and encourage craftsmen to improve themselves (achievement motivation encouraged), encourage the guilds or classes, and mingle with the people while maintaining the dignity and majesty expected of a ruler.[17] The prudent prince will also establish himself as a powerful yet not hated individual.[18] In the ruler-subject relationship, a number of role expectations exist. For example, the prince expects his subjects to be loyal, while the subjects expect the prince to rule justly and provide them with good government. However, if his subjects expect him to be cruel if they act against him, they are more likely to be faithful to him.[19] Discussing coalitions and alliances, Machiavelli noted that one's friends preferred one to be an active ally, while nations or rulers who were not friends expected one to be neutral in a conflict.

The concept of power has remained a central concern of writers on politics; it is frequently discussed in terms which indicate power is, in effect, an interaction process or role. For example, Robert Dahl states that "power is a relation, . . . it is a relation among people."[20] The relationship can be described in terms of a number of factors, including the source or base of the holder's power, means or instruments used to exert it, the amount or extent of power, and the range or scope of power (the responses of the subject). For example, we could examine a governor's power base and the means he would use in a power relationship with the state legislators. Dahl asserts that the amount of power can be represented by a probability statement of the chances of the governor obtaining the responses he prefers in voting on key issues which, without this exercise of power, would not otherwise be forthcoming.

[17] Niccolo Machiavelli, *The Prince* (New York: The Modern Library, 1950), p. 85.

[18] *Ibid.*, p. 63.

[19] *Ibid.*, p. 60.

[20] Robert A. Dahl, "The Concept of Power," *Behavioral Science*, 2 (July, 1957), p. 203.

If one wanted to compare the relative power of several governors using Dahl's formulation, one would calculate their base, means, and scope, as well as the number of respondents each could affect, and changes in probabilities of the amount of power. Harsanyi has suggested that measurements must also be made of the costs to the power wielder of attempting to exert influence over another and of the cost to the intended object of resisting the attempted power exertion.[21]

If we refer back to the dimensions of the role expectations discussed at the beginning of this chapter, we see certain similarities with the aspects of power as discussed by Dahl and Harsanyi. Consider Dahl's statement that A has power over B to the extent that he can get B to do something that B would not otherwise do. The exercise of power may be conceptualized as the resolution of a conflict in role expectations; when a power relationship exists, the definition of the role prescriptions which is accepted is that of the power wielder. Viewing power from this perspective makes it an individual role rather than a group phenomenon, and presents us with one approach to more precise consideration of one type of role relationship.

USES OF THE ROLE CONCEPT IN THEORY BUILDING

The concept of role could be used in analysis of political behavior in three ways; as an independent variable, as a dependent variable, or as an intervening variable. However, most of the writing about politics utilizing the concept of role has focused extensively on describing the distribution of role orientations among political actors rather than using the concept in testable hypotheses.

Role has been used as a dependent variable, with the emphasis on accounting for the choice made among alternative role orientations or for the distributions of political role orientations found in different environments. For example, are county chairmen in political party organizations more likely to be campaign-oriented in competitive districts or in those in which their party is in a dominant or subordinate position? Another use of the role concept is as an intervening variable, helping to explain and specify the relationship between an independent and a dependent variable. For example, a legislator's attitudes on taxes are such that he is opposed to an increase in his state's sales tax, yet he votes

[21] John Harsanyi, "Measurement of Social Power, Opportunity Costs, and the Theory of Two Person Bargaining Games," *Behavioral Science*, 7 (January, 1962), pp. 67-80.

in favor of a bill raising the tax. The legislator's role orientations toward his party leadership, his constituency, the governor, or an interest group may be useful in accounting for behavior at variance with his basic attitude on the issue.

An example of the development of a descriptive typology using role concepts was provided by a study of the state legislatures of California, New Jersey, Tennessee, and Ohio. The authors argue that the role concept is particularly useful for political science because it ties together the concerns of institutional, functional, and behavioral analysis.[22] The focus of their study is on the norms of behavior perceived by occupants of the position of legislator, distinguishing among different legislative roles. One type of role is that applying to a legislator in his relations with all other legislators; thus one can elaborate the norms or "rules of the game" to which legislators expect other legislators to adhere. Among the other roles is the purposive role, which refers to behavior which the legislator perceives as appropriate to the accomplishment of legislative goals. Five purposive role types are identified: the ritualist who perceives the legislative process in terms of the technical aspects of committee work, rules, and the procedures for enacting legislation; the tribune, who views his job as acting as the spokesman for popular opinion; the inventor, who perceives his role as that of creating and initiating public policy; the broker, whose role perceptions focus on achieving compromises between conflicting interests; and the opportunist, who meets only minimum requirements of the role and uses his legislative office to maximize his non-legislative interests, either personal or political. Another set of legislative role orientations focuses on orientations toward interest group activity; the role alternatives include facilitators (knowledgeable about group activity and friendly to it); resistors (knowledgeable about group activity and hostile to it); and neutrals (those who either have little knowledge or no strong reaction to group activity). A third set of role relationships is based on the way a legislator believes he should decide on an issue, regardless of the geographic focus of his role orientation; these are labelled his *representational role orientations*. A legislator who considers himself to be a free agent deciding on the basis of principles is termed a *trustee*. In contrast, a legislator who believes he should always vote his district's will, is labeled a *delegate*. The legislator who expressed both trustee and delegate role orientations is called a *politico*. Other role orientations are also held by legislators; these include role orientations toward the political parties, the executive, and

[22] John C. Walhke, Heinz Eulau, William Buchanan, and Leroy C. Ferguson, *The Legislative System* (New York: John Wiley and Sons, Inc., 1962), p. 7.

the bureaucracy.[23] Taken together, these form a system of role orientations on the part of the legislator; of course, occupants of the counter positions to the legislator have sets of role orientations also.

This set of role typologies is based on legislators' perceptions of their role enactments, rather than their perceptions of others' role expectations. In a more recent study the role expectations for legislative behavior held by the mass public and by attentive constituents (persons nominated by legislators as those district residents whom the state legislators considered to be politically knowledgeable and whom the legislator would turn to in seeking advice on legislative matters) were examined. Four types of role orientations — procedural, purposive, representational, and policy oriented — were found to exist, but the distributions of the expectations were different in the attentive public and the mass public. Only a general evaluation was obtained of the extent to which the respondents' expectations about legislative role enactments were satisfied. The samples of attentive constituents and mass public were asked if they thought the Iowa legislature had done an excellent, good, fair, or poor job. Unfortunately, this question does not directly assess the extent of perceived compliance with the respondent's explicit legislative role expectations.[24]

However, problems exist in analyzing political behavior in terms of the role concept and research using the role concept has not usually acknowledged or dealt with these problems. For example, we must ask whether a legislator's role orientations are consistent over time and in application to all issues or to all who occupy the same type of counter position. For example, does a member of a legislature serving in his third or fourth term have the same set of role orientations as he had in his first? In addition, a legislator's role orientations may evolve over the course of a legislative session. A state political leader implied this by asserting that it was difficult to manage a legislature with a large number of freshmen legislators in it. When the session first started the freshmen were aware of the dimensions of their ignorance and would do as instructed. However, after a few weeks and at about the time

[23] *Ibid.* See Chs. 11-15.
[24] G. R. Boynton, Samuel C. Patterson, and Ronald D. Hedlund, "The Missing Links in Legislative Politics: Attentive Constituents," *Journal of Politics*, 31 (August, 1969), pp. 700-02; See also G. R. Boynton, Samuel C. Patterson, and Ronald D. Hedlund, "The Structure of Public Support for Legislative Institutions," *Midwest Journal of Political Science*, 12 (May, 1968), pp. 163-80; Samuel C. Patterson, G. R. Boynton, and Ronald D. Hedlund, "Perceptions and Expectations of the Legislature and Support for It," *American Journal of Sociology*, 75 (July, 1969), pp. 62-76; Samuel C. Patterson and G. R. Boynton, "Legislative Recruitment in a Civic Culture," *Social Science Quarterly*, 50 (September, 1969), pp. 243-63.

important legislation was being reported out of committee, the freshmen legislators could find their way around and thereupon started acting as if they had all the answers. What was occurring and arousing the party boss's complaint was an evolution both in the relative importance placed by freshman legislators on different role orientations among the role set (representational, purposive, interest group, party, etc.) and in the freshman's selection of the appropriate role with respect to the party leaders in and outside of the legislature.

Other questions must be raised. As a legislator develops ambitions for higher political office do his role orientations change? Secondly, does he perceive the same representational role orientations regardless of the nature of the issue (whether it is to increase the sales tax or revise the state's laws concerning the construction of farm drainage ditches). Furthermore, perhaps a representative from a middle class, suburban, Republican district has one interest group orientation toward representatives of the state AFL-CIO and a second toward representatives of the state manufacturers association.

This question raised about role theory is its capability to contribute to predictive theory whereby we could predict legislative behavior and policy decisions. The four-state legislative study referred to previously did not attempt to formulate such a theory. What is needed is an elaboration of the scheme so as to make it useful for predicting role enactment or role behavior. Admittedly most researchers have focused on norms and expectations held and have not attempted to predict behavior from knowledge of role expectations. For example, in the four-state legislative study and in Kornberg's study of the Canadian Parliament, the legislators' own generalized expectations — and, to a limited extent, their perceptions of the expectations held by others — have been the research focus.[25] Where the actual expectations of others were evaluated, as in the Iowa study, expectations were evaluated only in vague and very oversimplified terms. Role expectations are undoubtedly specific to both situation and object, yet this has been ignored in political science research using the role concept. However, several problems are engendered by increasing specificity. First, a proliferation of role types will result. In addition, one cannot assume, as researchers have frequently done, that role orientations are stable over time. Role orientations form, are altered, and elaborated through the ongoing process of interaction with others, yet studies tend to be cross-sectional, studying the political actors at only one point in time.

[25] Walhke, Eulau, Buchanan, and Ferguson, op. cit.; Allan Kornberg, *Canadian Legislative Behavior* (New York: Holt, Rinehart, and Winston, 1967).

Francis has suggested that the concept role be elaborated and made useful for political science research through developing role topologies defined in terms of attitude dimensions. One can then build a set of probability statements to define the role set. Francis, using three of the sets of role orientations elaborated by the four-state study, has indicated the form such a theory would take.[26] Using the district, representational, and interest group orientations, Francis suggests a probability model of role behavior. He considers the probability that a legislator will accept instruction, consult interest group leaders, and consult leaders at the state and district level. From legislators' general orientations on these factors he develops a model to predict the probability of seeking instruction. In summary, the role typologies were used to specify attitude dimensions and the transition then made from attitude dimensions to probability statements. Francis points out that in order to evaluate the probable pattern of a series of interactions, one must know the legislator's cognitive structure, meaning "the way in which people, events and ideas are organized in his own mind."[27] Whether and who a legislator consults is then a function of his cognitive structure.[28] Legislators could be expected to initiate interactions and consult others in a priority ordering determined by their cognitive structures. Thus, in order to account for role behavior, one must have knowledge of relevant cognitive structures.

However, problems of operational definition and research procedures evolve out of formulation of role as attitude dimensions expressed through probability statements. What attitude dimensions are appropriate for the definition of particular political roles? In more practical terms, can one collect the data necessary for testing hypotheses utilizing this approach to role theory? Practically, it could be done as Francis has demonstrated.

Additionally, Zeigler and Baer emphasize that the role approach such as used in the legislative studies ignores the total environment within which political behavior is occurring. Thus, one must study the expectations and cognitive structure of those occupying positions counter to the political actor.[29] The Iowa study previously mentioned is a limited

[26] Wayne Francis, "The Role Concept in Legislatures: A Probability Model and A Note on Cognitive Structure," Journal of Politics, 27 (August, 1965), pp. 567-85.
[27] Ibid., p. 582.
[28] Ibid., pp. 583-84. The elaboration of the role has not gone uncriticized. For one critique, see Benjamin Walter, "Of Complements and Empirical Probabilities: A Critical Note on Francis' Paper," Journal of Politics, 28 (May, 1966), pp. 419-24. See also Francis' rebuttal, "The Utility of Probabilities in Models: A Reply to Walter's Critical Note," Journal of Politics, 28 (May, 1966), pp. 425-28.
[29] Hamon Zeigler and Michael Baer, Lobbying: Interaction and Influence in American State Legislatures (Belmont, California: Wadsworth Publishing Company, 1969), pp. 6-8.

and partial step in that direction as is the Zeigler and Baer study of lobbying.

Another use for the role concept and various typologies of role orientations is in description of the characteristic role orientations of political actors in different political systems. A recent study of predominant political role orientations of citizens in five western democratic countries (United States, West Germany, Great Britain, Italy, and Mexico) found substantial differences in the distribution of orientations in these countries.[30] The concept has also been used in comparative analyses of political recruitment and party organization.[31]

In a study of local party officials in five communities in Massachusetts and North Carolina, Bowman and Boynton found an emphasis on campaign-related activity, with sixty per cent describing this kind of activity as the most important job.[32] This type of analysis reflects the individual's definition of his role, not his behavior nor others' expectations about his behavior in the position of precinct leader. Eldersveld found considerably less emphasis on campaign activities among precinct leaders in Detroit;[33] he also found that both parties' precinct leaders in the precincts controlled by the county's minority party were much more likely to emphasize getting-out-the-vote activity.[34] Detroit precinct leaders who were party regulars were also much more likely to focus on increasing voting turnout. Apparently the career pattern of the activist within the party contributed to the activist's role definition; those who held other party office or aspired to it tended to place less emphasis on vote mobilization. Differences also occurred between the Republicans and Democrats in their role perceptions.[35] Crotty, in a study of county party organizations in North Carolina, also found a tendency for leaders' reported role behavior to vary with the majority or minority status of their party.[36]

One of the pressing problems of political science is to develop methods for studying the processes of social change. This is crucial if political science is to contribute to the development of public policy,

[30] Gabriel Almond and Sidney Verba, *The Civic Culture* (Princeton: Princeton University Press, 1963).

[31] Louis Bowman and G. R. Boynton, "Activities and Role Definitions of Grassroots Party Leaders," *Journal of Politics,* 28 (February, 1966), pp. 121-40; William J. Crotty, "The Party Organization and Its Activities," in *Approaches to the Study of Party Organization,* ed. William J. Crotty (Boston: Allyn and Bacon, 1968), pp. 217-46; James David Barber, *The Lawmakers* (New Haven: Yale University Press, 1965).

[32] Bowman and Boynton, *op. cit.,* p. 128.

[33] Samuel J. Eldersveld, *Political Parties: A Behavioral Analysis* (Chicago: Rand McNally, 1964), p. 254.

[34] *Ibid.,* p. 259.

[35] *Ibid.,* p. 260.

[36] Crotty, *op. cit.,* pp. 266-67; 273.

for much of the government's concern is with either stimulating or channeling social change, whether that change is concerned with alleviating poverty in the United States through promoting manpower training, black business ownership, and educational advancement, or with adoption of technological innovations in education, health care, transportation, or other areas of policy concerned.

How can role theory aid in the study of social change? How can it be useful in bringing about social or political change? Role theory provides a perspective from which we can study varieties of political and social change, whether it is the political modernization of a country such as Iran, the alteration in a developed country's governmental institutions as occurred in France in the shift from the Fourth to the Fifth Republic, or the slow development of a competitive party system in the South. Using role theory we can examine the development of new sets of expectations or changes in the expectations applied to existing roles, the development or alteration in sanctions for violation of norms, and consequences of these changes. As an example of just one type of political change, the political role system of a country tends to become more differentiated as the country modernizes. In a tribal society the political leader may also be religious, economic and social leader, all combined in the position of tribal chief. As political development occurs, new roles and systems of role relationship develop and the political system tends to become more independent of the economic, social, and political system. This differentiation and secularization of the political system is thus a study of the evolution of political positions and the development of role expectations applicable to them. This does not mean, of course, that all developed systems have a similar role structure.[37]

In another example, the fight against poverty in the United States has focused on the development of a particular set of role orientations among those who are the victims of the cycle of poverty. The acquisition of both general and specific orientations and their accompanying skills have been promoted and are related to the role of worker in general and to a more specific role, such as television repairman, electrician, or mechanic. As a first step, the role orientations appropriate to a trainee are emphasized. Much of the policy debate has centered around the most effective methods and the more appropriate bureaucratic organization for developing these orientations. An accompanying problem has been in deciding on and developing the appropriate role orientations among the bureaucrats, corporate officials, and instructors administering these manpower training programs.

[37] Gabriel Almond and G. Bingham Powell, *Comparative Politics: A Developmental Approach* (Boston: Little, Brown and Company, 1966), pp. 306-10.

The role concept has proved useful in developing typologies for the classification of political actors in different types of political systems. However, one cannot say that it has been used substantially in the development of explicit, predictive propositions. One definition of theory is "a set of interrelated constructs (concepts), definitions, and propositions that presents a systematic view of phenomena by specifying relations among variables, with the purpose of explaining and predicting the phenomena."[38] Obviously, such a role theory of politics does not exist. Can the role concept and the aspects of it discussed in this chapter be used to develop theories of politics?

Role expectations can be used as independent variables to explain variations in the dependent variable of role enactment. Thus, differences in representational style and focus could in part be accounted for by differences in the role expectations perceived by various legislators. Role expectations could be used in developing predictive theory if adequate measures of variables affecting the perception of role expectations and appropriate measures of the different dimensions of role expectations can be developed. The work by Francis in creating a model of legislative instruction seeking indicates that the possibility exists. However, much greater attention to formulating researchable hypotheses and operationally defining concepts will be required.

What is the relationship between role and other concepts useful in studying individual behavior? A link between role and personality has been suggested by Kenneth P. Langton, who pointed out that the importance of the relationship of social institutions to attitudinal characteristics is a function of their implications for behavior. It has been argued that attitudes should be treated as intervening variables in behavior where the same initial stimuli are present but behavior varies. Resulting theories developed should have greater predictive values and also be more parsimonious. However, research results have not always supported the thesis that personality characteristics are an important intervening variable.[39] Langton points out that role theory can help account for this finding. The expectations others have about how an individual occupying a certain social role should behave help to explain the discrepancies. "Role is related to the individual to the extent that he internalizes appropriate attitudes and behavior, and it is related to the society in that group expectations exist, however ambiguously."[40]

[38] Fred Kerlinger, *Foundations of Behavioral Research* (New York: Holt, Rinehart, and Winston, 1965), p. 11.
[39] Kenneth P. Langton, *Political Socialization* (New York: Oxford University Press, 1969), pp. 13-14.
[40] *Ibid.*, pp. 14-15.

Group-Level Analysis

7

INTRODUCTION

How are people organized for political action? Do group memberships have a bearing upon political values, attitudes, beliefs, and opinions? Does group membership really have a bearing upon political action, or can we dismiss broad membership groupings as mere conveniences used for unjustifiable generalizing by pollsters and those who are prone to shallow political analysis? Is it profitable to examine political behavior in units larger than the individual but smaller than the political system? The group-level approach to political analysis has had a long and honorable tradition in political science, although it has undergone sharp revision and refinement in recent years. The importance of this approach lies not so much in the convenience it affords in the categorization of individuals, but in the ways it can be used to draw together diverse research in several areas and lead us toward more useful explanation and prediction. We know that the "group" concept "implies that the members . . . have something in common; they share, perhaps, a set

144

of values or they have identifiable characteristics which distinguish them from the rest of the population of a social system."[1]

DEFINITIONS

Although there are numerous definitions of groups, one of the most common is that which classifies groups according to their proximity to the individual member, as primary, secondary, and categoric. The *primary group* may be taken as that group or groups with which an individual has most frequent face-to-face contact. Included in this would be one's family, neighbors, work groups, friendship cliques, and so forth. The contact need not be continual in a day-to-day context, as long as the individual has had and may expect to participate·in a more or less regularized high frequency of personal interaction. *Secondary groups* are those in which the relationship is usually of a less personal nature, and with considerably lower interaction of a variety that does not involve frequent personal contact. Thus, the American Medical Association, AFL-CIO, and the American Political Science Association would serve as secondary groups for doctors, union members, and political scientists, respectively. *Categoric* or *tertiary groups* are those which have no organization at all, but are merely conveniences for classification, such as race, sex, age, or ethnic groups. By this definition, everyone belongs to several categoric groups, whether consciously or not.

All three of these classifications may be subsumed by another concept, that of the *reference group*. This particular category has been defined as "a group to whose standards people refer" in developing their opinions, attitudes, and beliefs.[2] This is usually a group from which one seeks approval, in which case we refer to a positive reference group. Thus, if one seeks the approval of one's family, the family acts passively as a positive reference group. If one is in a rebellious mood against the family, then we can think of the family as a primary negative reference group, providing cues as to how not to act. For conservative Republicans who are in business for themselves, the National Association of Manufacturers or the Chamber of Commerce may act as secondary positive reference groups, whereas these two groups may act as negative reference points for a union member. Thus membership is not a prerequisite for

[1] Don R. Bowen, *Political Behavior of the American Public* (Columbus, Ohio: Charles E. Merrill Publishing Company, 1968), p. 41.

[2] Bernard R. Berelson and Gary A. Steiner, *Human Behavior: An Inventory of Scientific Findings* (New York: Harcourt, Brace, and World, Inc., 1964), p. 558.

a group to assist in the organization of one's perceptions.[3] A reference group can be also of a categoric or tertiary nature as well. For those who "don't trust anyone over 30," the so-called "generation gap" is a very real thing, symbolized by the negative cues supplied by the categoric group of over-30's. Ethnic groups are prominent examples of positive and negative reference groups.

GROUPS' INFLUENCES ON INDIVIDUALS

Political scientists are especially eager to demonstrate relationships, and one area in which considerable effort has been expended has been that of group influences, particularly upon individual members and non-members. Others have turned to inter-group relationships or to influences of groups upon the political system itself. We have already paid some considerable attention to group influences upon members, especially in the chapter on political socialization. We turn now to considerations of why individuals join groups or organizations in the first place, following which we discuss group influences upon members and non-members, other groups, and the political system.

In reviewing research on group memberships, Berelson and Steiner noted that there is a tendency to join organizations which express attitudes and values consistent with those already held by the individual. By joining such an organization, it can be expected that the new member will receive not only a reinforcement of his value positions and opinions, but may also have latent beliefs awakened, as new information and opinions are brought out by respected members of the group. The interaction of group members is likely to lead to the expression of values and opinions of which the new or old member might have been only dimly aware, if aware at all. Discussion of new issues and events may be based upon either previously expressed opinions or upon those beliefs which are fundamental to the group's purpose and/or membership.[4] Thus, if the government announces a new program to re-vitalize the cities, a member of the group might mention it in passing, with some critical comment, pro or con. This in turn could lead to further discussion, whether informed or not, which would act as a cue for other group members, even if they had not participated in the discussion. The issue itself might not even be germane to the group's purpose. Members of

[3] Robert E. Lane and David O. Sears, *Public Opinion* (Englewood Cliffs: Prentice-Hall, Inc., 1964), p. 34.
[4] Berelson and Steiner, *op. cit.*, pp. 331-39.

a bowling team, which meets primarily for athletic and social purposes, could briefly mention the federal government's new cities program in the course of an evening, thus awakening and crystallizing beliefs which the members might never have discussed before. One does not necessarily make a conscious effort to seek out and join groups which are similar in value and opinion-holding to one's own pre-existing positions. Nonetheless, it is fairly easy for an individual to ascertain if thus-and-such a group is "like us," and whether or not it would be pleasant to affiliate with the group. In other words, there is a tendency for persons to seek out homogeneous group memberships.[5] It is the rare individual who will consciously affiliate the other way, because he enjoys a good argument. Rather, most of us enjoy receiving reinforcement of our positions, political and otherwise, and our group memberships tend to reflect this.

Factors which affect the influence of a group upon its members are several and were described in Chapter Four on attitudes. Among those we listed as operating to increase conformity to group standards and norms are smallness of size, frequency of contact, homogeneity of opinion, and internal cohesion. If a group is small, meets frequently, is comprised of individuals who generally hold the same beliefs, and has a great deal of solidarity, it can be expected that pressures to conform will be present to a high degree. Another factor affecting conformity is that which relates to democratic decision-making. If an individual feels that he has participated in the making of some decision, he is likely to be more committed to the group's opinion than one who has merely been a bystander. Similarly, if an issue is ambiguous and the results of a position are difficult to predict, the group may act as a supplier of cues to opinion and action.[6] An example of this might be the difficulty of predicting every four years which presidential candidate might take positions and actions basically in accord with one's own position. In this respect, even though the outcomes are ambiguous and distant in time, it is common to rely upon the political party of the candidate as a source of positive or negative reference cues before one casts his ballot.

An example of the importance of groups in the formation and crystallizing of one's opinions may be found by examining the characteristics of those who most often have been found to answer survey questions with a reply of "no opinion." Although they may be described by categoric or tertiary group descriptions such as "poorly educated" or "of rural residence," they are often found to be deficient in primary and

---

[5] Berelson and Steiner, op. cit., pp. 327-31.
[6] Lane and Sears, op. cit., pp. 34-36.

secondary group memberships to which they can refer for cues. They may also be unaware of the stand which their appropriate reference group has voiced on a given issue, or have been unable to predict how that group might feel, for that matter.[7]

All of this is not to suggest, however, that there are not individual differences within groups, and that such differences as may exist are unimportant. An example of a primary group, within which one may detect considerable differences, is that of the Supreme Court. The "nine old men" meet regularly with each other, in the hearing of cases, in consultation with one another individually, and as a group to discuss cases before them. Yet, there has not been a history of abandoned unanimity of opinion, or 9-0 decisions. Eloise Snyder has examined the Supreme Court for the 1921-1953 period, in which time over 1,100 cases involving constitutional amendments were presented for decisions in more than 10,000 cases.[8] Certainly, it would seem that a functional group of as few as nine men would have considerable influence upon its individual members. Yet, Snyder's evidence is such that even smaller groups or cliques were found to exist. One was more given over to broader interpretations of the Constitution; another to somewhat restrictive interpretations; and the third was pivotal between the two, depending upon the issue or case at hand.[9] But, there was little evidence to suggest that any of these cliques, comprised of just a few persons, were necessarily the determinants of behavior among their member justices. Rather, a new member "tended to be 'ingested' by the Supreme Court through the pivotal clique and then, after a period of functioning with the Court, found his place in the group by joining one of the two opposing cliques."[10] Indeed, as numerous later studies have developed the theme, it would appear that the justices are guided in their decisions by ideology, presumably brought in before pre-Court days as well as developed through Court experience. Further, while one might impute a single ideological leaning to a given justice, this would be a rather simplistic approach. A justice might have a presumably liberal attitude on certain broad types of issues (civil rights, civil liberties, etc.), and still be consistently conservative on other issues (property rights, federal expansion of powers, and the like). In other words, while groups may very well affect the holding of opinions, attitudes, values, and beliefs, they are not necessarily pervasive, and considerable latitude exists

[7] Lane and Sears, op. cit., p. 40.
[8] "The Supreme Court as a Small Group," Social Forces, XXXVI (March, 1958), pp. 232-38.
[9] Ibid., p. 234.
[10] Ibid., p. 238.

for individual variation. This is, indeed, a basic weakness of the group-level approach to political analysis.

One example of the way in which political scientists have employed the group concept is in the study of voting behavior. In a sense, this represents a bridge between group influences on individuals, and group influences on politics. An early and often-cited version of such research is that by Angus Campbell and Homer C. Cooper, *Group Differences in Attitudes and Votes.*[11] Several demographic variables such as race, sex, religion, and education are considered, very much in the same way as earlier studies of voting behavior had concentrated on such variables.[12] They find, predictably enough, that these variables are strongly related to voting patterns, that party identification itself is a more valid indicator of future political action than demography alone.[13] Related to this is the phenomenon of ethnic voting behavior. Wolfinger has shown what many political candidates either have known or should have known for some time, that ethnic voting continues to be a persistent and important theme in American politics.[14] Although the last major waves of immigration ended just before the First World War, "national origins continue to be a salient dimension in many people's perceptions of themselves and of others."[15]

The "melting pot" thesis which we all learned in grade school has been largely dispelled by political scientists and sociologists who have investigated the impact of immigration and ethnic groups in this country.[16] We may speak of the "black vote," or the "Jewish vote," quite frequently, in describing the support provided by these groups to one party or another. Although it is ridiculous to imply that all voters of these ethnic or categoric groups will and do vote for any single candidate, these and others may well throw their support to disproportionate numbers behind a single party or aspirant. Among the more extreme examples of this are the 92.1 per cent vote by Jews for Roosevelt in

[11] (Ann Arbor: Survey Research Center, Institute for Social Research, University of Michigan, 1956).

[12] Most notably, Paul F. Lazarsfeld, Bernard R. Berelson, and Hazel Gaudet, *The People's Choice* (New York: Columbia University Press, 1948), and Bernard R. Berelson, Paul F. Lazarsfeld, and William N. McPhee, *Voting* (Chicago: University of Chicago Press, 1954).

[13] Campbell and Cooper, *op. cit.*, pp. 35-37.

[14] Raymond E. Wolfinger, "The Development and Persistence of Ethnic Voting," *American Political Science Review*, LIX (December, 1965), pp. 896-908.

[15] *Ibid.*, p. 896.

[16] Two good examples, using different approaches, are Nathan Glazer and Daniel Patrick Moynihan, *Beyond the Melting Pot* (Cambridge: M.I.T. Press and Harvard University Press, 1963), and Edgar Litt, *Ethnic Politics in America* (Boston: Scott, Foresman and Company, 1970).

1944[17] and the N.B.C. sample precinct analysis which showed 94 percent of blacks voting for Humphrey in 1968.[18] The same patterns are present to some extent in many of the identifiable ethnic groups in America, and political parties are not insensitive to this. For years, New York City parties have attempted to have a "balanced ticket," with a clearly identifiable candidate of Irish, Italian, and Jewish extraction on the ballot. Lately they have taken to adding blacks and Puerto Ricans to their slates, and city-wide candidates have been famous for taking the mandatory "Three-I" tour (Ireland, Italy, and Israel) immediately before the election.

Without going any further into the rich area of research which ethnic politics affords, we might well ask whether such patterns will necessarily continue. Parenti cites a major body of literature which suggests that ethnic voting and politics will continue for some time to come. Despite non-homogeneity of residential patterns, differential s-e-s levels within each group, and a host of other factors which seemingly work toward "assimilation," ethnicity is still a major force to be reckoned with in political behavior.

> That many urban and suburban politicians persist in giving attentive consideration to minority social groupings in American-born constituencies, then, may be due less to their inveterate stupidity than to the fact that ethnic substructures and identification are still extant, highly visible, and, if handled carefully, highly accessible and responsive. The political practitioner who chooses to ignore the web of formal and informal ethnic substructures on the presumption that such groupings are a thing of the past does so at his own risk.[19]

Evidence that at least one of the major parties is not of a mind to take such a risk is the recent *The Emerging Republican Party* by Kevin P. Phillips.[20] Regarded by some as the Republican blueprint for victory beyond the end of this century, Phillips' analysis is based largely on regional and ethnic bloc voting tendencies, such as those we have described here.

[17] Wesley Allinsmith and Beverly Allinsmith, "Religious Affiliation and Politico-Economic Attitudes," *Public Opinion Quarterly*, XII (Fall, 1948), p. 387.

[18] *Congressional Quarterly*, November 29, 1968, p. 3218.

[19] Michael Parenti, "Ethnic Politics and the Persistence of Ethnic Identification," *American Political Science Review*, LXI (September, 1967), p. 725.

[20] (New Rochelle, N.Y.: Arlington House, 1969).

GROUP INFLUENCES ON POLITICS

Do majorities rule? What *is* a majority, for that matter? Is it related
to a single issue? a candidacy? If it exists, does its composition and/or
preferences change over time? Robert A. Dahl has addressed himself
to these and a series of related questions. In considering the political
process in America, he states that "the making of governmental decisions
is not a majestic march of great majorities united upon certain matters
of basic policy. It is the steady appeasement of relatively small groups."[21]
If Dahl is right, how then are groups heard in the first place, and why
do governments feel the necessity to appease them at all?

One explanation, which is relative to individuals as well as groups,
is that which relates intensity to political participation. "All other things
being equal, the outcome of a policy decision will be determined by
the relative intensity of preference among the members of a group."[22]
If a few members of a group feel quite intense about their side in an
issue, it is expected that their preferences might prevail in any discussion. Similarly, if a particular group, engaged in pressure activity vis-a-vis
the government, feels and acts intensely about its position, it has a
valuable resource which may be employed to impress legislators and
administrators alike. Certainly, a desultory approach, lacking in con
viction, could hardly be expected to impress governmental decision-
makers with the urgency or necessity of a given solution to a problem.
Hence, groups which operate on the basis of ideology may have a distinct advantage on their side, if they are competing with other groups
which are not impelled to action in an intense manner.

However, even before intensity of conviction and action can be
brought to bear upon the political system, a necessary precondition
would appear to exist, namely access to those in power. One of the
foremost students of group activity has been David B. Truman. In discussing how groups may obtain access to a legislature, he suggests that
two types of factors affect the process. These are of the formal variety,
such as rules governing apportionment or the structure and operation
of the legislature; or they may be of the informal type, where the
"effect is somewhat more subtle but of at least equal significance."[23]

[21] *A Preface to Democratic Theory* (Chicago: Phoenix Books, The University of
Chicago Press, 1956), p. 146.
[22] *Ibid.*, p. 147.
[23] *The Governmental Process: Political Interests and Public Opinion* (New
York: Alfred A. Knopf, Inc., 1951), p. 322.

Examples of the latter might include the need of the legislator for opinions and information relative to pending legislation, or to how well he relates to other members of his chamber in their differing roles. For instance, if a congressman is uncertain as to the potential effects of a yea or nay vote on a bill, groups which could supply him with such information, especially as to its political consequences, could be expected to have greater access to him.[24] In short,

> The degree of access to the legislature that a particular group enjoys at a given moment is the result of a composite of influences. . . . Depending on the circumstances and the relative importance of these factors in a given situation, some groups will enjoy comparatively effective access, and others will find difficulty in securing even perfunctory treatment.[25]

But, Truman cautions us not to accept the point of view that government in general or the legislature in particular is at all "just a sounding board or passive registering device for the demands of organized political interest groups."[26] In sum, groups can be highly effective in obtaining certain ends from government. However, they operate in an environmental context, the variables of which they may be unable to control. Groups in the Truman view are therefore essentially contributory to rather than determinative of governmental policy and direction, if only because there may well be competing groups in the system.

Studies of group influence upon politics abound. The conventional approach, and one which has contributed greatly to the literature on policy-making, is that of the case study. Examples are those which have explored in depth the making of a particular bill, such as a new employment act,[27] a civil rights act,[28] ratification of the nuclear test ban treaty,[29] and so forth. In such an approach, the researcher carefully weighs the effects and contributions of various individuals and groups who have contributed to the final decision, bill or policy. A recent example of this approach is *Smoking and Politics*[30] which examines, among other things, the contribution of the tobacco industry in hindering and resist-

[24] *Ibid.*, p. 335.
[25] *Ibid.*, p. 350.
[26] *Ibid.*
[27] Stephen K. Bailey, *Congress Makes a Law: The Story Behind the Employment Act of 1946* (New York: Columbia University Press, 1950).
[28] Daniel M. Berman, *A Bill Becomes a Law: Congress Enacts Civil Rights Legislation* (2nd ed.; New York: The Macmillan Company, 1964).
[29] Ronald J. Terchek, *The Making of the Test Ban Treaty* (The Hague: Neijhoff, 1969).
[30] A. Lee Fritschler (New York: Appleton-Century-Crofts, 1969).

ing legislation which requires effective labeling of cigarette packages. Other groups participated in the decision-making process as well, including doctors, the Surgeon General's office, and citizens who were aroused enough on either side of the issue to write or otherwise petition their congressman.

GROUP PRESSURE TECHNIQUES

The popular version of pressure group activity is that which has been offered in the press; slick-talking people who represent big-money interests button-hole legislators, and cross their palms with silver, bribing them with huge sums to do the bidding of those who are, more likely than not, corporate "fat cats" who puff away on big cigars, all the while manipulating political power. While we may have overdrawn the image, it is indeed the impression that one can get from the occasional "revelations" which presumably help sell newspapers. This is not to say that bribery or even coercion is not attempted, but it would be simplistic to assume either that this is the only way in which groups bring their influence to bear upon the government, or that it is necessarily effective, for that matter. It is true that most pressure activity tends to be obscured from the national headlines, but several reasons may be offered for this. For one, lobbyists on behalf of the various interest groups do not openly solicit votes from congressmen in the presence of reporters. Furthermore, a great deal of legislation is of the minor variety, affecting a minimal number of persons or groups, so that the popular press might have little reason to publicize efforts to affect such legislation in the first place. This is related, of course, to the concern of the general public with specific policy legislation. To expect the average individual to be concerned with a broad spectrum of governmental activity, when some of it doesn't directly affect him, might very well be too much to ask. Hence, we may speak of "attentive" and "general publics."[31] The attentive public may be defined as including those who normally follow the course of government in a close and intimate manner, as well as those who are aware that they may be directly affected by potential or actual governmental activity. Thus, these persons and groups would be more likely to have an interest in pressure group activity, and might very well participate in such activity themselves.

[31] Gabriel A. Almond, *The American People and Foreign Policy* (New York: Frederick A. Praeger, Inc., 1960), p. 138.

A useful point of departure in any discussion of pressure group activity would be to specify the object(s) of pressure. It is commonly assumed that legislatures are the only bodies of government subject to pressure, a point which is wholly without substantiation. This would imply that the other two major branches of government, executive and judicial, would be immune from influence and potentially unresponsive to demands. Further, we must account for the activity of groups which have no constitutional foundation, such as political parties, if we are to consider objects of political pressure and influence. Vose, for instance, has shown that courts are particularly susceptible to pressure groups, through litigation if nothing else. Groups may bring cases before the courts if issues are involved that directly concern or affect them. They may also enter court cases on behalf of individuals, where some fundamental principle is at stake, affecting more than the person directly involved in the immediate issue. Test cases and amicus curiae (friend of the court) briefs can also be used to spell out a particular position held by the group in an attempt to influence the courts.[32] This point has also been made by Truman, in his study of formal and informal group processes.

> The activities of the judicial officers of the United States are not exempt from the processes of group politics. Relations between interest groups and judges are not identical with those between groups and legislators or executive officials, but the difference is rather one of degree than of kind.[33]

In a similar vein, we may also expect to find that interest groups find it appropriate in given circumstances to bring pressure to bear upon those in the bureaucracy charged with carrying out legislative intentions and policies. For instance, the American Medical Association no doubt would find it in its own best interest, having lost the battle over Medicare, to cooperate with the Department of Health, Education, and Welfare in promoting specific policies which were most favorable to the medical profession. Another example of bringing pressure to bear upon the bureaucracy would concern school integration. Southern interests opposing integration, and black militants favoring a separatist position might well find it to their advantage to offer reasons to the Office of Education as to why the pace of integration should be slowed, Supreme Court decisions to the contrary notwithstanding.

[32] Clement A. Vose, "Litigation as a Form of Pressure Group Activity," Annals of the American Academy of Political and Social Science, CCCXIX (September, 1958), pp. 20-31.
[33] Truman, op. cit., p. 479.

Lobbying, or pressure activity, is not necessarily restricted to groups outside of government, for that matter. When the administration takes a position and transmits it to Congress in the form of a presidential special message, it is acting as a lobby in its own way. Most of the major governmental agencies maintain what are euphemistically known as "legislative liaison officers," whose function is nominally to keep both Congress and their own agencies informed as to what the other is doing and thinking on specific legislation. In reality, these persons can and do perform significant pressure activity for their specific agency, seeking to get the Congress to enact legislation which is most in accord with administration and/or agency wishes. Thus, the interaction of various departments and agencies of government can result in the performance of pressure functions upon a branch of the government, by another part of the government. In this case, the pressure group may well be classified as of a primary nature, inasmuch as it involves work functions of a daily interactive face-to-face nature.

One of the better students of pressure activity by Washington lobbyists has been Lester W. Milbrath. He found that there were essentially three basic categories of influence technique. The first of these, "direct personal communication," involved the personal presentation of arguments (considered to be the most effective), personal presentation of research results, and testimony at committee hearings. Lobbyists may also work through intermediaries, using such devices as contact by constituents and close friends, mass letter and telegram campaigns, public relations campaigns, and the publicizing of voting records. The final technique is that with which the public is presumably most familiar; "opening communications channels," a euphemism which covers such methods as bribery (hardly if ever used, according to the lobbyists he interviewed), entertaining, campaign work, and collaboration or logrolling with other groups.[34]

Although in this section we have focused primarily on lobbying, or a specific set of means of bringing group pressure to bear upon the political system, pressure activities are not necessarily restricted to lobbying alone. Groups may make their wishes known through a variety of other techniques, consciously or unconsciously. A recent example of such activity, and one could scarcely term it "lobbying" in the conventional sense, is that of the mass demonstration. When protesters march on the Pentagon, or on the Department of Justice, they are engaging in a form of group pressure activity that has had a long history. In the

[34] "Lobbying as a Communications Process," *Public Opinion Quarterly*, XXIV (Spring, 1960), pp. 32-53.

United States alone, violent protest activity has been traced back as far as the early seventeenth century, when Indians sought to prevent white settlers from invading their property and individual rights. Farmers, city dwellers, white Southerners, women, and others have occasionally resorted to protest, violent and otherwise, in order to press their demands for recognition and to stress the legitimacy of their positions.[35] When protest takes on violent aspects, special problems are raised for the political system. One has been of such a nature that it could result in the dissolution of the protesters as a group.

> . . . the official approach to the problem of mass revolt has been to offer the rebels the benefits of individualism — reforms which promise members of the insurgent group fairer treatment, more votes, more jobs, and so on — provided only that they give up "unrealistic" demands for control of territory, recognition of collective political and economic interests, and the like. Naturally, such offers are rejected by the insurgents.[36]

Inasmuch as conflict may be a technique used by a group to achieve its ends, we now turn to the role played by groups in politics as conflict.

GROUPS AND POLITICAL CONFLICT

One school of thought in political science has it that groups are the basis of politics. Truman asserts that ". . . even in its nascent stages government functions to establish and maintain a measure of order in the relationships among groups for various purposes."[37] Indeed,

> Unless one denies, first, that the notion of differentiations in the habitual interactions of men is synonymous with the notion of groups and, second, that government is made up of just such patterns of habitual interaction, acceptance of groups as lying at the heart of the process of government is unavoidable.[38]

[35] *The Politics of Protest*, A Report Submitted by Jerome H. Skolnick, Director, Task Force on Violent Aspects of Protest and Confrontation of the National Commission on the Causes and Prevention of Violence (New York: Clarion Books, Simon and Schuster, 1969), pp. 10-15.
[36] *Ibid.*, p. 20.
[37] Truman, *op. cit.*, p. 45.
[38] Truman, *op. cit.*, p. 45.

Another view of politics is one which is essentially compatible with group theory, a view that politics is concerned with the allocative process. As Lasswell's formulation put it, *Politics: Who Gets What, When, How.*[39] Froman has stated that politics is "concerned with the distribution of advantages and disadvantages."[40] Easton defines the political system "as those interactions through which values are authoritatively allocated for a society; . . ."[41] All three of these definitions implicitly offer the opportunity for conflict, inasmuch as resources, advantages, and values may be scarce. These definitions further accommodate the group view of politics since groups may actively compete for the rewards to be distributed by the political system, on their own behalf as well as for individuals.

A study which examines the roles played by groups in political and social conflict is that offered by James S. Coleman in his *Community Conflict.*[42] Examining the ways in which conflict has been made evident in American communities in recent years, Coleman proceeds to develop a theory of conflict which is largely based upon the role of groups in competition for scarce resources and values. Four examples of issues which have been raised in local communities are examined by Coleman: school policy, fluoridation, industrialization, and libraries. While these issues may appear to be prosaic enough to the average reader, they are frequently typified by high intensity and involvement of the local citizenry. To bring this into better focus, Coleman states that there are essentially four types of issues with which communities are concerned, above and beyond the immediate ones he selected for study. These include issues concerning economics, the power or authority of public officials, cultural values, and personality reactions. The type of controversy, in turn, is likely to be related to the nature of the city; central or self-contained cities are more prone to issues which are economic; dependent or satellite cities, such as a suburb, tend to have disputes over cultural issues; and "service cities," such as resorts, frequently have personality disputes.

The size and nature of the community, according to Coleman, also has a bearing on how individuals participate. In larger cities, there is a

[39] Harold Lasswell (Cleveland: Meridian Books, World Publishing Company, 1958).

[40] Lewis A. Froman, Jr., *People and Politics: An Analysis of the American Political System* (Englewood Cliffs, N.J.: Prentice-Hall, Inc., 1962), p. 6.

[41] David Easton, *A Systems Analysis of Political Life* (New York: John Wiley & Sons, Inc., 1965), p. 21.

[42] James S. Coleman (Glencoe, Ill.: The Free Press of Glencoe, 1957). The following discussion relies heavily upon Chapter 2 of this work, "The Dynamics of Controversy," pp. 9-14.

tendency for individuals to express themselves through intermediary organizations, whereas in smaller communities where more personal arguments take place, existing voluntary associations frequently act on behalf of the individual. But, before we get to the various roles played by groups, it is necessary to elaborate on how issues arise and change in the process of conflict.

Coleman notes that there are essentially three major changes in issues over time. The first of these is a tendency for specific issues to give way to those which are more general. If a dispute arises over the placing of certain books on the library shelves, it may be expected that the more general issue, such as censorship or First Amendment freedoms, will emerge shortly. A notable exception to this tendency is for political issues, especially those which involve fewer people for the most part, to remain essentially specific. "Political controversies, for example, exhibit the pattern much less than do disputes based primarily on differing values or economic interests."[43] The reasons for this must remain hypothetical for the time, but one of the more consistent findings in the literature is that there is a notable tendency, in this country at least, towards minimal popular involvement in politics. Milbrath cites and reviews a considerable body of literature on this point.[44]

> About one-third of the American adult population can be characterized as politically apathetic or passive; in most cases, they are unaware, literally, of the political part of the world around them. Another 60 per cent play largely spectator roles in the political process; they watch, they cheer, they vote, but they do not do battle.[45]

A second major change is that which brings in different issues, however unrelated to the original issue they may be. This may happen because of two factors; for one, the relationships inherent within the community are susceptible to change themselves as soon as the original issue is raised. If relationships are upset, however, issues which had been previously suppressed or accepted as the normal way of things may be expected to arise, as the equilibrium of the community is now disturbed. Secondly, and especially so in the realm of political issues, "the diversification of issues is more a purposive move on the part of the antagonists, and serves quite a different function: to solidify opinion and bring in

---

[43] *Ibid.*, p. 10.
[44] Lester W. Milbrath, *Political Participation: How and Why Do People Get Involved in Politics?* (Chicago: Rand McNally and Company, 1965), pp. 16-22.
[45] *Ibid.*, p. 21.

new participants by providing new bases of response."[46] The third element in the ways in which issues change is a movement from disagreement to hostility or antagonism, from fairly reasoned or dispassionate argument to less rational forms of discourse. A summary of the three steps involved may be "flow-charted" according to Coleman as follows:

1. Initial single issue.
2. Disrupts equilibrium of community relations.
3. Allows previously suppressed issues against opponents to appear.
4. More and more of opponent's beliefs enter into the disagreement.
5. The opponent appears totally bad.
6. Charges against opponent as a person.
7. Dispute becomes independent of initial disagreement.[47]

It might superficially appear that Coleman has presented us with a statement which has its basis primarily on individual action, with no special functions to be performed by groups. However, groups, and the roles they play, are found by Coleman to be central to the entire community conflict process, inasmuch as they form the basis for the community's social organization, and also act to upset local equilibrium by performing several of the steps outlined above.[48] For instance, as the controversy begins to expand in scope, individuals will seek allies, and ad hoc organizations emerge which are polarized on the initial and then subsequent issues.

The controversy literally serves to create groups, according to Coleman, inasmuch as shared values and attitudes are given voice, when they might have otherwise been suppressed. New leaders are brought into the controversy as well, particularly as these highly charged partisan organizations emerge.

> . . . often they are men who have not been community leaders in the past, men who face none of the restraints of maintaining a previous community position . . . In addition, these leaders rarely have real identification with the community.[49]

As existing community organizations are drawn into the controversy, their leaders frequently find themselves polarized against the new mili-

[46] Coleman, op. cit., p. 10.
[47] Ibid., p. 11.
[48] See also George C. Homans, The Human Group (New York: Harcourt, Brace, and World, Inc., 1950), pp. 459-60.
[49] Coleman, op. cit., p. 12.

tants, a factor which should not prove unfamiliar to those students who have followed black politics in recent years. Organizations in the North and South alike which had not taken an overt position on school integration, for example, found themselves drawn into the controversy, whether or not it was fundamental to their purpose. For instance, such groups as the American Legion or the Lions, normally looked upon as social-interest organizations, were not founded to take positions of national interest, with the exception of patriotism and national social norms. Nonetheless, they may have been drawn into the school segregation controversy in selected communities because of the other interests of their leaders and members.

Existing community organizations are, however, not necessarily drawn into a controversy. There may be significant pressures from within the community as well as from within the group to remain neutral or to disengage from the conflict. If this is to happen, the consequences to the group may result in group maintenance, but at some costs, as the newer or "combat" ad hoc groups may pre-empt the field of battle. In either event, the controversy is more likely than not to be expressed through groups which can become important new means of communicating views and shared attitudes, however distorted they may be. Indeed, if the conflict gets out of hand at all, those organizations and elements in the community which might normally play a conciliatory or "dampening" role are neutralized.[50]

One factor cited by Coleman as contributing to a minimum of tension is that of overlapping memberships in various groups, a point often mentioned by sociologists concerned with group activity.[51] We use the term "cross-pressured" to refer to situations in which individuals are subjected to two or more sets of attitudes, opinions, or beliefs which conflict with one another. Cross-pressures may be derived from individuals directly, or from groups. An example of the first might be feelings towards one's parents, and the attitudes that derive from them as well as the feelings themselves. One's father might be a die-hard Democrat, a union member with a strong penchant for political activism; if one's mother is equally intense and active as a Republican, we can describe this situation as one of extreme cross-pressures on the individual. Similarly, one belonging to two or more primary groups, such as

---

[50] *Ibid.*, pp. 12-13.
[51] *Ibid.*, p. 13. See also Seymour Martin Lipset, *Political Man: The Social Bases of Politics* (Garden City, N.Y.: Anchor Books, Doubleday and Company, Inc., 1963), pp. 75-82. "The available evidence suggests that the chances for stable democracy are enhanced to the extent that groups and individuals have a number of crosscutting, politically relevant affiliations." p. 77.

the family and peer group, which hold differing viewpoints on the same issue, is therefore also in a situation of cross-pressures. Milbrath's review of the literature on voting and political participation states the role of groups in cross-pressure situations as a general proposition. "Persons belonging to two or more groups which pull in opposite directions (cross-pressured persons) are likely to have diminished political interest." [52] Thus, if one lives and works in a homogeneous situation, it could be expected that cross-pressures would not be present to a significant degree. If this is the case, reinforcement of existing positions might occur and intensify political participation and political conflict. In a heterogeneous situation, on the other hand, cross-pressuring would be more likely, thus serving to diminish participation and perhaps minimizing conflict. But, as suggested earlier, when individuals are pressured out of participation in conflict situations, they may be forfeiting the chance to voice possibly moderate positions in favor of those who are not cross-pressured, and are more prone to taking extremist positions. The role of groups in community conflict, in both suppressing and raising issue stands, can therefore be fundamental to community equilibrium and the patterns which conflict follow.

Examining some of the major propositions of Georg Simmel, sociologist Lewis A. Coser demonstrates the essential role of groups in conflict situations. [53] A major part of this review is his assertion that conflict essentially creates and helps to identify groups. [54] This is not to assume that all groups necessarily have their bases in conflict, but only to point out that shared interests may very well involve the taking of positions which are mutually acceptable and may be opposed to those of others. Conflict within a group can also take place, despite the common basis of shared attitudes or interests. If this is so, and there is a formal or informal provision within the group for the expression of hostile viewpoints, as well as for "clearing the air," it might be said that conflict can then perform a "safety-valve" function, and act to preserve the group in the long run. "Conflict is thus seen as performing group-maintaining functions insofar as it regulates systems of relationships." [55] In this line, Coser adds that those groups which are relatively flexible and are loosely structured are more likely to have some provision for allowing conflict to arise rather than be suppressed. In other words, they "institute safeguards against the type of conflict which would endanger

[52] Milbrath, *Political Participation, op. cit.,* p. 55.
[53] *The Functions of Social Conflict* (Glencoe, Ill.: The Free Press of Glencoe, 1956).
[54] *Ibid.,* pp. 33-38.
[55] *Ibid.,* p. 39.

basic consensus and thereby minimize the danger of divergences touching core values."[56]

Conflict with other groups, whether direct or in competition with each other, as for scarce values, can serve to increase internal cohesion and solidarity, according to Coser.[57] Just as conflict helps to identify groups for others, it also increases internal identification of the group for its constituent members. Under such conditions, centralization of group authority may take place, provided the conflict is of a protracted or violent type, and if the nature of the group is such that differentiated labor is required. An example of this might be when a nation goes to war with another nation, and finds that, in order to mobilize its resources, even on the home front, greater authority is necessary at higher levels. Thus, rationing may take place, under some central office, and the free market economy which might otherwise prevail is displaced at least temporarily. Another example might be drawn from the experience of black groups in this country in the 1960s. Numerous black organizations grew and withered in this decade, some more militant than others. Some of the older and less militant organizations, such as the N.A.A.C.P. or the Urban League, were challenged by the newer groups for not being militant enough. These newer organizations, such as CORE, tended to have both a greater militancy and a higher degree of centralization of effort. The Black Panthers, probably the most militant of the newer black organizations, explicitly took the position that they were engaged in combat, although not necessarily of a violent nature. The militancy of their attitudes is revealed in a tight, almost para-military form of organization, exceeding in centralization of command that seen in any of the other black groups. When the conflict did assume a more violent nature, such as the 1969 shooting by Chicago police of Fred Hampton, chairman of the Illinois Black Panthers, the black community responded in various ways to increase their identification with the Panthers, even if they were not members. A characteristic of groups engaged in continuous struggle, such as the Panthers, is not only that internal centralization takes place, but that they may also become quite intolerant of deviations by members. "Such groups tend to assume a sect-like character: they select membership in terms of special characteristics and so tend to be limited in size, and they lay claim to the total personality involvement of their members."[58] Groups of this nature, according to Coser, may also be more inclined to seek out

[56] *Ibid.*, p. 80.
[57] *Ibid.*, pp. 87-95.
[58] *Ibid.*, p. 103.

"enemies," or to create them if needs be.[59] As their internal cohesion and unity may rest in part upon the existence of opposing groups, they may very well be unconsciously inclined to view other groups as necessarily opposing them. Such a view may actually serve to create opposing groups, whether or not they existed in the first instance. An example of this might be the way in which "law and order" forces in this country have occasionally created a picture which suggests that the poor, the black, and the young are forces of social dissolution. If members of these categoric groups feel that they are attacked unjustifiably, they may coalesce to form primary and secondary organizations to express their point of view, that they themselves are not necessarily against the social order at all. Rather, they may suggest that it is the "law and order" element in society which chooses to ignore basic social and moral obligations, and would sweep aside First Amendment protections of free speech and assembly.

Thus, the constant forming and re-forming of groups may be taken as being fundamental to political and social conflict. The means by which such conflict takes place is a subject sufficiently rich in potential to occupy political scientists for years to come.

SUMMARY AND CRITIQUE

There can be little doubt but that group-level analysis can and has provided some important clues to the study of political behavior. In our earlier chapter on political socialization, for instance, we found evidence to suggest that the family, as a primary group, can have a meaningful influence upon future political behavior. The study of attitudes is refined by the use of various categoric groups, such as age, sex, and regional groupings. Political activity often, as we have seen, finds its expression through groups, as individuals coalesce with others to attempt to achieve political and social ends. The literature of political science has had frequent recourse to group analysis. When we discuss parties, legislatures, courts, and bureaucracies, we are discussing groups, and not merely isolated individuals. Political science, in other words, simply cannot afford to ignore the group. Certainly, as we have demonstrated, any discussion of political conflict will almost inevitably involve the group concept, inasmuch as conflict often finds its expression through

[59] *Ibid.*, pp. 104-10.

groups, and may even have its roots in group antagonisms. Modern theories of democracy, such as those elaborated by Dahl, rely heavily upon the group as an organizing concept. Truman's application of the group concept also demonstrates its utility in studying the manner in which the United States government works.

Obviously, however, we have not been dealing with a single operational definition of "group." We have treated it in the sense of memberships (primary, secondary, and categoric) and perceptions (positive and negative references). There is little here to suggest a single theory of politics or human behavior. The study of ethnic politics, for instance, can be said to rely upon the group *approach*, employing basic sociological concepts to further understand how and why ethnicity is manifested in voting behavior or different styles of political participation. It would be fallacious to assume that this approach is embodied in a group *theory* of politics, however.

How else is the group concept operationalized? An alternative approach has been that taken by a large school of political scientists, who look upon the group as a collectivity of interests and action. Eckstein has summarized this whole approach, which devolves largely from Arthur F. Bentley's *The Process of Government,*[60] in the following manner:

> Politics is the process by which social values are authoritatively allocated; this is done by decisions; the decisions are produced by activities; each activity is not something separate from every other, but masses of activity have common tendencies in regard to decisions; these masses of activity are groups; so the struggle between groups (or interests) determines what decisions are taken.[61]

It is obvious here that we are dealing with something less than tangible, and not totally susceptible to empiricism. Yet, a considerable deal of research has been done in the name of group "theory," all from this frame of reference. A common error, according to Eckstein, has been to assume that the referent of "interests" necessarily implies that group theory, if it is indeed a theory, must concern itself with pressure groups.[62] This would seem to be an understandable error, considering the con-

---

[60] (Chicago: University of Chicago Press, 1908.)

[61] Harry Eckstein, "Introduction: Group Theory and the Comparative Study of Pressure Groups," in Eckstein and David E. Apter (eds.), *Comparative Politics: A Reader* (New York: The Free Press of Glencoe, 1963), p. 391.

[62] *Ibid.*

siderable stress placed upon the interest concept by Bentley and his followers.

If not just pressure groups, then what groups? in what circumstances? possessing what characteristics and what concerns over what interests? Group theorists have been notorious in their failure to come to grips with these definitional problems, and critics of "group theory" have had a field day demonstrating tautologies and imprecisions in the group approach. Odegard, for example, finds that "equilibrium" is used in the context of several different arguments by group theorists, all without any clear empirical reference.[63]

If group theory is to be regarded as a theory, then the group concept itself must be sufficiently clear that all can know what the theory purports to explain and predict. Yet, this is the main thrust of the criticisms directed at what passes for group theory. If we define groups in terms of certain sociological characteristics, such as primary, secondary, and so forth, we are fundamentally assuming that some form of activity or at least shared interests or attitudes defines that group. The shared activity may be nothing more than overt hostility among its members. In other words, the members are identifiable as a coherent unit because of something which they do, or something they are. Even when we can clearly identify the nature of the activity which underlies the group's existence, and can do so with many groups, do we have a group theory of politics? It may indeed be useful to look at political behavior by categorizing individuals into any number of groups, but such an endeavor

> . . . gives little information as to the pattern of group politics in a given society. Thus, it cannot tell us why and how individuals will do or behave politically. The superficial plausibility of the group approach rests upon a certain partial reading of American politics which enables group theorists to ignore the real premises from which they operate. If this is so, there is no warrant to assume that the study of politics is the study of groups. Rather groups are reduced to the status of one kind of political actor.[64]

[63] Peter H. Odegard, "A Group Basis of Politics: A New Name for an Old Myth," Western Political Quarterly, XI (September, 1958), pp. 296-97. The arguments put forward by Odegard on this point were apparently ignored by various systems analysts as well, who use and change the meaning of this term extensively. See Chap. X, "Systems Analysis."

[64] Stanley Rothman, "Systematic Political Theory: Observations on the Group Approach," American Political Science Review, LIV (March, 1960), p. 32.

An even more damaging attack on those who would hold that the group approach properly falls within the realm of theory is offered by Eckstein. He returns to the requirements of theory, and suggests that group "theory" can never be empirically tested because "it does not relate any variables to one another, nor specify any relations between variables."[65] Given this, and no amount of academic rhetoric by those who follow the group approach can deal adequately with the charge, we can see that "group theory" is thus lacking in testable explanatory or predictive capacities.

Another difficulty with the group approach is that of generalizability. If we do not accurately and precisely define the nature of the activity which supposedly characterizes the group, it is difficult at the least to assume that such activity may be engaged in by other groups. If the activity is ill-defined, we can never be at all certain that similar patterns of political behavior and actions exist in other or larger groups, or that any patterns exist at all, even within the one group under study. Fundamental to the approach taken by those of the group school is the assumption that some form of interest underlies the group itself. But, if interest and activity are defined in a circular sense, what is left for us to examine? And, can we assume that the interest is similar enough to that held by other groups to warrant generalization and prediction?

Related to this problem of generalizability is the manner in which group theorists have over-interpreted their own findings and approaches. If the group is an essential component of politics, as writers since Aristotle have maintained, can we really assert that they are anything more than components? Are they really "the stuff of politics"? In other words, the nature of the beast is such that, although the group may be properly treated as a major building block of the system, it is necessarily limited to being just an organizing concept, and not a broad-gauge theory at all. As Young points out, "the fundamental perspective of group theory precludes any substantial deviation from a subsystem orientation."[66] On the other side of the coin, one may examine the joining of organizations as possibly providing a clue to the group basis of politics, as Truman has done. But Rothman shows that even this can be over-interpreted, and cites a large body of evidence which thus far shows that Americans are not "joiners" in the popular sense of the word at all. Further, since group politics is not necessarily pressure politics upon the polity, and there is little overt joining of organizations, we are left with "very little evidence that these associations have an appreciable effect

[65] Eckstein, op. cit., p. 392.
[66] Oran R. Young, *Systems of Political Science* (Englewood Cliffs, N.J.: Prentice-Hall, Inc., 1968), p. 92.

upon the attitudes of their membership."[67] In short, the claims made for "group theory" far outweigh any empirical evidence which has been mustered in its behalf.

Another criticism of the group approach, if not of what purports to be group theory, is that it has by and large been applied in a parochially American fashion, almost exclusively to problems involving American politics. If we are to be able to develop empirical theory which is truly generalizable, then it must also apply to non-American and non-Western nations as well. Admittedly, we are all prone to studying that which is closest to us, and travel grants to study abroad are not always available. Nonetheless, there has been all too little attention paid to the supposed group basis of politics, although American political scientists have been studying abroad for many years. Where groups have been the focus of attention, there has been little if any attempt at replication. For instance, one volume deals with pressure groups on a cross-national basis.[68] However, the results of the studies it contains are essentially single-nation studies, non-comparative in nature, lacking in any single set of propositions which were tested uniformly in each of nine countries studied. While it may be pleasant to know that political scientists abroad are examining one facet of the group approach to the study of politics, we thus far have little evidence that what passes for theory possesses any qualities at all admitting to generalization.

But, if not theory, and lacking in generalizability, then what is left? We have suggested that groups may be used as an organizing concept, as a starting point for the study of politics. To ignore the concept of groups, in its many variations of definition, would be an omission of serious proportions. This has, unfortunately, been the case off and on for some time. Golembiewski, Welsh and Crotty rightly point out that there has been an almost cyclical or circular history of the group concept in political science. Bentley discusses the concept at some length, and then it is laid aside, to be discovered anew by someone or other. It then becomes the focus of any number of researchers until its problems become evident, and it is laid aside only to be rediscovered again at some later date.[69] Why is this so? What has caused political scientists to periodically ignore this organizing concept which, as the authors claim, supposedly "takes us right to the very heart of the disci-

[67] Rothman, op. cit., p. 22.

[68] Henry W. Ehrmann (ed.), Interest Groups on Four Continents (Pittsburgh: University of Pittsburgh Press, 1958).

[69] Robert T. Golembiewski, William A. Welsh, and William J. Crotty, A Methodological Primer for Political Scientists (Chicago: Rand McNally and Company, 1969), p. 122.

pline"?[70] One may very well suggest that academic faddism has its place in such an explanation, and this would not be totally in error. Political scientists are no less prone than members of other disciplines to jumping from one field of exploration to another as the occasion warrants. However, another explanation might lie in some of the fundamental problems of the group approach, which we have elaborated above.

What is ultimately left then is not a theory at all, but a set of concepts, poorly defined, with little basis for comparison between them in the development of more elaborate models or theories of political behavior. As we have demonstrated, the group approach is a major tool of descriptive analysis, and it thus plays an important role in the development of other models and theories. It will continue to be used, if not as the grand and general theory of politics which some of its more enamored adherents might hold, at least in the sense of classifying individuals into useful categories for description. Its potential is necessarily circumscribed, as we have demonstrated, but it can play a major role in the development of other would-be paradigms for political science.

[70] *Ibid.*, p. 121.

Decision-Making

8

INTRODUCTION

The decision-making approach is taken by many political scientists in the organization of their findings and in an attempt to deal with politics on a broad-gauge level. This approach takes the decision, and the events surrounding it, as the basic and stable unit of analysis fundamental to political life. However, the concern of those who belong to the decision-making school is not necessarily to establish quite literally how specific individuals arrive at decisions, although this may be implied from some of their classificatory schemes. Rather, there appears to be a concern with how whole systems operate in the decisional area. The system may be an administrative agency, a community, or the foreign policy apparatus of a nation. Regardless of the level of a political regime toward which attention is directed, however, the fundamental category is and remains the decision.

Among the leading proponents of this school is Harold D. Lasswell.[1] In several works he has laid a foundation for the decisional school.

[1] *The Future of Political Science* (New York: Atherton Press, 1963), esp. pp. 15-26; and, with Abraham Kaplan, *Power and Society* (New Haven: Yale University Press, 1950).

The approach he takes is one which is characterized by the process of fulfilling seven functions, which he describes in the following manner:

> Think of any act of decision. We conceive it as beginning in an influx of information from sources at the focus of attention of participants in the decision process, some of whom perceive that their goal values have been or may be affected in ways that can be influenced by community decision. We refer to this as the *intelligence* phase.
>
> The next phase is *recommending*, or promoting, which refers to activities designed to influence the outcome. The *prescribing* phase is the articulation of norms; it includes, for instance, the enacting of enforceable statutes. The *invoking* phase occurs when a prescription is provisionally used to characterize a set of concrete circumstances. When a prescription is employed with finality, we speak of *application*. The *appraisal* phase characterizes the relationship between policy goals and the strategies and results obtained. The *terminating* phase involves the handling of expectations ("rights") established when a prescription was in force.[2]

These classifications are used by Lasswell not merely for the convenience they afford in delineating the decision process, but to describe structures which are particularly involved with the fulfillment of the functions. Specialization by a structure does not necessarily imply that it is essential to the forms of analysis posited by Parsons and Almond.[3] For example, a field worker in the Head Start program might very well be involved in gathering and processing information as to the effects the program is having on pre-school children. He is not limited solely to the intelligence function, but might make recommendations and preliminary evaluations for consideration by Head Start officials in Washington. He would then be in the position of applying a new policy which could result from the information which he and others had gathered, and would naturally be involved in the appraisal function as well. While his position in the field for Head Start nominally requires that he be involved in the application phase as a primary function, he would inevitably perform several other functions as well.

Richard C. Snyder has clearly indicated the dynamic nature of decision-making analysis, involved as it is with "*time plus change* — change in relationships and conditions."[4] Given this, the decision-making ap-

---

[2] *The Future of Political Science*, pp. 15-16. Emphasis in original.

[3] See Chapter 9 — Systems Analysis.

[4] "A Decision-Making Approach to the Study of Political Phenomena," in Roland Young (ed.), *Approaches to the Study of Politics* (Evanston: Northwestern University Press, 1958), p. 10. Emphasis in original.

proach affords one the opportunity "to help identify and isolate the 'crucial structures' in the political realm where change takes place — where action is initiated and carried out, where decisions must be made; and to help analyze systematically the decision-making behavior which leads to action and which sustains actions."[5] Snyder then posits the process by which decisions are made, and suggests that the process may be broadly classified as one involving a sequence of "(a) pre-decisional activities, (b) choice, and (c) implementation."[6] Thereafter, his classificatory scheme becomes more elaborate, providing a similar yet alternative approach to that of Lasswell. In any respect, both approaches, Lasswell's as well as Snyder's, may be used for the systematic analysis of behavior to which Snyder refers.

It is this concern with behavior proper that distinguishes Snyder's work. Prior to the publication of the essay to which we have had reference, he authored, with H. W. Bruck and Burton Sapin, the small classic, *Decision-Making as an Approach to the Study of International Politics.*[7] In this work, careful attention is paid to the development of a conceptual scheme whereby one could account for the various influences on national actors, those who engage in the actual decision process relative to foreign policy-making. Included in this analysis was the importance of perceptual processes, and how members of the policy-making groups individually and corporately define the problem with which they are faced.

The role of perceptions in decision-making, particularly as it relates to the foreign policy process, is illustrated by Karl Deutsch in his outstanding *The Nerves of Government: Models of Political Communication and Control*[8] to which we shall refer more in Chapter Ten. In the Appendix to this work,[9] Deutsch presents a model of the foreign policy decision process, in terms of information flow. Information is not received or processed in a value-free sense at all, according to Deutsch's viewpoint. Instead, we find that individuals and groups alike in the decisional process pay selective attention to information and engage in an unconscious process of selective recall.

An excellent example of the means by which classification and categorization may assist in the development of empirical theory is the ap-

---

[5] *Ibid.,* p. 15.

[6] *Ibid.,* p. 20.

[7] (Princeton: Foreign Policy Analysis Series, No. 3, 1954). A distinguished follow-up to this was authored by Snyder with James A. Robinson, *National and International Decision-Making,* (New York: The Institute for International Order, 1961).

[8] (New York: The Free Press of Glencoe, 1963).

[9] *Ibid.,* pp. 258-61.

proach to decision-making taken by Lewis A. Froman, Jr.[10] Froman defines politics as being "concerned with the distribution of advantages and disadvantages among people,"[11] a definition which places decision-making at the core of any political process. Thus, political systems may be defined themselves in light of the means by which decisions are arrived at, and who participates in the reaching of decisions. Four types of decisional systems are possible, involving the interaction of leaders with leaders (Bargaining), leaders with followers (Hierarchy and Democracy), and followers with followers (Discussion).[12] Each of these processes may then be characterized according to the concerns of the actors involved, their attitudes, rewards involved, and the direction in which it may evolve, as shown in Figure 1.

Froman's models of decision-making are obviously oriented toward Snyder's concern with behavior per se, and yet offer a wider perspective than each model might suggest, taken alone. Instead, if we concentrate on the aspect of "system changes," the final column in Figure 1, we may be able to operationalize the dynamic aspects of decision-making more readily than with the models suggested earlier. In consideration of this problem of operationalization, we turn now to several studies of political influence and decision-making conducted at the local level, in order to determine to what degree decision-making approaches present a viable option for the building of empirical theory.

THE COMMUNITY POWER CONTEXT

In the proliferating studies of community power structures, we have an excellent illustration of several phenomena. For one, we can study decision-making itself, in a readily recognizable and presumably relevant context. It is not at all uncommon in our society to make assumptions about "the Establishment," or to fail to take decisive individual action because "you can't fight city hall." The assumption underlying these examples of conventional wisdom is that power, as a political phenomenon, rests someplace (certainly not with oneself), and is associated with the making of binding decisions themselves.

We can also see, by a close reading of the literature on community

[10] *People and Politics: An Analysis of the American Political System* (Englewood Cliffs: Prentice-Hall, Inc., 1962), esp. pp. 49-66.
[11] *Ibid.*, p. 6.
[12] *Ibid.*, p. 52.

Figure 1 A General Model of Politics[a]

Type of Decision-Making	Actors	Interest and Information	Issue Orientation	Type of Issue Concern	Type of Attitudes	Type of Rewards	System Changes
Bargaining	Leaders	High	High	Position	Utilitarian and Knowledge	Material	Hierarchy and Democracy
Discussion	Non-leaders	Low	Low	Style	Value-expressive and Ego-defensive	Symbolic	Hierarchy
Democracy	Leaders and non-leaders	High for leaders — low for non-leaders	High for leaders — low for non-leaders	Style	Utilitarian and Knowledge for leaders — Value-expressive and Ego-defensive for non-leaders	Material for leaders — Symbolic for non-leaders	Hierarchy
Hierarchy	Leaders and non-leaders	High	High	Position	Utilitarian and Knowledge	Material	Bargaining

[a] Lewis A. Froman, Jr., *People and Politics: An Analysis of the American Political System* (Englewood Cliffs, N.J.: Prentice-Hall, Inc., 1962), p. 79. Reprinted by permission.

decision-making, the development of several conceptual schemes, through scholarly interaction. In fits and starts, over the last several decades, the ways in which we conceive of and examine our political environment have changed drastically, in a continual process of refinement.

The link between theory and methodology is also well illustrated in this line of development. Without becoming avowed methodologues, and knowing quite little about the various research methods which are employed, we can see how theory tends to lead methodology, and to demand innovative techniques to assist in the verification of theory. We can also, unfortunately, find far too many examples of the way in which method and approach can virtually dictate findings which are presented as conclusive when indeed they are not so at all. Indeed, the study of community power is a prime example of not only methodological refinement, but failure as well.

The conceptualization of community power, finally, also leads us to an examination of the means in which normative and empirical works clash in their assumptions of values. Certain early approaches implicitly ask the question, who *should* rule? In what ways *should* power be exercised, and for whose benefit? Later approaches seek to determine who *actually* rules. In this process of normative/empirical conceptual conflict, we see an almost classical example of the very real differences which can and do emerge in scholarly debate over descriptions of and prescriptions for the real world.

First Generation Models: Reputational/Elitist

The study of community power is not necessarily a uniquely American phenomenon, as scholars have for centuries commented on apparent tendencies for power to concentrate in the hands of a few instead of the many. However, a coherent picture of the ruling elite model, as it may be called, began to emerge in studies conducted by American sociologists starting with the 1920s. The landmark studies of this era were conducted by Robert S. and Helen M. Lynd.[13] These studies, conducted in Muncie, Indiana, were to become the classics which pointed not just to elite control, but to virtually monopolistic control — and by a single family at that. The Middletown reports were not intended to be an examination of just control processes at work, although this has been a central theme of their undertaking. Rather, they were a comprehen-

---

[13] *Middletown* (New York: Harcourt, Brace and World, Inc., 1929); *Middletown in Transition* (New York: Harcourt, Brace and World, Inc., 1937).

sive attempt to examine a community in depth, to examine the culture of a single community, and how that culture interacts with its members. The dominance of a single family, which controls a small business elite, has, however, a fascination about it which is hard to lay aside. Methodologically there is little doubt today that their work was unsound, drawing unevenly from a wide variety of observations, records, and interviews. In a conceptual sense, there is much to be desired in the work of the Lynds and in other elite studies. For instance, there is a tendency to assume that reputed power is actual power.[14] That is, one finds as a constant thread throughout the reputational/elitist school the assumption that if people *feel* a given person or persons have either power or its resources then the power is *actually* possessed and employed. As tenuous as their work may appear to be, however, the impact of a single family upon a total culture, if valid, is not easy to ignore. For instance, one of the more striking passages in the Middletown studies is that which shows how the "X family" either owns, operates, or reputedly influences virtually all of the industry and essential services. These include a bank, hospital, department store, brewery, churches, political parties and the newspaper, to name but a few.[15] In this early portrait of a single town, therefore, however questionable the methodology appears to be, we get a picture of a small, coherent, and presumably cohesive elite with an all-pervasive impact on the life of a community. If this description has any value at all, the X family has a control over various decisional and allocative processes and institutions which is scarcely short of total. And, one might add, even if it is not entirely accurate, the attribution of such power to a single group may in and of itself, if held widely enough, provide sufficient latitude for an elite to attempt to influence the decisional processes of the town. In short, other potentially competitive groups which feel ineffective in the face of such power, real or imagined, may be non-participative by default.

Numerous additional studies of community power which use the reputational approach and result in elitist findings appear in the literature. A useful if occasionally intemperate guide to these is Nelson Polsby's *Community Power and Political Theory*,[16] which surveys elitist or what he prefers to call "stratification theory." For several reasons, not the least of which is that political scientists have chosen his work as

[14] Peter Bachrach and Morton S. Baratz, *Power and Poverty: Theory and Practice* (New York: Oxford University Press, Inc., 1970), p. 5; see also Nelson Polsby, *Community Power and Political Theory* (New Haven: Yale University Press, 1963), pp. 480-81.

[15] *Middletown in Transition*, p. 14.

[16] *Op. cit.*

a touchstone for criticism and the proposal of alternative approaches, Floyd Hunter's *Community Power Structure*[17] is a work of especial importance in the development and refutation of elitist theory. It may be that Hunter has been over-interpreted by his critics, as there is a tendency to take his elitist findings of political power concentrated in the hands of a few and generalize them to a pervasive picture of power, à la Middletown. Briefly, Hunter's examination of "Regional City" (Atlanta) commenced with a reputational form of methodology. Four lists of leaders were provided by the Chamber of Commerce, the League of Women Voters, "newspaper editors and other civic leaders,"[18] and the community council. In other words, the findings were begged in advance by starting with these closed lists, limited to those who were ascribed by these four groups with the reputation of being potentially powerful in the community. A panel of fourteen persons selected from these lists a total of forty individuals, presumably the pre-eminent leaders of Regional City in business, politics, society, and general community leadership. As Polsby points out so well,

> . . . consider the question Hunter asked, first of his original list-makers, then of the panel. He wanted them to name the community's top leaders which presupposed that a group of top leaders exists . . . this presupposition causes great methodological difficulties. First, how many "top leaders" are there? Second, what differentiates "top" from "nontop" leaders? Third, how do we know the judges are applying standards of "topness" consistent with one another and with Hunter? Fourth, how do we know the judges are correct, that in fact there are "top leaders" in the community, and that, if there are, they have been correctly identified?[19]

In short, the methodology which Hunter employed presumed in advance that an elite did exist, and his job was simply to identify this elite and its characteristics. Alternative assumptions were apparently not considered or included in his research design, and findings of elitism are literally dictated by his methods. The findings are therefore obvious, but bear at least a brief repetition here. A relatively permanent set of individuals, operating in a pyramidical fashion, were found to dominate the life of Atlanta. This group, largely derived from the business and commerce world, had no blacks and only four from local government,

[17] (Chapel Hill: University of North Carolina Press, 1953.)
[18] *Ibid.*, p. 269.
[19] Polsby, *op. cit.*, pp. 48-49.

including two from the school system. Another criticism by Polsby concerns the extent to which

> Hunter limits the role of the alleged decision-makers to the relatively innocuous task of "getting consent." He specifically denies that the top members of the pyramid had special opportunities either to *innovate* or to *execute* policies.[20]

This latter criticism, referring to the means by which one operationally defines power and its use, is central not only to the criticism by Polsby but also to the approach taken by Robert Dahl and his followers, to which we now turn.

Second Generation Models: Decisional/Pluralist

As part of the attack on the elitist model, derived in large part by reputational methods, Robert A. Dahl proposed that the definition of "ruling elite," as employed by such as Hunter, lacked the requisites for complete operationalization. The definition, he claimed, is normally embedded in an implicit hypothesis, to the effect that

> "Such and such a political system (the U.S., the U.S.S.R., New Haven, or the like), is a ruling elite system in which the ruling elite has the following membership." Membership would then be specified by name, position, socio-economic class, socio-economic roles, or what not.[21]

Such an hypothesis, claims Dahl, is particularly subject to improper tests, such as confusing "a ruling elite with a group that has a high *potential for control*," assuming that the elite is "a group of individuals who have more influence than others in the system," and generalizes "from a single scope of influence."[22] On the other hand, he states,

> The hypothesis of the existence of a ruling elite can be strictly tested only if:
> 1. The hypothetical ruling elite is a well-defined group.
> 2. There is a fair sample of cases involving key political decisions in which the preferences of the hypothetical ruling

[20] Polsby, op. cit., p. 55.
[21] Robert A. Dahl, "A Critique of the Ruling Elite Model," *American Political Science Review*, LII (June, 1958), p. 465.
[22] *Ibid.* Emphasis in original.

elite run counter to those of any other likely group that
might be suggested.
3. In such cases the preferences of the group regularly prevail.[23]

In his now-classic *Who Governs?*[24] Dahl essentially tests the ruling
elite hypothesis in New Haven by the means which he had earlier
proposed. Implicitly, involved in his second point, the examination of
political decision-making was to be the core of his approach, instead of
relying upon reputationally-derived models such as those employed by
Warner, Hunter, and others. In the examination of decision-making, the
pluralists fall subject to the same criticism which Dahl and Polsby had
offered to describe the elitist position. A subjective bias must inevitably arise in selecting "key political decisions" for study. How are issues
to be considered "key" or central? Cannot groups disagree over what is
important? Certainly one group may consider an issue to be vitally important, perhaps even essential to its own continuance or survival, while
another group may choose to ignore the issue entirely.[25] In discussing
this fault with the pluralist approach, Bachrach and Baratz go on to suggest that Polsby, as well as other pluralists, are

> . . . guilty here of the same fault he himself has found with
> elitist methodology; by presupposing that in any community
> there are significant issues in the political arena, he takes for
> granted the very question which is in doubt. He accepts
> as issues what are reputed to be issues. As a result, his find-
> ings are fore-ordained.[26]

Returning to the means by which Dahl attempted to study decision-
making, we find that he adopted what he refers to as an "eclectic" methodology. Thus, he used the following considerations, instead of merely
limiting himself to an examination of the "key political decisions" to
which he had earlier referred. He determined the nature and extent of
"changes in socioeconomic characteristics of incumbents in city offices";
examined a single category of individuals, the "Social and Economic
Notables, to define their nature and extent of participation in local affairs"; surveyed "samples of participants in different issue areas in order
to determine their characteristics"; surveyed registered voters for the

[23] *Ibid.,* p. 466.
[24] (New Haven: Yale University Press, 1961.)
[25] Bachrach and Baratz, *op. cit.,* pp. 10-16.
[26] *Ibid.,* p. 10.

same purpose; and studied changes in voting patterns among varying community strata, such as ethnic groups.[27]

The result of such a comprehensive approach to community power was a sweeping rejection of not only the methods but the conclusions of the elitists as well. Different issues, according to Dahl, tend to evoke the participation of different individuals and groups, with some degree of overlap, but not noticeably so. Central to this finding is the conclusion that decision-making is a group-involving process, with different groups concerned with different issues. Thus, the major issue areas which he chose to examine, those of urban renewal, education, and nominations for office, tended to involve different groups, with only a minimal overlap. Decision-making was considered by Dahl to extend beyond the loose definition of ruling offered by the elitists, as it involved the processes of initiation, modification, and veto, thus greatly expanding the potential for inclusion of individuals and groups ignored by the elitist school of thought. As might be expected, this broadened definition of decision-making, along with the varied approaches used, led ultimately to the finding of political office-holders participating to a greater degree than suggested by Hunter.

The pluralist school, following in Dahl's footsteps, argues that power is necessarily tied to issues, and real issues at that. In order to study power, they claim, we must at least examine the actual decisions themselves, and determine who was involved in the process, from beginning to end. It is not enough to claim, as do the reputational/elitists, that certain individuals have the potential for control. Rather, one must find out whether or not they actually engage in the decision-making process. This approach was also used by Jennings in Atlanta, in an attempt to replicate, using the decisional approach, the findings of Hunter.[28] As might be expected, he rejected the elitist conclusions of Hunter and found decision-making patterns in Atlanta similar to those in New Haven. A decisional approach was also taken by Wildavsky,[29] in Oberlin, Ohio, with similar results again, reinforcing the claims of the pluralist school that New Haven was not unique in its dispersion of authority, and that economic notables do not play the central role claimed for them by Hunter. A different methodological approach, employing primary documents such as public records, memoirs, personal letters, biographies

[27] Dahl, Who Governs, p. 331. A detailed and useful guide to Dahl's methodology may be found in pp. 330-40.

[28] M. Kent Jennings, Community Influentials: The Elites of Atlanta (New York: Free Press of Glencoe, Inc., 1964).

[29] Aaron Wildavsky, Leadership in a Small Town (Totowa, N.J.: Bedminster Press, 1964).

and the like, revealed that even large cities, such as New York, may be characterized as pluralistic in nature.[30] Indeed, New York might well be the ultimate case for pluralism, inasmuch as political power and decision-making there are highly fractionated through diverse political and non-political organs of influence.

> The city's political system is, in fact, vigorously and incessantly competitive. The stakes of the city's politics are large, the contestants are numerous and determined, the rules of the competition are known to and enforced against each other by the competitors themselves, and the city's electorate is so uncommitted to any particular contestant as to heighten the competition for the electorate's support or consent. No single ruling elite dominates the political and governmental system of New York City.[31]

With the volume of replicative attempts conducted by the pluralists, one might well expect that the debate over community power, who rules, or who governs, or who makes decisions, might well have ended right there, and that social scientists could have moved on to other areas of concern. However, the same questions might be asked of the pluralists as were asked of the elitists. Did anything in the methodology ultimately prejudice or bias the findings? Did the examination of decisions, with the broad interpretation of decision-making offered by Dahl and his followers necessarily imply that political notables as well as political and non-political groups would and should participate? Is there a normative bias to the decisional approach, or for that matter, in the implication one often gets from reading the works of this school which suggests that decision-making *should* be diversified? that the decisional process *should* involve shifting groups rather than coherent elites?

One example of the critical point of view taken of the pluralist model is that of Thomas J. Anton,[32] which questions the fundamental assumptions about power which seemingly underlie their research. These

> . . . *begin* with a view of society (or community, or any other social unit) as an aggregation of different individuals motivated by self-interest, predominantly rational (in the sense that they are conscious of their interests and active in seeking

[30] Wallace S. Sayre and Herbert Kaufman, *Governing New York City: Politics in the Metropolis* (New York: Russell Sage Foundation, 1960).

[31] *Ibid.,* pp. 709-10.

[32] "Power, Pluralism, and Local Politics," *Administrative Science Quarterly,* VII March, 1963), pp. 425-57.

their fulfillment), and free from any permanent relationships with anyone or anything else.[33]

Further,

> ... there is the question of whether persons using pluralist methodology could recognize issues. Issues can be defined either by the observer's commitment to an ideological outlook that defines important problems or by his ability to comprehend fully the issue definitions of the people he studies. The pluralist literature, however, claims no ideology, other than commitment to empirical science — a commitment which emphasizes that which is rather than that which ought to be. And interestingly enough, pluralist ability to get "into the heads" of its subjects appears to be hampered by a similar acceptance of the existing political order.[34]

This attack by Anton on the works of other political scientists is not entirely without justification, and serves in part to point up some of the weaknesses of the decisional/pluralist school of thought.[35]

Bachrach and Baratz have pointed out additional difficulties involved in accepting the work of the pluralists. Not the least of these is the attention paid to overt decisions. As we have earlier pointed out, such a conceptual approach requires one to decide in a subjective manner the issues that are central to the political process, thus lending an immediate bias to the research. For, if we are to look for such issues, we are inevitably going to decide that some issues will be excluded, and we will be left only with those which can point to politicals, as compared to those who are involved in the business or social worlds. But, in a more meaningful manner, Bachrach and Baratz assert that decisions alone will not suffice in locating community leaders. If an issue is suppressed from emerging in the public arena, then power is exercised, through a "non-decision."

> Of course power is exercised when A participates in the making of decisions that affect B. Power is also exercised when A devotes his energies to creating or reinforcing social and political values and institutional practices that limit the scope of the political process to public consideration of only those

[33] *Ibid.*, p. 447. Emphasis added.
[34] *Ibid.*, p. 454.
[35] Other useful critiques of the pluralist position may be found in Charles A. McCoy and John Playford (eds.), *Apolitical Politics: A Critique of Behavioralism* (New York: Thomas Y. Crowell Company, 1967). See especially the selection by Todd Gitlin, "Local Pluralism as Theory and Ideology."

issues which are comparatively innocuous to A. To the extent that A succeeds in doing this, B is prevented, for all practical purposes, from bringing to the fore any issues that might in their resolution be seriously detrimental to A's set of preferences.[36]

In an excellent discussion of a set of politically potent issues in Baltimore, involving race and poverty, the authors show just how effective the "nondecision" may be in stopping real grievances from emerging in the public forum. In one particular instance, organizers from the Congress of Racial Equality had announced that Baltimore was to become a focus of their activity. Acting with unusual speed, the mayor organized biracial "task forces" to make recommendations regarding possible programs which could be developed for the city's black population.

> Whatever his motives, the Mayor made an extremely effective nondecision. Before CORE's organizers stepped off the train in Baltimore, their planned campaign was aborted. Whatever hope they may have had of forming a local alliance with local liberals, black and white, was shattered by successful pre-emptive co-optation on the Mayor's part. . . . CORE thus found itself without access to the political system and with no resources, other than the inert mass of impoverished Negroes, for the exercise of power.[37]

Thus, in describing and showing how the decisional approach, taken alone, is subject to serious faults which cannot be ignored, Bachrach and Baratz, along with Anton, have shown that conceptual and methodological refinement was still needed in the study of community power. Such refinement may be found in the next study we consider.

Third-Generation Models: Combinatorial Approaches

The refinement of approach, conceptually and methodologically, of the community power problem, is well illustrated through the study conducted by Robert Presthus,[38] which appeared only a year after Anton's critique of the pluralist school. Rather than accepting or rejecting, a

[36] Bachrach and Baratz, op. cit., p. 7.
[37] Ibid., p. 71. See especially Chaps. 5 and 6 of this work for practical applications of the non-decision concept, pp. 124-45.
[38] Men at the Top: A Study in Community Power (New York: Oxford University Press, 1964).

priori, either or both of the two previously used approaches, Presthus chose instead to test them simultaneously in a comparative study of two small upstate New York communities. The decisional approach involved the selection of five decisions, each broadly affecting the appropriate community, with concentration on those involved in primarily the initiation phase of decision-making. Attention was also paid, however, to those who either assisted in implementation or opposed the decision.[39] The reputational method was employed by asking respondents in a sample survey to name those persons whom they would include in a group of leaders to make a decision on some community-wide project.[40] The two methods were thus conceived of as being *"mutually supportive"* in the determination of relationships between overt (decisional) and potential (reputational) power.[41] Finally, Presthus employed "Verstehen — the use of a combination of intellectual and subjective frames of thought in . . . synthesizing, weighing, and modifying the evidence provided by the two methods. . . ."[42] The use of this final technique, while methodologically appalling to those who prefer to "let the data speak for itself," is an admission of the necessary and ultimately subjective role of interpretation in even the most complex data analysis.

The approaches taken resulted in findings which could not give great cheer to either the elitists or the pluralists exclusively, for Presthus found something of merit in both schools of thought. A small number of individuals, representing .005 per cent of the populations, was found to "play the central active role in initiating and directing major community decisions."[43] At first glance, the limited proportion of participating individuals would appear to support the elitist school, especially since Dahl's expanded definition of decision-making, encompassing the initiation phase, is included within the finding. However, there are essentially two decision-making centers within the towns studied by Presthus. One of these is political in nature, and is largely related to the electoral process. The other deals with economic affairs, largely in the private sector, and draws its membership from those holding high positions in local business and society. As might be expected, this second group, with a firmer grasp on the necessary resources than that of politicians upon votes, has a greater continuity of leadership and position. The two elites, political and economic, do not exist in a vacuum, but must compete and cooperate with each other on matters of mutual interest. Further, these two

[39] *Ibid.*, pp. 52-57.
[40] *Ibid.*, p. 57.
[41] *Ibid.*, pp. 59-60. Emphasis in original.
[42] *Ibid.*, p. 37. Emphasis in original.
[43] *Ibid.*, p. 405.

elites compete with as well as rely upon the expertise of specialists, those who are concerned with single issues, such as education or welfare. Such specialists must be counted upon to participate in the total decision process, although they lack the continuity and cohesiveness which occurs in the other two bodies of participants. The comparative approach taken by Presthus also goes far to suggest that no single pattern of decision-making, or dominance by any single group, can be expected to occur from town to town, nor does each elite "play the same role" from community to community.[44]

A substantial proportion of the leaders identified by the two methods were found to be involved in more than one decision. Considering the size of the towns studied (6000 and 8500), as contrasted with the size of other cities studied as regards community power, Presthus determined that "there is an inverse association between overlapping (elitism) and size.[45] Thus, the larger the city, the more likely one is to make a case for pluralism, for the "existence of multiple competition among leaders, i.e., little overlapping among the local elites in terms of their participation in major issues. . . ."[46] A generally low rate of participation by the citizenry-at-large was found, even through normal electoral channels of influence such as referenda, elections, and public meetings. Participation through group memberships was also sharply limited. After studying fifty-two voluntary organizations, it was found that approximately forty per cent of the groups were active in any decision-making process affecting the community on the issues studied, and most of these were single-issue concerns. For that matter, the notion of Americans as "joiners" receives short shrift as about half of the individuals surveyed in both communities belonged to either no voluntary organizations at all, or only one, excluding church memberships. Hence, the potential for participation through group participation is sharply curtailed by limited memberships to begin with, minimal participation by voluntary organizations in community-wide decision processes, and single-issue participation for the most of those groups which participate at all. It was further suggested that the extent of social integration in a community is positively related to the ability of the wider base of citizenry to participate in decision-making. For instance, communities which are low in social cohesion and are characterized by sharply variant and operational values are more prone to have limited or elitist decision centers.[47]

On a methodological level, Presthus found that his assumptions regarding the utility of the reputational and decisional methods were largely

[44] *Ibid.*, p. 407.
[45] *Ibid.*, p. 408. Italics in original.
[46] *Ibid.*
[47] *Ibid.*, pp. 409-12.

borne out. Granted the imperfections of the reputational method, and they are many, this approach, based primarily upon the potential for power, was able to duplicate fifty-two percent of the list arrived at by the decisional method, which focuses upon behavior itself. The use of both methods also provides clues as to why individuals, who may properly be reputed as having the potential for participation, fail to exercise that potential or are not identified by the decisional method, for that matter. Hence, the two approaches are not to be considered as mutually exclusive at all, but are more truly complementary instead of being contradictory.

Fourth-Generation Models: New and Expanded Concerns

One of the concerns to which Presthus addressed himself was the distribution and holding of ideological positions within the communities studied. However, this was not as central to his approach as it was to that taken in *The Rulers and the Ruled: Political Power and Impotence in American Communities*, published in the same year as Presthus' study.[48] This study, like that conducted by Presthus, was comparative in nature, examining four communities, two in "Western State" and two in "Southern State." The communities studied varied widely in size, history, politics, and life-styles. In addition to these variables, the authors introduced another dimension, that of change over time. This is a highly critical element in empirical studies which frequently focus on a single session of Congress. Thus, the authors were able to determine the relative stability of the community power structures studied, instead of concluding that one was necessarily and immutably elitist, for instance. In elaborating a six-stage decision-making model, the authors also operationalized, in a sense, the Lasswellian model to which we referred earlier, although there are distinct differences between the two. By referring to their model as relating to political decision-making, the authors suggest that the process involved "is political only in the sense that those engaged in action at any stage are acting consciously, in some measure, in reference to the scope of government."[49]

But what is this scope of government? Rather than introducing their own normative biases in this direction, the authors suggest that this question itself is fundamental to the study of leadership and citizenry ideol-

[48] Robert E. Agger, Daniel Goldrich, and Bert E. Swanson (New York: John Wiley & Sons, Inc., 1964). For a useful review of the Hunter, Jennings, Presthus and Agger works see Lyman Kellstedt, "Atlanta to 'Oretown' — Identifying Community Elites," *Public Administration Review*, XXV (June, 1965), pp. 161-68.

[49] Agger, Goldrich, and Swanson, *op. cit.*, p. 40.

ogies, which they conceive of as being the central question in community
power structures. Thus, the ways in which leaders and others norma-
tively view the role of government, in either "expansionist" of "contrac-
tionist" terms, operationally defines political ideologies.

By political ideology we mean a system of interrelated
ideas about the polity that includes general answers to the
following questions:

(1) What sorts of general interests exist in a community, personal or group? If the latter, are the interests
community-wide public interests or are they those of less inclusive sectors of the community?

(2) Who ought to make the decisions about the proper
scope of government and in whose interests?

(3) What share of available socio-economic and cultural values is a person currently being allocated relative to
others in a community?

(4) What role should the government play in allocat-
ing values produced in the economy, in the society, and in
the governmental institutions themselves?[50]

Given these questions, it is apparent that we can therefore describe
political leaderships as either agreeing on their preferences as to the
scope of political activity, in which case they are "convergent," or dis-
agreeing, in which case they are "divergent." Similarly, the distribution
of political power among citizens may be classified as either broad or
narrow, particularly as regards opportunities to participate meaningfully
in the decision-making process. Presented in the form of a 2 x 2 matrix,
the various types of possible power structures emerge as in Figure 2:

Political leadership's ideology	Distribution of political power among citizens	
	Broad	Narrow
Convergent	Consensual Mass	Consensual Elite
Divergent	Competitive Mass	Competitive Elite

Figure 2 Types of Power Structures[a]

[a] Robert E. Agger, Daniel Goldrich, and Bert E. Swanson, *The Rulers and the
Ruled: Political Power and Impotence in American Communities* (New York: John
Wiley and Sons, Inc., 1964), p. 73. Reprinted by permission.

[50] *Ibid.*, p. 16.

Given this typology, regardless of Agger's concern in his research design with the time dimension, it is easy to see why time itself must be accounted for as an important variable. To assume that any one given community is, and must be for all time, a single form of power structure, is to assume a totally static situation. Thus, if Hunter's Regional City were to be pictured as a consensual elite structure, can we assume that this is fixed and unchanging? To do so would be to ignore the potential impact of events, powerful leaders, and changes in the political climate which might act to redistribute political power, even if we were to assume Hunter's findings as necessarily valid for that point in time when he studied Regional City. Recognizing the difficulties inherent in any typology, we can still posit the conditions under which decisional structures in communities may vary over time, and suggest some of the characteristics of these structures, as well as of the communities themselves.

The authors take an analytic approach, derived from some of the considerations we have raised. To present even a summary of their findings would do an injustice to this altogether impressive work. However, we might include a brief summary of the "primary perspectives" they used, and which they suggest for future analyses. These include, in

> ... viewing a community as a polity: (1) the patterns of decisional preferences; (2) the patterns of political participation; (3) the patterns of political influence relations; (4) the patterns of power relations that constitute the community's power structure; (5) the patterns that constitute the formal institutions of local government; (6) the patterns of decisional outcomes produced by the power structure; and (7) the type of regime.[51]

Given these considerations, and the properly guarded and tentative nature of their conclusions, we can suggest that Agger, Goldrich and Swanson have indeed laid the groundwork for further empirical studies of community power structures, at a minimum, as well as of the complex interaction which exists in political decisional structures.

CRITIQUE

As can be seen, the concern with decisions as stable units of analysis offers several distinct advantages in the development of empirical theory. For one, attention is paid to the centrality of decision-making in the value-

---

[51] *Ibid.*, pp. 112-13.

allocative process. By focusing on the decision, it is easier for the concerned student of politics to sweep away the superfluous, and finally begin to answer the questions imposed by the Lasswellian formulation of politics: "who gets what, when, how." Several approaches may be taken in this context. For instance, one may trace a decision through the various steps outlined by Lasswell, from intelligence through termination, examining the individuals and agencies involved. It is possible, through this method, to determine if each of the functions is performed in an optimum manner, or whether minimal performance by involved agencies may lead to less adequate decisions. In any analysis of policy-making, this approach would appear to have much to commend it, as it offers analytically distinct and perhaps operational categories of performance in the political arena.

The infant nature of political science, despite its ancient roots, is shown by the multiplicity of decision-making schemes alone. Snyder's concern with behavior, especially in the foreign-policy process, is highly suggestive of the ends to which decision-making analysis may be applied. Certainly, Froman's explicit concern with the behavior of individual leaders and followers demonstrates that decisional analysis represents a major breakthrough in attempting to develop a macro-theory of politics. Yet, certain problems remain before we can proceed further.

If decision-making is to serve as the focus for the study of political behavior, and there is certainly excellent evidence to suggest that it may very well be a useful tool of analysis, can we afford to ignore external influences? If we restrict our attention to just the legally defined government, we run the risk of assuming that there are no individuals elsewhere who are concerned with decisional outcomes, and that they might not apply pressure to achieve their ends. Yet, we know that pressure groups play an important role in the formulation of public policy at all levels of government. What function do they play in the scheme of Lasswell, or Snyder, or Froman, and how? In the performance of this function, are they facilitative or obstructive in nature, and under what conditions? These questions have been asked and answered elsewhere, but there appears to be little in decisional analysis thus far to integrate these findings.

An alternative approach which we have examined is that offered by Bachrach and Baratz. Their concern with "nondecisions" deftly shows that power may be exercised in meaningful ways by actors who are not always visible to the public eye. It may also serve to gratify the needs of those who are certain that someone, somebody, must be wielding power in the back room someplace. By acting on issues before they emerge publicly, power has been exercised and a nondecision has taken place.

There are two basic problems with this approach. The first is one of generalizability. Although the Baltimore study is revealing and offers some fascinating insights, it is a case study, and that is all. It is impossible to generalize from a single instance, and yet that is what Bachrach and Baratz have done. Their form of analysis requires replication, in short. But, is this possible? Can one study something which is essentially a "nonevent," something which in effect does not happen?[52] Merelman points this out quite well when he states that such a form of analysis in essence posits the presence of an elite, for if an event which might threaten the presence of an elite never arises, then we must presume an elite.[53] Bachrach and Baratz concede the difficulty of empirically verifying the non-observable, but maintain that not all non-decisions are by nature non-empirical as well. In essence, they place the non-decision in a different light, by implying that if conflict is not present, one can go behind the scenes to observe non-decisions.[54] The problem is obviously moot. If non-decisions are defined as non-events, then they are obviously non-empirical as well. What Bachrach and Baratz have done in effect is redefine the non-decision, in a manner which implies the presence of an elite or at least of a single individual who can make a "non-decision" to suppress or bury an issue.

The Problem of Integration

One area of concern is that which centers on the development of typologies and approaches to the study of decisions. We have presented three approaches which are not unlike each other; those by Lasswell, Snyder, and Froman. Yet another approach has been adopted by Lamb and Smith in their examination of the ways in which decisions are made in political campaigns. Focusing on the 1964 presidential election, they have adopted the approach suggested by another major theorist of decision-making, Herbert Simon. Simon has suggested that the decisional process is essentially three-fold. The first step is a decision as to which

[52] Richard M. Merelman, "On the Neo-Elitist Critique of Community Power," *American Political Science Review*, LXII (June, 1968), pp. 451-60. See also the reply by Bachrach and Baratz, and Merelman's rejoinder, *ibid.*, (December, 1968), pp. 1268-69. Merelman suggests in his rejoinder, "The situation is analogous to a jury forced to convict on circumstantial evidence. It is always nice to have a *corpus delecti* around. We must, otherwise, make leaps of faith that are usually too great for most political scientists, as scientists and not as citizens, to attempt." (*Ibid.*, p. 1269.)

[53] Merelman, "On the Neo-Elitist Critique of Community Power," pp. 453-55.

[54] Bachrach and Baratz, *op. cit.*, p. 46.

problems merit attention; this is the "focus of attention" phase. The second step requires that different options or alternatives be searched out and developed. The third phase is the actual making of a choice.[55] These phases are cast in the framework of two decisional models, comprehensive and incremental. The comprehensive model is tested against the Goldwater organization and requires centralized decision-making in an hierarchical organization. In such a model

> ... each decision-maker [should] have a clear perception of his goals, including their relative value or rank; an equally clear understanding of the scope and purposes of his own and others' decision-making authority; and full knowledge of the relationship of his decisions to a consequence of goals to be attained.[56]

The incremental model, under which the Johnson campaign organization operated, is "exploratory, means-oriented, serial, remedial, fragmented," requiring a constant adjustment in the process. In short, it operates under the assumption that the decision-maker frequently "must act with less than complete information at his command."[57] As useful as the approach taken by Lamb and Smith might be, how might it be integrated into a larger theory of decision-making? Which of these might be more applicable to the study of political behavior? In other words, various approaches have been proposed at one time or another, yet we lack evidence as to their generalizability at the present time. Merely because we have presented three such approaches does not imply that these are the only such means offered in the literature for studying decision-making. Certainly Lasswell, Snyder, Froman and Simon are not the only theorists of decision-making, but this compounds the problem even further. For, if we have difficulty seeing how these might be used, how might others be fruitfully employed? For that matter, how may we integrate these various approaches one with another and still develop an empirically operable tool of analysis?

This is not to belittle the work done by those who have involved themselves with decisional processes, especially in approaching the prob-

---

[55] Karl A. Lamb and Paul A. Smith, *Campaign Decision-Making: The Presidential Election of 1964* (Belmont, Calif.: Wadsworth Publishing Company, Inc., 1968), pp. 18-19. Their three-fold breakdown of the decisional process is drawn from Herbert A. Simon, "Political Research: The Decision-Making Framework," in David Easton (ed.), *Varieties of Political Theory* (Englewood Cliffs, N.J.: Prentice-Hall, Inc., 1966), p. 24.

[56] Lamb and Smith, *op. cit.*, pp. 20-21.

[57] *Ibid.*, p. 33.

lem of community power. Indeed, in these works we see a very real concern with the political environment as affecting decisional outcomes. Part of the problem would appear to be, however, that each student of political power has had to grapple with the central question of what it is that is political. Most of the students of community power have evaded this to some degree by taking broad definitions, loosely related to the allocative process, or "who gets what, when, how."

The one work of those we have examined which addresses itself most specifically to this problem is that by Agger, Goldrich, and Swanson. They admit to the difficulty of arriving at a definition which adequately encompasses the political, but suggest by implication that this is not so much the task of political scientists but of decision-makers themselves, and those who are capable of bringing the loosest form of pressure upon them. Thus, the many questions concerning the scope of government, as they are answered in each context, provide our key to defining politics itself. In *The Rulers and the Ruled* we see the development of a scheme which incorporates just such an approach, paying careful attention to environmental pressures which are addressed to the definition of the proper scope of government, and the results thereof. Further, they employ a scheme of analysis which differs from Lasswell's seven specific functions, but which may result in the final analysis in the same results sought by Lasswell. Their concern with such factors as types of issue concern, issue-orientation, attitudes, rewards, and especially system changes as posited by Froman show that theory can be grounded in solid empirical work, and can literally be operationalized. It would appear that they have demonstrated not only the utility of the decisional approach to analysis, but may have gone considerably beyond that step towards the formulation of macro-theory.

Rosenau has provided an interesting review and critique of the decisional approach in a wide variety of areas.[58] One of his concerns deals with the widespread usage accorded this approach in recent years, without any apparent coherence to the findings. Thus, the decision or decision-maker has been central to analyses of foreign policy, legislators, members of the military, the press, and so forth. Because the concerns of political scientists have spread over a broad number of questions, little in the way of theory has yet emerged. "Few analysts probed different aspects of the same problem and even fewer built upon the findings of others."[59] In line with our earlier criticism which suggested that the ap-

[58] James N. Rosenau, "The Premises and Promises of Decision-Making Analysis," in James C. Charlesworth (ed.), *Contemporary Political Analysis* (New York: The Free Press, 1967), pp. 189-211.
[59] *Ibid.*, pp. 204-06.

proaches taken by various theorists of the decisional school have not been integrated with each other, Rosenau finds that this has seriously hindered the development of empirically testable theory. In sum, there is an absence of hypotheses which suggest that "*if* certain circumstances are operative, *then* certain decisions and actions are likely to ensue."[60]

However, it should be pointed out that theory-building is more likely to take place, through an integration of existing models, when researchers attempt to ascertain the validity of those which already exist. It may well be that a thorough-going attempt at validation of the various models we have discussed may lead to their rejection. Certainly, we have an excellent example of how this process works in the community power sector of study. Where attempts have been made to replicate the work of others, we have noticed a continual refinement in our conceptions of how community power is exercised, and by whom. If further testing were to take place along the lines of existing typologies, we might be better able to say that we have developed an operable theory of decision-making which can cover diverse areas such as campaigns, community power, and the making of foreign policy. Students of decision-making have been too content to merely describe, to identify, rather than lay the foundations for testable predictive theory. Until this is done, we can expect that the decisional approach will remain limited. Thus, as with other approaches, more research is obviously needed. We feel that the approach taken by Agger may offer the greatest possibilities for those who would study decisions. However, it remains to be seen whether this model, already tested in one context, may assist in the development of a paradigm for political science. For instance, can it be further integrated with other decisional approaches? Is it applicable to the consideration of other questions such as the analysis of national economic policy? of foreign policy? of educational policy? Or, must we yet draw from other approaches such as systems analysis and communications theory, before we can state that political science as a discipline has finally begun to arrive at its needed paradigm?

[60] *Ibid.*, pp. 208-09. Emphasis in original.

Systems Analysis
9

INTRODUCTION

It should be abundantly clear to the student by now that classification and categorization are processes underlying the behavioral movement to an unusual degree. The reasons for this are manifold, but essentially relate to the necessity of developing guidelines for research, as well as tying together in some orderly fashion the research findings which are products of the behavioral movement. Of the several different models and theories examined thus far, it can be said that there is something of a natural progression of generality from groups to decision-making. An even more general scheme is that offered by systems analysis. For reasons which shall be elaborated in the discussion which follows, systems theory will be shown as being of a sufficiently general nature that it can subsume the various models and theories just mentioned and discussed in the two preceding chapters.

In 1965, David Truman, then president of the American Political Science Association, addressed his fellow political scientists, tracing the development and rise of behavioralism in America. In so doing, he made reference to Thomas Kuhn, a physicist, on the necessity of a paradigm or working model which incorporates the assumptions and guides further research in that branch of science. As Truman points out, Kuhn was not speaking directly to the problems of the social and behavioral sciences, but his words have particular relevancy for political scientists at this time.[1] Political science, in the view of some, has gone through a nonviolent revolution in changing the direction of its concerns and the means of answering the questions raised by those concerns.[2] For others the success and even the desirability of the "revolution" are yet to be determined.[3] But, in every sense, it is apparent that major changes in the discipline are under way. One of the hallmarks of that change in more recent years has been the emergence of systems theory as a paradigm-in-development, as a means of organizing our knowledge and of fulfilling one of the functions of models as well, the generation of additional hypotheses.

Systems theory, like communications analysis, owes a considerable intellectual debt to the work done in cybernetics, particularly that by Norbert Wiener.[4] Systems has also drawn heavily from the work of Ludwig von Bertalanffy, a biologist who first began exploring the possibilities of broad-gauged explanations of behavior in the 1920s.[5] Following the New Deal and World War II, it became increasingly apparent to a number of academicians that the various disciplines need not stand in splendid isolation from one another, and that the artificial restraints imposed by rigid disciplinary boundaries could hinder rather than aid research. Increasing attention was paid to means by which disciplines might be drawn together. Among the many conferences, formal and informal, held by researchers in various areas was a series held at the Reese Hospital in Chicago, starting in 1951. The scope of their concerns was broad indeed, if revealed by only one of the works which emerged from those conferences.[6] A major contributor in the direction pointed to by these conferences is David Easton, a political scientist whose work has been highly influential in the discipline in the last several years.

[1] David B. Truman, "Disillusion and Regeneration: The Quest for a Discipline," *American Political Science Review*, LIX (December, 1965), pp. 865-66.

[2] Robert A. Dahl, "The Behavioral Approach in Political Science: Epitaph for a Monument to a Successful Protest," *American Political Science Review*, LV (December, 1961), pp. 763-72.

[3] For instance, Herbert J. Storing (ed.), *Essays on the Scientific Study of Politics* (New York: Holt, Rinehart and Winston, Inc., 1962); Christian Bay, "Politics and Pseudopolitics: A Critical Evaluation of Some Behavioral Literature," *American Political Science Review*, LIX (March, 1965), pp. 39-51.

[4] Norbert Wiener, *Cybernetics* (New York: John Wiley & Sons, Inc., and the Technology Press, 1948). See the next chapter for a discussion of communications.

[5] Ludwig von Bertalanffy, "General Systems Theory," *General Systems*, I (1956), pp. 1-10.

[6] Roy R. Grinker (ed.), *Toward a Unified Theory of Human Behavior* (New York: Basic Books, Inc., 1956).

EASTONIAN ANALYSIS

We will not attempt to provide a complete statement of the theory and implications of Eastonian systems analysis. Rather, for the sake of simplicity as well as for clarifying the relationships between Easton and other systems theorists, we shall deal with the main burden of his argument as well as with the principal concepts which he has elaborated.

Political systems are defined by Easton as "a set of interactions, abstracted from the totality of social behavior, through which values are authoritatively allocated for a society."[7] Underlying this seemingly straightforward definition are, however, a number of assumptions which lend direction to systems analysis. For one, the emphasis is upon *interaction* as a variable. Interactions may take place between individual actors, institutions, or actors and institutions taken together. Easton does not specify which actors or institutions engage in these interactions which are engaged in the value-allocation process. Indeed, if we stress interactions in Easton, we must therefore stress process as well, for Easton's is not a stable but a dynamic model, in which the system and its individual actors engage in processes designed to secure the maintenance and dynamic equilibrium of the system itself.

Easton recognizes[8] that no single way of conceptualizing human behavior can properly encompass all the variety and complexity of that behavior, at least for the time. Any attempt to conceptualize and describe behavior, therefore, must be quite general and broad in nature. This being the case, Easton's model is one which uses, as its major unit of analysis, the political system itself, in which political life is viewed as a system of behavior. Presuming a system implies that it may be analytically distinguished from its surroundings, or what Easton refers to as the environment. It must be stressed, however, that although an analytical distinction is made between the system and its environment, the system will be open in varying degrees to influences from the environment. Indeed, the nature of environmental influences and the ways in which the system responds to them is one of Easton's major concerns. In separating a system from its environment, however, we must refer at least symbolically to the system's *boundary*. The nature of systemic boundaries,

[7] David Easton, A *Framework for Political Analysis* (Englewood Cliffs: Prentice-Hall, Inc., 1965), p. 57.
[8] *Ibid.*, passim. The following discussion relies heavily upon this work as well as upon Easton's *A Systems Analysis of Political Life* (New York: John Wiley & Sons, Inc., 1965).

how they are defined, and their degree of flexibility or rigidity are major problems facing systems theorists. It might be said that there is a distinct parallel between the controversy over the proper boundaries or scope of political science and that which involves those political scientists working with systems theory itself. Are the boundaries such that the political system encompasses a broad or narrow proportion of the total social system? Are they subject to changing definition? Will they admit to the presence of external influences and, if so, to what degree? Should boundaries be defined in a legalistic sense, or is there behavior in the real world to which we may have reference in isolating the system from its environment?

The point of view taken by the authors, and one with which some may disagree, is that it is useful to look at the boundary problem as one of mutual perceptions. These involve the outlooks of the internal actors of the system who are engaged in the interactions themselves, as well as actors in the environment, who may belong to other political systems or interlocking systems such as the economic and cultural spheres of activity. An example of this may be shown in Figure 1, in which the Congress and the presidency are viewed as distinct but related systems. In Figure 1A we see a virtual non-system. That is, the Congress and the presidency are not interacting with each other at all. This is a situation which, in real life, might exist quite infrequently. An example might be congressional consideration of its own organization (procedural rules, committee chairmanships, member ethics, etc.), in which there is no evidence at all that the president or his executive office has communicated preferences to the Congress. Figure 1B represents a tangential relationship, in which provision is made for minimal contact between the two systems. Such a situation might arise in purely legal or constitutional relationships, such as that of fulfilling the legislative function. As all students of political behavior are aware, and as introductory texts in American government continually stress, there is no constitutional provision for the president's role as "chief legislator," a role which is often imputed to him.[9] Rather, the only constitutional provision for presidential involvement in the legislative process is that of approval, by signing a bill into law, or veto. The "advice and consent" provision relating to presidential appointments might nominally fit this category, again in a purely legal sense. In Figure 1C we see a relationship which is probably more nearly like that which exists in real life between the two systems. That is, there is a degree of constitutional and legal overlap between them, in-

[9] Many works on the presidency follow the pattern of describing the office in terms of possible roles. One such is Clinton Rossiter's *The American Presidency* (New York: Harcourt, Brace & World, 1960).

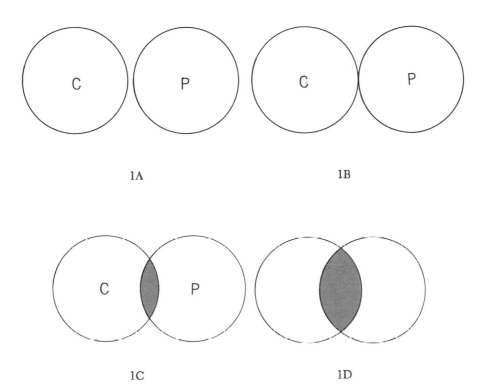

1A   1B

1C   1D

Figure 1 Boundary Relationships Between the Congressional and Presidential Systems

volving some considerable interaction. The shaded area represents the potential for political conflict and compromise, in legal and constitutional terms alone, a reality which is reflected by our frequent usage of the term "checks and balances." To use the example to which we just referred, presidential appointments may lead to considerable political conflict. In the constitutional sense, the Senate simply gives its "advice," as it were, and then either approves or disapproves presidential nominees. However, as President Johnson found out in 1968, and President Nixon in 1969, the nomination of a Supreme Court justice can be anything but pro forma. The Fortas, Carswell, and Haynsworth nominations led to considerable political infighting before they were rejected by the Senate. Finally, in Figure 1D, we make allowances not only for boundaries of legal dimensions, but for boundaries of a behavioral and perceptual nature as well. That is, the president, in this instance, may view his proper scope of action in quite flexible terms through broad interpretations of the powers which are legally granted him, perhaps because of his own proclivities, or because the nation is in a state of crisis which he sees as requiring greater freedom of action on his part.[10] Continuing our example of the Supreme Court justice nominations, if either President Johnson or Nixon took the point of view that the Senate was obliged to merely a *pro forma* approval of their nominee, they might have increased the tension of the conflict in a concerted attempt to secure approval.

The potential for political conflict (the darkened area) is thereby considerably broadened, through the perception of boundaries by one of the actors. Such conflict need not always come about, however, in a period of crisis especially, if other actors feel that such an expansion is required. Instances of this might be the first one hundred days of Roosevelt's New Deal, or the months immediately following President Kennedy's assassination. However, it can generally be assumed that there will be actors present, in one system or the other, who will view such boundary interpretations with a jaundiced eye. Strict constructionists of the constitutional prerogatives of the president abound, however, notably when he proposes some major extension of either federal powers or of his own. An example might be of civil rights legislation, a subject which inevitably leads to extended rhetoric by some congressmen and senators who view it with disfavor.

Input-Output Analysis

If we assume, along with Easton, that systems are susceptible to varying degrees of influence from the environment, and that the system itself may affect its surroundings, we must make reference to the *inputs*, *outputs*, and *feedback* variables. In short, Easton tells us that a political system cannot exist unto itself. Surrounded as it is by a physical, cultural and economic environment, not to mention other political systems, it must functionally interact with these potential sources of influence. Inputs from the environment as well as from within the system may be classified as basically of the *demand* or *support* variety. Without inputs, the system can do no work and cannot sustain itself. An analogy may be made to the human biological system. It is difficult for a person to survive for long without such basic physical supports, as food, clothing and

[10] See Rexford Tugwell, *The Enlargement of the Presidency* (First ed.; Garden City, N.Y.: Doubleday, 1960), for an extended statement on this point.

shelter. To varying degrees, determined in part by the physical environment, clothing and shelter may or may not be needed (although cultural influences may abound regarding these requirements). Minimal caloric requirements must be met in order for the system to continue functioning. However, demands are also necessary as they lend purpose and direction to the system. For the human to exist in a state of pure support, receiving excessive calories, would ultimately lead to organic breakdowns, as the internal demands generated by such an existence would place too great a strain upon one's body. Thus, external demands, in the form of exercise, may place a required and systemically desirable form of stress upon the system.

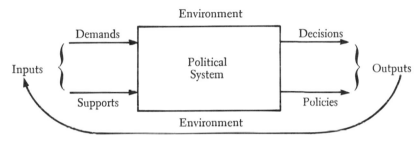

Figure 2 Basic Eastonian System[a]

[a] David Easton, "An Approach to the Analysis of Political Systems," *World Politics*, IX (April, 1957), p. 384. Reprinted by permission.

Comparably, the political system receives demand inputs from its environment, reacting to cultural and economic problems, plus those raised by the nature of interaction with other political systems. Demands are generally concerned with matters relating to the allocation of resources, material or positional. Problems for the system are raised here in that the various sources of demands, be they individuals or groups within or external to the system, are likely to have different views as to how those resources should be allocated. It must be stated that there is never any assurance that demands will be met in a one-for-one ratio with regard to outputs, or allocations of resources. In other words, the system is not as mechanistic as it might appear at first glance. This is especially the case if the resources to be distributed by the system are scarce and are highly valued by competing groups; then it is less likely that demand input X will result in output X; especially if the sources of demand possess sufficient and relatively balanced resources to promote alternative demands as well. For instance, demands for tax reform do not arise from one sector of the economy alone. Those favoring a closing of tax loop-holes such as the oil depletion allowance must compete with the oil industry before Congress. The result (output), may be a temporary but protracted stalemate, which is to the advantage of the oil industry, which opposes any cuts in the depletion allowance. Or, after extended conflict on the matter, the result may be a compromise, such as the cutting, in 1969, of the allowance from twenty-seven and one half per cent to twenty-two per cent.

Obviously, therefore, demand inputs result in stress upon the system, stress which may be functional as it activates the system as an allocator of resources. However, stress can only go so far in any system. Just as a physician may recommend jogging to an over-weight patient, he will also recognize that jogging a minimal distance represents healthy stress. Advising the obese patient to run a four-minute mile could lead to total collapse. James G. Miller has discussed this point with reference to living systems, suggesting that overcompensation or reaction to stress will generally follow a lag in response, and may precede collapse, assuming that stress is increased over time.[11]

We have, however, pointed out that stress can be taken as functional to the system. As Miller states the point, "While extreme stress always worsens performance, moderate stress can improve it above ordinary levels."[12] In the Eastonian model, system maintenance or survival is a primary goal, the one which must precede all others. In discussing demand inputs (and support inputs for that amatter), we can therefore pay attention to such additional variables as the substance, source, intensity, and quantity of demands. Such factors, as related to the demand and support problem, will be indicative of the ability and capacity of a system to modulate stress, which in turn will suggest the ability of the system to both perform its tasks and survive as well. Since the questions of system equilibrium and survival are implicit in all systems theory, we discuss them from the viewpoint of conflict and violence later in this chapter.

Crucial to the consideration of input/output analysis is the learning and corrective capacity of a system. As in communications theory, we refer to this as *feedback*. In short, it is recognized that system outputs or decisions do not automatically solve all problems. Indeed, they may raise additional problems which were not initially foreseen in the making of decisions or policies. Those whom Easton refers to as the authoritative decision-makers, or the allocators of values, therefore must receive information as to the effect and effectiveness of their decisions. This

[11] James G. Miller, "Toward a General Theory for the Behavioral Sciences," *American Psychologist*, X (September, 1955), pp. 527-28.
[12] *Ibid.*, p. 528.

information or feedback acts as new input to the system, whether or not the information comes from outside the system or from other actors within the system ("withinputs"). Feedback can have several results. It may provide not only increased or altered demands, in which the process continues somewhat cyclically; it may also provide information that the outputs have essentially solved a problem and thereby may be viewed as a potential source of supports. Feedback may also reveal that the outputs are not accomplishing the purposes desired by the authoritative decision-makers, and thus lead to "corrective" action.

From the foregoing, it would appear that there is little overt concern in the Eastonian model for support inputs. However, as we have suggested, no system can survive if it is subject only to demands. Support inputs for the political system can assume many forms. In the physical sense, a system needs material resources to support itself. These material values can also be transformed into allocatable resources. Earlier, we pointed out that the human system has several basic needs, such as food, clothing, and shelter. Additional intangible supports may be needed as well, such as affection, respect, and acceptance by others. So, too, a political system requires certain intangible supports, such as a recognition of legitimacy by system and environmental actors, as well as allegiance and obedience by those internal to the system. Tangible supports for a political system may include such resources as money and personnel, derived from taxes and varying recruitment processes. In attempting to derive such resources, the system may ultimately provide, however unwittingly, sources of potentially dysfunctional demand inputs. For instance, it is not difficult to relate demands by taxpayers for an easing of their burden to reduced governmental services in certain areas. Feedback from these areas could result in the necessity for greater resources. An example of this might be a reduction in welfare services, including those related to public health and sanitation. Should disease increase, as a result, the government might well have to expend even greater funds in order to abate the problem. Similarly, the U.S. government may have become accustomed to compliance in the administration of the Selective Service System. In pursuit of a policy which became increasingly unacceptable to the American public in the 1960s, the draft came to provide problems for the government which, as a normal vehicle for supports, might never have been expected otherwise.

Summary Statement

In the Eastonian model we see a "system" which is not unrelated to the broad communications models discussed in the next chapter. Greater attention is paid to problems of boundary, in that this helps to define the system and isolate it, at least analytically, from its environment. Provision is made for considerations of feedback, as in communications theory, but to a less explicit degree. Indeed, in many respects systems analysis may be considered a definite analogue of communications. Both are heuristic rather than predictive, and lend themselves to comparative analysis. In both, however, there is the problem of further definition. Inasmuch as the various communications theorists and Easton have chosen to elaborate a carefully-refined set of models, with definitions and classifications of variables to be considered, then both must bear the burden of carrying this scheme out to useable lengths. It is not as easy to level this charge against the communications theorists, notably Deutsch, as one can against Easton. For instance, the system is denoted by its ability to allocate values authoritatively, but Easton spends comparatively little time and space suggesting testable hypotheses about the nature of the allocative process or of the actors involved. It must be pointed out, however, that the problems inherent in "broad-gauge theory" can also be of value. We suggested earlier that systems analysis may be considered as subsuming such approaches as group theory and decision-making models. If we examine Easton, we see that the considerations raised by these various schools of thought may be properly applied as well to the questions which Easton poses. Decision-theory, for instance, may properly "flesh out" the bare bones of the resource-allocating function of the political system. Group theory can more explicitly specify sources of demand and support inputs as well as reactions to outputs. The complementarity of these approaches is one of the factors which may yet lead to a broader theory of political life, which can both explain and predict at a high level of accuracy.

PARSONIAN STRUCTURAL-FUNCTIONALISM

Another theorist who has addressed himself to the major task of developing a broad-gauged theory of behavior, although not specifically political, is the sociologist, Talcott Parsons. His works[18] are landmarks in the development of such theory, and help to lay the foundations for the so-called school of structural-functionalism. Without intending to

[18] Notably *The Social System* (Glencoe, Ill.: Free Press, 1951), and, edited with Edward A. Shils, *Toward a General Theory of Action* (Cambridge: Harvard University Press, 1951). Also, with Robert F. Bales and Edward A. Shils, *Working Papers in the Theory of Action* (New York: The Free Press, 1953).

slight other important members of this school, we shall concentrate on Parsons as having a relationship to Easton which is developed by Gabriel Almond, the last systems theorist with whom we deal in this chapter.

Basic Concepts

Readers familiar at all with the works of Parsons will recognize the difficulty of abstracting his work in a few pages, as he is generally recognized as not only one of the most influential contemporary social theorists but also one of the most abstruse. In a brief overview, we may start by taking Parsons' basic scheme, relating its various parts one to another, before we detail its specifics. To begin with, Parsons asserts that all systems have four basic *functions* to perform (see below). These are performed by *structures*, within which are multiple *actors* each of whom has *roles* to play, which are performed according to five *pattern variables*. This basic scheme is considered operative for all social systems, of both the macro and micro varieties. Thus, the total social system has the same basic functions as do particular societal or political subsystems.

A common way of looking at the functions which Parsons ascribes to systems is the so-called G-A-I-L approach, standing for the four functions which he sees as necessary to system survival. Goal Attainment or specification is the first of these, and is that function which is most concerned with the preservation of the society or particular system. In the total social system, this function is performed primarily by the polity. If the system is to survive, resources must be mobilized in support of those goals which have been specified. This is the function of Adaptation and, in the social system, is performed primarily by the "structure" we call the economy. We have stressed in this discussion the point that certain functions are performed primarily by given structures, as no single structure performs all functions alone, nor is any structure necessarily uni-functional. Because structures, as well as individual actors, tend to be multi-functional, to deal with functions other than the one with which they are primarily concerned, a third major function must be performed, that of Integration. As no one agency can perform all functions equally well, a means must be found to integrate the functional performance of individual actors and institutions. This is a function performed by the various institutions of societal or systemic culture, such as education, in which information as well as norms are passed on. Finally, and distinctly related to this latter function, is that of Latency, or Pattern Maintenance. As the secondary title for this function suggests, it deals with the maintenance of conformity to the norms of the cultural system. Values are passed to succeeding generations, and sanctions may be applied for non-observance of values or norms. In the societal system, this function is performed primarily by the family.

At this point it might be wise to examine these constructs in a schematic sense. In Figure 3 we see the basic Parsonian scheme relative to functions and structures in the total societal system. (In this and succeeding figures relative to Parsonian structural-functional analysis we do not take into account the additional concepts of actors, roles, and pattern variables, but these will have to be taken as given. For more extensive discussion of these, see especially the works cited in footnote 13).

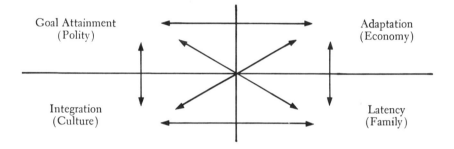

Figure 3   Parsonian Scheme for Total System[a]

[a] Adapted from Talcott Parsons and Neil J. Smelser, *Economy and Society: A Study in the Integration of Economic and Social Theory* (New York: The Free Press, 1956), p. 53. By permission.

Multi-functionality and interaction between the various structures is indicated by the several arrows between the functional quadrants. A problem with this form of conceptualization is understanding the relationship of the various functions and structures to other systems. One approach to this is that indicated in Figure 4, in which we can more clearly see not only the relationship of particular functions to selected environments, but the central positions of two of them, Goal Attainment and Integration. The complexity of the environment is also suggested more clearly by the schematic representation, and offers some idea of the problems which face those not only in the central goal-setting arena (who may be likened to Easton's "authoritative decision-makers") but to other actors as well.

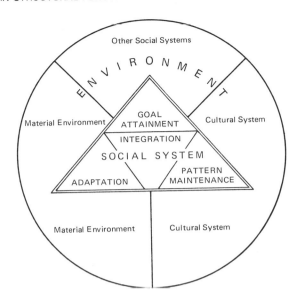

Figure 4   Relationship of Parsonian Functions With Environment[a]

ª From *The Political Basis of Economic Development* by Robert T. Holt and John E. Turner. Copyright © 1966, by Litton Educational Publishing, Inc., by permission of Van Nostrand Reinhold Company.

The Parsonian approach is not restricted to one of analyzing the total social system, but may also be adapted to examining particular subsystems. For instance, as political scientists we are most concerned with examining the polity, that structure which is concerned primarily with Goal Attainment. In Figure 5 we see how this structure, supposedly concerned primarily with a single function, is indeed multi-functional.

Goal Attainment (Executive Functions and Roles)	Adaptation (Administrative Functions and Roles)
Integration (Party-Political Functions and Roles)	Latency (Legislative-Judicial Functions and Roles)

Figure 5   Parsonian Functions in the Political System[a]

ª Adapted from William C. Mitchell, *Sociological Analysis and Politics: The Theories of Talcott Parsons* (Englewood Cliffs: Prentice-Hall, Inc., 1967), p. 104. By permission.

In pursuing its major function of goal attainment on behalf of the total system, the polity performs added functions, and has more specialized structures which assist in this task. Thus, the generalized function of Goal Attainment is supported not only by institutions such as the economy, culture, and family, which are concerned with supporting the total system, but has particularized structures which assist in this endeavor as well, such as the judiciary and the administration. The idea of multi-functionality is demonstrated still further by Figure 6, which shows how one subsystem, that of the legislature which assists in the performance of the latency function within the polity, may be further sub-divided.

Goal Attainment-Leadership
    party leaders
    committee chairmen
    bloc leaders
    delegation deans
	Adaptation-Information
	    committees
	    office and committee staff
	    informal study groups

Integration-Ideological
    ideological blocs
    friendship cliques
    political parties
	Latency
	    informal groups
	    formal procedural rules
	    friendship groups

Figure 6   Parsonian Functions in the Legislative Subsystem[a]

[a] David Leege (unpublished seminar paper, Indiana University, 1960). By permission of the author.

We can also, from Figures 5 and 6, develop an idea of the complexity of the Parsonian scheme, in that actors may exist in several quadrants, to greater and lesser degrees. For instance, relative to Figure 6, we may see a congressional leader, such as the Speaker of the House, operating in all four quadrants quite readily. As a party leader he is concerned with Goal Attainment; his role as speaker is clearly not limited to one function, for he may be an invaluable source of information, a major resource in Congress; he is a party member, a member of various blocs and cliques and is therefore involved in the Integration function; and he applies formal procedural rules, invoking sanctions if needs be, in fulfilling the Latency function. The ways in which he fulfills each of these often conflicting roles is indicated in part by the five pattern variables.[14]

[14] See Chapter 6, pp. 126-27, for a statement on pattern variables.

Problems and Applications

Although we have barely skimmed some of the essential concepts of the Parsonian approach, it should be apparent that we have no simple classificatory scheme of demonstrable utility. Parsons and his various interpreters offer numerous definitions of these concepts, often conflicting and often confusing. The essential step of classification has been provided for, but with definitions that may be difficult to apply in empirical analysis. Some utility of the approach is evident, for in delineating various functions, and in suggesting the institutions which might be expected to perform those functions, we may properly proceed to a more fruitful form of comparative analysis. For instance, if we can properly define the meaning and implications of the Integration function, we might ask what institutions in various western and non-western countries really perform this function. In other words, the ascription of a function to particularized institutions may be in error, and we may well find that various societies perform the same function (if these functions are universal) through different structures. If this is the case, we may be able to infer why some societies or polities are more or less prone to internal stability. In examining the Adaptation function on a cross-cultural basis, we would expect to find that some polities are more prone to become involved in economic planning than others, a factor which could be expected to aid or hinder in the Goal-Attainment function.

A recent examination of the Parsonian approach illustrates additional problems and promises of structural-functionalism as it is here conceived:

> First, Parsons does not adequately deal with a stratum of behavior that operates at a subcultural level and does not recognize the impact that this level of behavior may have on the culture and performance of systems . . . Second, political analysis should proceed at both the systemic and individual levels of analysis. Generalizations about the operation of systems must be supplemented with generalizations about individual decision-making. The behavior of individuals cannot be always inferred from data on the culture of social systems. . . . [however] Parson's image of social structure can be used with considerable effectiveness both as a foil and as a systematic statement about the cultural-institutional sources of social behavior.[15]

[15] Harold Kaplan, "The Parsonian Image of Social Structure and Its Relevance for Political Science," *Journal of Politics*, XXX (November, 1968), pp. 903-08.

ALMOND'S SYSTEMIC STRUCTURAL-FUNCTIONALISM

There are many approaches which fall under the general rubric of "systems analysis," in part because it is still in a developmental stage, and also because it represents a synthesis of the approaches previously discussed. Gabriel Almond, whose work has been primarily in the area of comparative politics, sought to suggest "how the application of certain sociological and anthropological concepts may facilitate systematic comparison among the major types of political systems operative in the world today."[16] In so doing, he helped to lay the groundwork for not only a more comprehensive analysis, but for systems analysis as well. He also delineated the various components of political systems, such as the role, which is taken as "the unit of the political system."[17] He then describes structures or patterned interactions among roles, and other characteristics of the political system, such as concern with the "scope, the direction, and the conditions affecting the employment" of "*ultimate, comprehensive,* and *legitimate* physical coercion" which is "the monopoly of states."[18] He also directs his attention to *political culture,* or a "pattern of orientations to political action."[19a] In so doing he then examines the role structure of several types of political system, such as the Anglo-American, pre-industrial, totalitarian, and continental European. The significance of this particular approach lies, relative to systems analysis, in the provision of more substantive definitions from which he and others of his school can work.

Almond later provides a clearer statement of his approach in a work issued several years after the article to which we have referred. He reiterates some of his earlier statements, and then proceeds to explore their meanings, consequences, and applications. Thus,

> . . . the political system is that system of interactions to be found in all independent societies which perform the functions of integration and adaptation by means of the employment, or threat of employment, of more or less legitimate physical compulsion . . . legitimate force is the thread which runs through the inputs and outputs of the political system.[19]

[16] Gabriel A. Almond, "Comparative Political Systems," *Journal of Politics,* XVIII (August, 1956), p. 391.

[17] *Ibid.,* p. 393.

[18] *Ibid.,* p. 395. Emphasis in original.

[19a] *Ibid.,* p. 396.

[19] Gabriel A. Almond, "Introduction: A Functional Approach to Comparative Politics," in Gabriel A. Almond and James S. Coleman, *The Politics of the Develop-*

All systems, according to Almond, share certain characteristics. Thus, they all have structures, which may be compared for their degree of specialization. The same functions are performed in all systems as well, and we can examine the frequency with which they are performed, which structures perform them, and the style or manner in which they are performed. As with Parsons, to whom the relationship should be evident by now, all structures are multi-functional. Further, all systems are "culturally mixed," and may be examined for their levels of development, as well as to the extent to which they may be considered "modern."

All political systems perform certain functions, as we have noted. Input functions are initially stressed. These are "political socialization and recruitment, interest articulation, interest aggregation, and political communication." Requisite output functions are "rule-making, rule-application, and rule-adjudication." The output functions may, at first glance, appear to be a restatement of the classic legalist approach to political science. Indeed, they might almost seem like Montesquieu revisited. However, if the political system is at all concerned with the specification of goals (Parsons), or the allocation of values (Easton), then the fact that these functions are performed cannot be ignored. In point of fact, this statement of output functions can provide us a clear illustration of the multi-functionality argument. Hence, courts not only adjudicate, but legislate, in a very real sense. The bureaucracy initiates legislation, as well as administers rules under which it operates and which it enacts itself.

Each of the seven functions enumerated by Almond is performed by particular or special structures according to the pattern variables outlined by Parsons. As an example, the input function of political socialization and recruitment may be taken. This function is "the process of inculcation into the political culture" resulting in "attitudes, value standards, and beliefs towards the political system."[20] In a sense, this function may be considered as analogous to Parson's Latency function, which is performed in the total social system by the family. Almond recognizes this institution, along with others such as the church, schools and voluntary associations which perform a pre-political socialization function, by introducing the individual to patterns of authority and decision-making. Among the pattern variables which Parsons enumerates is the dichotomy of affective neutrality. This particular pattern vari-

---

ing *Areas* (Princeton: Princeton University Press, 1960), p. 7. The discussion which follows relies upon this work.
    [20] *Ibid.*, pp. 27-28.

able is especially important in political socialization, for the individual will presumably learn certain norms, such as loyalty towards and pride in his political system (affect). He may also learn to be objective, judging his system by its performance rather than its presumed attributes (affective neutrality). Similarly, political socialization may be either universalistic or particularistic, as an individual is an occupant of many roles, each with specific claims and demands upon the actor. The style of socialization may be specific or diffuse. Almond suggests that primitive and/or parochial systems will tend towards diffuseness, whereas totalitarian systems would tend towards rigid specificity in ways in which socialization is carried out.

This concern with the ways and means by which a system carries out the socialization and recruitment input function, and the consequences of such performance, is reflected in a major work co-authored several years later with Sidney Verba.[21] In this work, an empirical examination of attitudes and belief structures in the United States, Great Britain, Germany, Italy, and Mexico, the authors seek to examine some of the preconditions of the "civic culture," a "pluralistic culture based on communication and persuasion, a culture of consensus and diversity, a culture that permitted change but moderated it."[22]

The work is not without its faults, either conceptual or methodological, but it is a ground-breaking study in both of these areas, nonetheless. Conceptually, the authors address themselves to a series of questions about the political cultures of the nations involved, and the various input processes which apparently relate to the orientations held by the citizenry of these nations. While their work cannot be considered purely theoretical in the area of systems analysis, Almond and Verba have empirically examined the presence and effects of certain variables which had been posited previously by Almond, as we have discussed above. Methodologically, their work represents a new direction in means of comparison, employing survey research with presumably comparable questions and phraseology, given the problems of language and meaning within each of the five countries.

Almond has also, in a later work co-authored with Powell,[23] paid even more detailed attention to some of the questions raised in his earlier essays. Thus, interest articulation, interest aggregation, and politi-

---

[21] Gabriel A. Almond and Sidney Verba, *The Civic Culture: Political Attitudes and Democracy in Five Nations* (Princeton: Princeton University Press, 1963).

[22] *Ibid.*, p. 8.

[23] Gabriel A. Almond and G. Bingham Powell, Jr., *Comparative Politics: A Developmental Approach* (Boston: Little, Brown and Company, Inc.)

cal communication, which were earlier regarded as input functions, are examined in regard to their styles, means, consequences, and effects on political modernization. Governmental structures are examined not from the purely legalistic and/or historical standpoint which had characterized so much of early political science, but for the output functions which they perform (role-making, rule-application, rule-adjudication) and the effects which various structures have upon the political culture.

Summary Statement

Almond is not without his critics, least of all himself. His systemic approach to structural-functionalism has yielded a classification of input and output variables which can be highly useful to the researcher, especially one concerned with comparative analysis. Difficulties of operationalization abound, but this does not mean that they are insurmountable. However, does his work really represent a comprehensive theory of how systems operate? This would appear dubious, and Almond concurs, as he maintains that it really represents instead "a proposed first step towards constructing a theory of the political system and of the development of political systems."[24] Leonard Binder, shortly after Almond set forth his scheme of inputs and outputs, stated that

> Almond's "seven-function system" (really neither functionalist nor a system), despite its advance over institutional description, may be praised as interesting or perceptive, without compelling further attention. It will be useful, indeed, to those seeking a better way to define the problems they want to study, but it cannot serve as a foundation for the study of whole political systems.[25]

What we have with Almond, therefore, is what might be called an approach-in-development. As he and his followers continue to operationalize his categories and concepts, we will be better able to determine whether systems analysis, as employed by Almond, may yet serve the functions of theory, explanation and prediction.

[24] Gabriel A. Almond, "A Developmental Approach to Political Systems," *World Politics*, XVII (January, 1965), p. 205.

[25] Leonard Binder, *Iran: Political Development in a Changing Society* (Berkeley and Los Angeles: University of California Press, 1962), p. 10.

STABILITY AND CHANGE

One problem with which the three theorists we have treated are commonly concerned is that of stability. Easton, in particular, is concerned with stress upon and within the political system, its sources, mechanisms, and outcomes.[26] While some analysts have recently come to be concerned with the total system, others have turned in recent years to an examination of political development and change, or to the role of violence in our social and political life. These concerns, while nominally different, actually present an excellent opportunity for linking micro and macro theories of politics.

Almond has suggested that essentially four different types of groups perform the input function of interest articulation. Respectively, these are of the institutional, associational, non-associational, and anomic varieties.[27] The first three categories are such that they will be fairly familiar to the reader. The institutional interest group is one formed for purposes other than interest articulation, although it performs this function from time to time. It is characterized as having a relative degree of permanence and formal organization. An example of this type might be the professional bureaucracy; although created for other purposes, it has definite interests and articulates them from time to time. Associational interest groups approximate to some degree the pressure groups with which we are familiar. They are formed specifically to articulate their interests and do so on a much more frequent basis than the others. They also have a relatively high degree of organization and permanence and can serve as a major source of demand inputs to the political system. Non-associational interest groups are most like the categoric or tertiary groups to whom we had reference in Chapter Eight.[28] That is, there is no degree of organization or structure to speak of, yet interests are there nonetheless and are expressed by various individuals or groups who claim to speak for the larger group. Thus, a senator can claim to speak for the disenfranchised, the poor, the black, and the young, while he is none of those things himself. Anomic interest groups are the final category, and are those most likely to contribute to system instability. These are temporary groups, coalescing without any real structure as a result of

[26] See especially A Systems Analysis of Political Life, Chapter IV, pp. 57-69; Chapters 14-21, pp. 220-340.

[27] Almond, in Almond and Coleman, op. cit., pp. 33-38.

[28] See pp. 145-46.

an event, personality, issue, or combination of these. Their particular importance to the political system lies in their essential "normlessness," their lack of attachment to the social and/or political system. In a sense, the presence of such groups in the system is suggestive of a basic weakness in the system which might lead to greater instability or the ultimate overthrow of the system itself.

Huntington has suggested by inference that this is one of the keys to violent political change. "The vulnerability of a traditional regime to revolution varies directly with the capability of the regime for modernization."[29] If institutions, created for specific functional ends, cannot adapt themselves to changing conditions, then the system must expect change to take place, however violent this may become.[30] An increasing concern of political scientists in recent years has been the incidence of violent and non-violent disruptions in political systems. Terchek has examined the means by which non-violent tactics have emerged in India, the United States, and Czechoslovakia.[31] These tactics are viewed as tools to gain access and to lead to bargaining situations, but with different results. For instance, the Gandhian approach in India contributed to the eventual displacement of the colonial system by independence. In contemporary India, however, non-violence has often been superseded by the articulation of "non-negotiable demands," which are seen by Terchek as being opposed in spirit and practice to the Gandhian ideal, with less success on the whole than that experienced in colonial days, for the most part. Gandhian campaigns in the United States have been exemplified by those led by the late Dr. Martin Luther King, Jr., such as his Birmingham, Alabama, bus boycott, which had a substantial economic impact on the bus company. Although the non-violent approach has been used with considerable success in the South, there is not yet enough evidence as to its potency in the North. In Czechoslovakia non-violent resistance to the Soviet invasion of August, 1968, did not repel the Soviet armies by any means, but it is questionable as to whether the techniques were completely unsuccessful, for they served in part to limit the Soviets. The Czechs, although at an obvious disadvantage militarily, were able to stop the Soviets from dividing their country, and were able to assume a bargaining posture, however unequal, through non-violent tactics.

[29] Samuel P. Huntington, "Political Development and Political Decay," *World Politics*, XVII (April, 1965), p. 422; also his *Political Order in Changing Societies* (New Haven: Yale University Press, 1968).

[30] *Ibid.*, p. 397.

[31] Ronald J. Terchek, "Theory Application of Gandhian Tactics in Three Disparate Environments: India, the United States, and Czechoslovakia" (paper prepared for delivery at the annual meeting of the American Political Science Association, New York City, August 31–September 4, 1969).

Lipsky has taken a similar approach in examining protest in political systems, by viewing such activity as an attempt to mobilize resources. A specific "target" of protest is assumed, and those engaged in activity of this nature attempt to win rewards, generally of a material nature, through forming coalitions with other groups which are either as powerless as the protest group itself, or those who control certain resources, such as money and access to the media. Lipsky concludes that protest, by groups which are relatively deficient in political power, is not highly likely to lead to success, especially in a short time span. Nonetheless, the activity itself may be useful in the building of more coherent groups with a greater chance of acquiring and managing their own resources.[32]

A successful attempt has been made to deal with the problems of civil strife in terms of developing a model which might predict system instability.[33] In an analysis of 114 polities, various measures are employed, such as political and economic deprivation, the level of institutionalization of the polity, and past history of instability. Gurr finds that he can account for sixty-four per cent of the variance among these nations in terms of the magnitude of civil strife, and concludes that there is a direct relationship between the potential size and previous history of coercive forces and the magnitude of eventual violence. When coercive forces are so large that they can be utterly repressive, then and only then does strife diminish. He concludes, "The adage that force solves nothing seems supported; in fact, force may make things worse."[34] Considerable work remains to be done in this area of research, but it is apparent that long strides are being taken which may have eventual importance not only for scholarly work, but for the making of public policy as well.

CRITIQUE

The authors may be faulted for combining under the general rubric of systems analysis several approaches which are, superficially, quite different. However, we see within Easton, Parsons, and Almond a distinct line of development and concerns. No single theorist has apparently offered us the "best" model, yet each has contributed to a process of

[32] Michael Lipsky, "Protest as a Political Resource," *American Political Science Review,* LXII (December, 1968), pp. 1144-58.

[33] Ted Gurr, "A Causal Model of Civil Strife: A Comparative Analysis Using New Indices," *American Political Science Review,* LXII (December, 1968), pp. 1104-24.

[34] *Ibid.,* p. 1124.

intellectual development. We have purposely kept our description of each approach to what may be considered its highlights. In so doing, we have not intended to oversimplify, nor to do injustice to each theorist. We have previously criticized some of the more salient points of each model, and we may now begin to tie these criticisms together in terms of the current state of systems analysis.

It is obvious that the type of analysis posited by Easton, Parsons, and Almond is of a considerably broader variety than that which is offered by group and decision analysis. Yet, each of our three theory-builders may be taken as being sufficiently broad that they can accommodate some of the very same concerns offered at narrower levels by theorists of the schools discussed in preceding chapters. Indeed, systems analysis and structural-functionalism are often described as "broad" or "middle-gauge" theory.

But, is it really theory of an empirical nature which we have been discussing? There are some fundamental problems with systems analysis which must be pointed out. The major one, as far as empiricists may be concerned, is a lack of testable hypotheses in any of the models we have described. Another problem is that of the normative sense which tends to underlie systems analysis and structural-functionalism. The first is one which is immediately apparent. Systems theory, such as it is, may be a fine pedagogical tool for offering a taxonomy of how the political system operates. As such, it is really what Easton meant by describing it as a *Framework for Political Analysis*.[35] The problem with frameworks or any bare-bones approach is that although a lot of wind can whistle through them, they afford no protection to their inhabitants. This is not to say that the various systems theorists have made no effort to flesh out their various systems. Those familiar with the works of Easton or Parsons, for instance, are all too aware of the infinite attention to detail paid by these theorists, and of the many concerns of systems theory.

However, one might search in vain for testable hypotheses in the works of the various systems and functional analysts. If we re-examine our earlier definition of any hypotheses, "general statements, suggestions of the connections between concepts,"[36] we might erroneously assume that systems analysis does indeed provide testable hypotheses. In a sense, Easton posits a system in which demand and support inputs operate and there are hypothetical relations between the two, but are they testable? The answer is an emphatic "no." One might, for instance, use input/output analysis to describe current poverty programs in the ghetto.

[35] *Op. cit.*
[36] Chap. Two, p. 20.

Eastonian analysis might be an admirable tool to describe and to order that which is observed, and to serve to raise questions about empirical phenomena. If one were to observe, for instance, that an infusion of federal dollars through a job-training program in a high-crime area was followed after some time lag by a reduction in certain types of crimes, one might infer a relationship between the federal aid (input) and the decreased crime rate (output). But this is a simple causal analysis, testable in its own right. Why, one might well ask, would one bother to put this in a systems framework in the first place? We have repeatedly made the point that the functions of theory are twofold, to explain and predict. Our overly-simplified systems model relating crime and job-training programs might help to explain such relationships, but it does nothing to predict future relationships, or how these two might obtain elsewhere. In this light it is proper to think of systems analysis not as a theory, but more as a model, one which may help to generate hypotheses[37] although it may not be comprised of hypotheses itself. Systems analysis proceeds under the assumption that it is useful to "view political life as a system of behavior."[38] Proceeding from this, Easton and others then construct elaborate models of the political process, some of which we have reviewed in this chapter. These models can serve the highly useful purposes of generating hypotheses, although systems analysts are generally loathe to do so. Further, these models can provide an interesting and useful taxonomy for the political process, providing a conceptual ledger for the presence or absence of variables which presumably enter into politics. Meehan has provided a thoughtful and concise critique of the problems raised by such "theories."

> A theory is not merely an "approach" to a discipline or topic — a suggested framework for explanation . . . . theories can function with any kind of generalization, whatever the terms they employ. But theories are definite and particular; they are attempts to explain real phenomena . . . . systems theories are research strategies, or statements about the content that political generalizations ought to include.[39]

While perhaps useful as an approach to research problems of one sort or another, systems analysis thus suffers from an absence of substantive

[37] Henry Teune, "Models in the Study of Political Integration," in Philip E. Jacob and James V. Toscano (eds.), *The Integration of Political Communities* (Philadelphia: J. B. Lippincott Company, 1964), pp. 294-97.
[38] Easton, *Framework*, p. 32.
[39] Eugene J. Meehan, *The Theory and Method of Political Analysis* (Homewood, Ill.: The Dorsey Press, 1965), p. 147.

content of its own. Whether it is more or less useful as a taxonomy is a moot point, dependent upon the preferences of each student. Readers of this work may be familiar with two texts for American Government courses, for example, which follow the systemic approach.[40] Others with more advanced training may have seen applications of systems analysis in other fields such as comparative politics,[41] or international relations.[42] As useful as the operationalization of systems analysis might be to some problems, there is no evidence to suggest that it is necessarily the best approach available to researchers.

On a more specific level, Meehan cites major flaws in the works of each of the three theorists we have discussed in this chapter. Eastonian analysis is immediately suspect, for it never attempts to define "political" in any meaningful sense.[43] "System" itself is defined in light of interactions, but is described in terms of its human components or as an actor, without reference to the interactions which supposedly define it in the first place.[44] In short,

> . . . one would really expect that criticism of a conceptual structure would be based largely on its adequacy or inadequacy in relating to the phenomena. Easton has no phenomena! The "political system" which he so busily dissects exists nowhere except in his mind; the closest empirical approximation is probably the sovereign national state.[45]

Parsonian analysis is similarly open to criticism according to Meehan. By aiming for a general theory, one which would be capable of explaining and predicting human behavior in all fields, Parsons essentially requires a static system, one which is incapable of meeting change. This fundamental error, for the rest of his work proceeds from this point, does not in and of itself mean that his work is entirely without value. However, Parsons is subject to the same criticism as that offered of Easton. He prepares an elaborate taxonomy, but one can search in vain

---

[40] Marian D. Irish and James W. Prothro, *The Politics of American Democracy* (5th ed.; Englewood Cliffs, N.J.: Prentice-Hall, Inc., 1971), and Stephen V. Monsma, *American Politics: A Systems Approach* (New York: Holt, Rinehart and Winston, Inc., 1969).

[41] A. J. Milnor, *Elections and Political Stability* (Boston: Little, Brown and Company, Inc., 1969).

[42] Morton A. Kaplan, *System and Process in International Politics* (New York: John Wiley & Sons, Inc., 1957).

[43] Eugene J. Meehan, *Contemporary Political Thought: A Critical Study* (Homewood, Ill.: The Dorsey Press, 1967), p. 172.

[44] *Ibid.*, pp. 172-73.

[45] *Ibid.*, p. 174.

"for adequate explanations of concrete phenomena."[46] Furthermore, there is a bias present toward the collectivity in his four-fold system, ignoring the individual, and thus raising some serious questions about the ultimate values upon which his work and others are premised.[47] This point is most important, and we shall conclude with it after a final critique of Almond.

In Almond's seven-function system, a meld of Eastonian and Parsonian analysis, we have another example of an attempt at a general all-encompassing theory. And, he too must necessarily fall subject to the same criticism of producing an elaborate taxonomy or a model, which fails to meet the requirements of theory. We have earlier made the point that Almond's approach has been used in comparative analysis, as systems in general appears to offer some points on which useful comparison can be made. Meehan suggests that this is not sufficient to warrant the label of theory.

> ... specialists in comparative government have for years taken it for granted that comparisons are always worth making even when there is no specific end in view. Now, inquiry may aim at description, explanation, or evaluation, or all three; and comparative government, as presently conceived, seems primarily concerned with description. But it is pointless to make endless comparisons unless the similarities and differences uncovered by the comparison are explained, and explanation does not necessarily depend on still further comparisons.[48]

If political science seeks to be more rigorous and empirical, it must be divested, as much as is humanly possible, of biases in its approaches. Can it be said that systems analysis leads us closer to this goal? From the works of the three we have examined there is considerable evidence that just the reverse is true. Concerns with "steady states," "equilibrium," and "system maintenance" all have a heavily loaded bias in favor of the status quo, as well as against the individual. If something is "dysfunctional" for the system in which it operates, is it to be implied that this is bad? To describe variables as functional or dysfunctional appears to place a higher value on system continuance than on system change or displacement. The functionality of some variable, person, or event is measured against whether it assists a system or one of its vital subsystems in the performance of its other functions. Implicitly, then, systems analysis is stating that maintenance or continuance has a higher

[46] *Ibid.*, p. 145.
[47] *Ibid.*, p. 150.
[48] *Ibid.*, pp. 180-81.

place in the order of things. Thus, if we continue this line of reasoning, stability to the systems analyst becomes a prime requisite, and variables which are described as "functional" may take on another meaning — they are good. Further, what is "functional" in the eyes of one analyst at the time might not be functional to another elsewhere, and might lead to unforeseen payoffs, some of which may be patently "dysfunctional."

A somewhat morbid example of this might be the occasional crop failures in China. To the more rabid individuals in this and other countries who are fearful of the "yellow peril," a famine killing five or six million Chinese might be functional — it lessens the imminent menace just so much. Leaders in communist China, forced to deal with the many problems of a famine may find that it is entirely dysfunctional to the economy as well as to the regime. The time element also casts some doubt upon the utility of such concepts as functional and dysfunctional. In 1933, one could argue, rabid anti-Semitism was entirely functional to the Third Reich in that it provided a convenient scapegoat for Germany's ills and gave a coherence to the ideology of National Socialism which was not otherwise present. But, strictly avoiding any discussion of human values, the loss of a significant element of Germany's professional and mercantile population in a short time, without adequate replacements, could have contributed in part to the eventual German losses in the Second World War. What was perceived as functional by the regime at one time may have been dysfunctional to the German nation at a later time. In short, by considering system maintenance or stability as a prime goal, by "measuring" variables against artificial and system-biased constructs such as functionality, analysts may fall prey to using a heavily value-laden scheme which ultimately interferes with instead of assists the goals of explanation and prediction. Functionality can take on the hue of a purely normative theology instead of an empirical social science. Much depends on the operationalization of systems models, of course, but the danger is no less there because of the use of abstract concepts with a seemingly empirical tone. Indeed, as Mechan pointed out, there is little evidence of empirical orientation in the work of our three model-builders, a criticism well worth bearing in mind in the evaluation of such approaches insofar as they do or do not contribute to theory-building.

In sum, considerably greater information is required at all levels, as we have suggested in our earlier chapters dealing with specific substantive topics of political science. We have stressed continually that theory and method must go hand-in-hand. The questions posed by those of the systems school are quite broad, perhaps too broad, but they could be taken as suggestive of new concerns of political scientists. An inescapable difficulty in the systems approach is the lack of clear empirical references. Some of the variables discussed by those of the systems school are taken further and operationalized by communications analysts in the development of more adequate predictors and more comprehensive explanation. It may well be that systems analysis, which has been in something of a vogue in recent years, will be supplanted by the communications approaches discussed in the next chapter. The constant interaction between theory and empirical findings will test the constructs of systems analysis and structural-functionalism, and may be expected to either refine or replace them. It is this constant process of development, which we have found throughout our survey of the directions in which political science has been moving in recent years, that is both the frustration and excitement of a developing discipline.

Communications

10

INTRODUCTION

A major step toward the development of broad-gauge theory in political science is that of communications analysis. This approach is an excellent example of the debt which political science has to other disciplines. Indeed, the father of communications analysis is probably Norbert Wiener, a physicist and mathematician. In his *Cybernetics*[1] we have one of the earliest models useful to political science in the analysis of political behavior in communications terms. A fundamental assumption of the communications approach is that "society can only be understood through a study of the messages and the communication facilities which belong to it...."[2]

In this chapter, we shall consider the various levels of communications analysis, and discuss some studies which have applied this ap-

---

[1] *Cybernetics: Or Control and Communication in Animal and the Machine* (New York: The Technology Press, John Wiley & Sons, Inc., 1948).

[2] Norbert Wiener, *The Human Use of Human Beings: Cybernetics and Society* (Boston: Houghton Mifflin Company, 1950), p. 9.

proach. The levels which we shall consider are interpersonal, sub-system, and system, respectively. But, before we discuss the means by which communications analysis has been applied, it is necessary to first clarify some basic concepts.

DEFINITIONS

The fundamental unit of analysis in communications is that of the *message*, regardless of content or meaning. Milbrath defines this as "any thought that is complete or stands by itself."[3] Messages, in turn, contain *information*. Wiener suggests that information is

> . . . a name for the content of what is exchanged with the outer world as we adjust to it, and make our adjustment felt upon it. The process of receiving and using information is the process of our adjusting to the outer environment, and of our living effectively under that environment.[4]

Deutsch adapts this definition by emphasizing that information also demonstrates a "patterned relationship between events."[5] The concept of patterns, be they relationships or interactions, is fundamental not only to communications but to systems as well.

Messages are *sent*, *received*, and *stored*. But, before they are sent, they must be *encoded*. The process of encoding, whether by an individual or a group, requires an attempt "to select and execute a response (R) to the environmental event (S). . . ."[6] The definition offered by North is suggestive of the way in which communications analysis can subsume other approaches, such as decisional analysis. The response requires several steps, all related to the very heart of the decisional process, how one reacts to stimuli. Quite literally, if one receives a stimulus, according to North, the response is necessarily a decision, and requires several steps in the encoding process before the message or response can be sent or transmitted.[7] Encoded messages are transmitted in a variety of ways, but we refer to their passing through communica-

[3] Lester W. Milbrath, *The Washington Lobbyists* (Chicago: Rand McNally and Company, 1963), p. 187. Italics in original.

[4] Wiener, *The Human Use of Human Beings*, p. 124.

[5] Karl W. Deutsch, *The Nerves of Government: Models of Political Communication and Control* (New York: The Free Press of Glencoe, 1966), p. 84.

[6] Robert C. North, "The Analytical Prospects of Communications Theory," in James C. Charlesworth (ed.), *Contemporary Political Analysis* (New York: The Free Press, 1967), p. 304.

[7] *Ibid.*, pp. 304-05.

tions *channels*, or "a transmission medium over which messages flow."[8] The messages, however, may not arrive at the intended recipient, as they may be blocked, or intercepted by others.[9] Distortion can take place, as there may be *noise* in the channels, or because the message was improperly encoded and/or *decoded*. Both encoding and decoding require the use of one's perceptions of the message or stimulus, increasing the possibility of misunderstanding or distortion.[10] Further, since encoding or decoding involves human brain activity, "a combination of electrochemical phenomena occurring within (individual) human evaluators, decision-makers, and the like, together with sign and symbol communications,"[11] we may describe the entire communications process as involving something less than objective reality.

In the process of transmitting messages over channels, it must be recognized that any channel, such as face-to-face oral communication, the mass media, or diplomatic couriers, ultimately has a given "*capacity*, which, if exceeded, creates a condition called *overload*."[12] In this case, the communications channel becomes totally ineffective as messages may not get through at all.

An example of the use of such concepts in political analysis might be fruitful. Assume, for instance, that action in a combat zone may require immediate notification of the president. The Tet offensive by enemy forces in Viet Nam in 1968 might serve as our illustration. Sensory information was perceived by our intelligence teams in such a way as to suggest that unusual conditions existed. They had visually or aurally received a message. However, our concern is with a hypothetical single message which ultimately reached the president. Each intelligence officer in a combat zone was literally incapable of gathering all the objective facts about the situation — what units of the enemy, with how many men, using what arms, were engaged in combat at any given moment with what purpose. On the basis of their preliminary reports, filtering into army headquarters in Saigon, various individuals received the messages, collated and sorted them, and then composed a wire for President Johnson. The individual messages received at headquarters had to be decoded, and their precise meanings arrived at by others. Before writing a message, they had to select information on the basis of a preliminary evaluation. The selection process involved recalling some information, from individual memory as well as the files, in order that

[8] Milbrath, *op. cit.*, p. 307.
[9] *Ibid.*
[10] North, in Charlesworth, *op. cit.*, p. 307.
[11] *Ibid.*, p. 306.
[12] Milbrath, *op. cit.*, p. 188. Emphasis in original.

pertinent information be transmitted. Action which appeared to be of a routine nature, and did not fit the apparent pattern of a coordinated enemy offensive, was rejected as being unrelated. The message was written, using ordinary language and symbols, all of which might be subjected to varying interpretations. Thus, the possibility of distortion from objective reality was introduced in several stages, even before the message was transmitted. A classified army message, it was then probably put into a top secret code for electrical transmission. This process could again introduce distortion, as a code clerk might have erroneously encoded certain letters or words. We will assume that the communications channel used was one which is normally reserved for high-priority messages, by radio-telegraph facilities. If enemy agents had been able to identify the channel, and had wanted to block the message from getting through to the president, they could have "jammed" the frequency with over-riding noise. Assuming that this was not done, the message was received over a special teletype machine, converting electrical energy into mechanical, and the message was typed out. Communications personnel would then have had to alert the appropriate officers in charge, one of whom presumably had the wisdom (or "stored" instructions) to notify the president, however indirectly. Ultimately the president received the message, composed thousands of miles away by people he had never met, on the basis of information provided by still others. In consultation with his advisers, all of whom had to read and interpret the message through their own value screens, the president was then prepared to make some sort of a response. The cycle was then restarted, with new messages from the White House to various officials in Viet Nam to the Congress, the Pentagon, the press, and ultimately, the average citizen in his home. We have not detailed all the possible steps in this example, but it is easy to see how distortion can take place at any point in the message flow. For instance, if there was only one channel for presidential messages from Viet Nam, and a high number of messages had to be passed, the equipment itself might have broken down. This is to say nothing of the capabilities of the president and his advisers in receiving and assessing a high number of messages, with complex information, in a short period of time.

Essential to the entire communications process is *feedback*. We define this as

> . . . a communications network that produces action in response to an input of information, and *includes the results of its own action in the new information by which it modifies its subsequent behavior.*[13]

[13] Deutsch, *op. cit.*, p. 88. Emphasis in original.

Expressed in another way, feedback refers to the process by which an individual, a group, or a system learns the consequences of its action(s), so that corrective behavior may be instituted. In the feedback process, particularly, we make use of four additional concepts. *Load* refers to the amounts of information involved in feedback and other channels; *lag* suggests the delay involved in responding to information transmitted by feedback channels; *lead* is the inverse of lag, and indicates the ability of a system to act on predicted and anticipated events; *gain* is literally the amount and speed of reaction to information.[14]

We may relate these feedback processes to our example, by examining additional channels involved in the presidential decision-making process. We have already suggested that load is a critical factor, as the channels carrying information have a limited capacity. How did the president respond to the initial messages bringing him information about the Tet offensive? Did he delay until further information was forthcoming? Did he request this information from Saigon? How detailed were these requests, and did they ask for the sort of information he needed to make a command decision? In other words, was there a lag in the decisional process introduced by faulty use of communications? Or, was the president prepared for the Tet offensive by having received advance warning and prediction of the event, thus requiring only his formal order to implement a planned response to the offensive? Finally, what was the reaction to the initial message from Saigon? Was it treated in a desultory fashion, and possibly overlooked by those responsible for alerting the president? Or did the lights burn overtime at the White House, as the meanings of the offensive were explored by the president and his advisers?

The use and elaboration of these concepts might seem at first glance to be superfluous, and to be merely redundant of what any astute political observer might be able to reason out for himself. However, by specifying the details of the communications process, it may be possible to develop more refined predictors of political behavior. The communications analysis approach to behavior has been with us for some time, but has only recently been developed in the context which we have outlined. We turn first to communications on the inter-personal level, and examine them in terms of how they influence behavior and attitudinal change.

---

[14] *Ibid.*, pp. 187-90.

LOW-LEVEL ANALYSIS: INTERPERSONAL COMMUNICATION

Long before communications analysis in its modern form became the
focus for many analysts, social scientists had been paying attention to
the effects of inter-personal communications on behavior and attitudes.
We see, for instance, that a considerable body of research on behavior
and attitudes had focused, prior to Wiener, on those aspects of political
behavior which most easily relate to inter-personal communications.
Thus, Chapter Four, on values, attitudes, opinions, and beliefs, is derived in part from those studies which have explored interpersonal
communications and relationships. Chapter Five, on political socialization, is also based on such work. To consider such objects of study as
socialization or attitudes without understanding the necessary role played
by communications would be to commit a glaring error.

In this vein, Milbrath suggests that a necessary antecedent for
political action is that "the political actor must pick up relevant stimuli
from environment. Stimuli likely to be perceived as political make up
only a small part of the total available."[15] There is little doubt that stimuli are available to some degree to most individuals, but the amount
present is a function of one's environment, needs, and training. Thus,
an individual who is in a situation which requires little knowledge of
current affairs might make little attempt to seek out political information, unless it was either personally relevant to some operative need
(e.g., if he is unemployed, and the government is considering a new
job-training program). The roles played by selective attention and
selective perception are therefore crucial if the communications process
is to be at all effective in altering or reinforcing behavior and attitudes.

A factor which enters the communications process and has a direct
relationship to the effectiveness of communications is the way in which
the communicator is perceived. As Cohen points out, "Who says something is as important as *what* is said in understanding the effect of a
communication on an attitude."[16] The source of a message or stimulus,
as perceived by the recipient, can thus be a major reason for a message
getting through in the first place. If one feels that the communicator
is an untrustworthy source, or otherwise unattractive, the message itself

[15] Lester W. Milbrath, *Political Participation: How and Why Do People Get Involved in Politics?* (Chicago: Rand McNally and Company, 1965), p. 39.
[16] Arthur R. Cohen, *Attitude Change and Social Influence* (New York: Basic
Books, Inc., 1964), p. 23. Emphasis in original.

may be screened out either consciously or unconsciously. Hovland, Janis and Kelley summarize research in this area, and suggest

> . . . the reactions to a communication are significantly affected by cues as to the communicator's intentions, expertness, and trustworthiness. The very same presentation tends to be judged more favorably when made by a communicator of high credibility than by one of low credibility.[17]

Group membership is another factor affecting the influence of communications. We have examined in Chapter Seven some of the means by which groups influence attitudes and behavior. Hovland, Janis and Kelley pay particular attention to the means by which group memberships can lead to resistance to communications. They refer to "counternorm communications," those which take a stand opposite to that held by groups to which individuals belong.[18] One factor which inhibits the effects of communications stimuli is the extent to which one values membership in the group. Counternorm messages would therefore be rejected in large part by those who have a high regard for some particular group and who rely upon that group for status or feelings of "belongingness." Indeed, the more one values a particular group membership, the more it can be expected that he will not only reject messages which oppose group norms, but he may rely more strongly on communications with other group members.[19] Status within the group is another factor which may be associated with resistance to counternorm messages. Those who have only average status in the group are likely to be more resistant to external stimuli than are those who have high status. Hovland felt at the time of his writing that popularity or value to the group is for the most part "positively correlated with conformity and resistance to counternorm communications," and that conformity was to be expected of those aspiring to leadership positions.[20] However, those holding leadership positions might be more prone to occasionally deviate from group norms, and these persons could be highly influential themselves in changing group attitudes.[21]

Some evidence for this may be found in the study by Samuel A. Stouffer.[22] In this pioneering work, two national cross-sections were

[17] Carl I. Hovland, Irving L. Janis, and Harold H. Kelley, *Communication and Persuasion: Psychological Studies of Opinion Change* (New Haven. Yale University Press, 1953), p. 35.
[18] *Ibid.*, pp. 134-35.
[19] *Ibid.*, pp. 137-44.
[20] *Ibid.*, p. 153.
[21] *Ibid.*, p. 154.
[22] *Communism, Conformity and Civil Liberties: A Cross-section of the Nation Speaks Its Mind* (Gloucester, Mass.: Peter Smith, 1963).

matched against a special sample of approximately 1500 local leaders holding certain community positions, such as mayors, county party chairmen, American Legion post commanders, and regents of the Daughters of the American Revolution. Stouffer was concerned with how the American public and its local leaders viewed questions of civil rights and liberties. Granted that the study was undertaken in the 1950s, prior to campus rebellions, ghetto uprisings, and the activist mood which dominated so much of the nation in the next decade, the questions asked and their answers are of intrinsic importance today. For those concerned with the persuasive effects of communications, and how to apply them, Stouffer offers some suggestions. Perhaps most importantly, especially as our civil liberties develop or are modified, he found that civic leaders were more prone to holding pro-civil liberties positions than was the national sample.[23] While this was not directly related to group memberships per se, it follows that these leaders, holding high formal status in their organizations, may be more susceptible to communications campaigns than are the members of their associations. The evidence for this is murky and inferential at best. For instance, Katz and Lazarsfeld suggest that conformity to group norms is essential for those who seek leadership positions and wish to maintain them.[24] However, the same authors report that the most successful group members in effecting attitude change or influencing others are those to whom are attributed high status or power in the group.[25] Thus, although group leaders tend to resist change in their attitudes and beliefs,[26] once persuaded, they can become successful message carriers. Formal and informal leaders therefore operate as "opinion leaders," and assist in the "two-step flow of communications." That is, they tend to expose themselves to more media than do most people, and pass on to others their own perceptions and interpretations of media messages. In this way, they can reinforce existing opinions, or assist in changing them.[27] Personal contact, therefore, is probably the most important phase of any communications process. A distinct advantage of personal contact is its flexibility as compared to the media, for it can be more effective in en-

[23] Ibid., especially Chap. 2.
[24] Elihu Katz and Paul F. Lazarsfeld, Personal Influence: The Part Played by People in the Flow of Mass Communications (New York: The Free Press, 1955), pp. 51-53.
[25] Ibid., p. 105.
[26] Lewis A. Froman, Jr., People and Politics: An Analysis of the American Political System (Englewood Cliffs, N.J.: Prentice-Hall, Inc., 1962), pp. 41-42.
[27] Katz and Lazarsfeld, op. cit., pp. 309-20; see also Paul F. Lazarsfeld, Bernard Berelson, and Hazel Gaudet, The People's Choice: How the Voter Makes Up His Mind in a Presidential Campaign (2d ed.; New York: Columbia University Press, 1948), pp. 151-52.

countering resistance and adapting to counterarguments or even passivity, than can the mass media.[28] As used by group leaders or opinion leaders, personal communications can provide stimuli of sufficient intensity that the likelihood of changing the listener's attitudes may be increased, not to mention the possibility of mobilizing the listener to action as well. In a political campaign, for example, personal persuasion may be at least as effective as mass media campaigns in arousing the voters to action and getting them to the polls. This is not, however, to dismiss the media as important participants in the communications process, which we next consider.

MIDDLE-LEVEL ANALYSIS: THE MASS MEDIA

One of the most significant statements of the role of mass media in influencing attitudes and behavior concerns the 1960 televised "debates" between Richard Nixon and John F. Kennedy. The first telecast on September 26 had a national audience of some seventy to seventy-five million viewers. The three succeeding broadcasts drew smaller audiences, but in no case less than forty-eight million persons watched the third and fourth debates. The impact of television was apparently one of the deciding factors in Kennedy's victory. A survey by the Roper organization showed that about fifty-seven per cent of the voters admitted to having been influenced in one way or another by the debates. About six per cent, representing potentially four million voters, apparently "decided to cast their ballots on the basis of the television performances, and their verdict was three-to-one for Kennedy, providing him with considerably more votes than the two one-hundredths of one per cent by which he won the popular count."[29] While it is questionable whether or not the debates actually were the cause of the Kennedy victory, there is no doubt but that they played a large part. They also suggest the importance of the mass media, in a striking and dynamic way. From this example, it is possible to overstate the case for mass media. V. O. Key has warned that this is a common fault, and suggests that dependence upon the mass media is limited by the fact that a listener, viewer, or reader is not "an automaton actuated by impulses transmitted by anonymous rulers" of the media.[30] In light of this warning, and as important

[28] Lazarsfeld, Berelson, and Gaudet, op. cit., pp. 153-54.
[29] Earl Mazo, The Great Debates (Santa Barbara: Center for the Study of Democratic Institutions, 1962), pp. 4-5.
[30] V. O. Key, Jr., Public Opinion and American Democracy (New York: Alfred A. Knopf, Inc., 1964), p. 344.

as interpersonal communications may be, there is yet a significant role for the mass media in politics, and an examination of that role is essential to understanding political behavior.

What roles do the media play? An obvious starting point is to employ the concepts we earlier defined. The mass media, such as radio, television, newspapers, and magazines, are transmitters of information. They gather information, through their own channels, encode it in styles peculiar to their own medium as well as to their particular format, and transmit it to viewers, listeners, and leaders. Other than *how* they gather their information, the means by which they encode their messages is of the most striking importance.[31] Assuming that some given event takes place, such as a campus sit-in, the media can be expected to give vastly different treatment to the event. Even if the radio and television networks are on the scene, and if wire service reporters are there as well, they may report different aspects of the same event. A radio reporter can roam about with his tape recorder, reporting the facts as he sees them and has them given to him by the campus public relations office, and offering a commentary which may or may not have a distinctly editorial "line" about it. Television cameramen are somewhat more restricted, but their filmed report of the event, with voice commentary and reporting as well, is a radically different means of encoding information. Home viewers may have the sit-in "brought into their homes," but only those scenes recorded by the camera can be received. The visual effect may heighten viewers' involvement, but possibilities for "objective" encoding and decoding are severely limited. If the cameras should record the presence of shouting long-haired students, even if they are a distinct minority, it is all too easy to receive the impression that only "hippie-types" are involved, that they are the only students at that college, or that all students are like that, for that matter. Newspapers would have to rely primarily on the written word, but may have a photograph or two of the event. The headline for the story may cue the reader as to whether or not he should actually read the story, and what he may get out of it. On the basis of a fast reading, a member of the paper's staff will write a short capsulized description of the story which follows. Weekly magazines will have a natural lag, or more time to cover the story, to provide an "in-depth" report, but may well allocate less space to the event. Thus, their encoding will involve considerable condensation, attempting to get more information in less space. Monthly magazines, or those which expressly hold some view-

---

[31] A recent and popular work which treats this aspect of communications extensively is Marshall McLuhan and Quentin Fiore, *The Medium Is the Message* (New York: Random House, 1967).

point, may not cover the story at all, but may make some passing reference to it in the context of a broader article on student unrest. Added to all this, each particular station, paper, or magazine may well have its own distinct style or reporting. For instance, it would be possible to read accounts of the sit-in in *The New York Times, Chicago Tribune,* and *Berkeley Barb,* and honestly wonder if their reporters had been covering the same event.

Thus, considerable distortion is likely to be present in the mass media, without this being anyone's intent at all. Furthermore, although the messages may be encoded and sent, there is no assurance that they are read or viewed by any great audience, or that once received they are decoded in the same manner as desired by those reporting the event. It is no small wonder, therefore, that the mass media are preoccupied with viewer or listener ratings, or that newspapers and magazines keep a careful eye on subscriptions and newsstand sales. Further, there is a pluralism in the media, which can inhibit any overwhelming influence. Even assuming that television sets are turned on, one can usually select three evening news programs, all of which may take different viewpoints. In the larger cities, there may be some choice of newspapers, although this has been declining in recent years. National news magazines of different persuasions are also available.

In addition to the varying vehicles within each medium from which the viewer or reader can select, he can also choose several of the media for his information, by subscribing to a newspaper and magazine, listening regularly to the radio and watching television as well. It behooves us, therefore, to distinguish among the media in terms of the amount of reliance the public places on them for political information. A 1968 national sample was asked which they used for information about the campaign.[32]

Newspapers	72%
Radio	39
Television	86
Magazines	35

Given the obvious reliance upon television as the widest used source of political information, to what extent does the public rely upon more than one source? The same national sample was asked a series of questions as to whether or not they used each of the media and a cumulative index was derived.

[32] Data Source: 1968 Election Study, University of Michigan SRC Study 523.

No media	4%
One	15
Two	32
Three	34
Four	14
Total	99%[33]

Although there is a strong tendency for the American public to receive political information from television, there is no evidence to suggest that this is a single source for any significant number of people. The pluralism of which we spoke, in terms of the availability of different types of media, is apparently operative, and there is an overlap between the audiences or receivers of the various communications channels.

Key has examined the relationships between types of media used for sources of political information and several variables relating to political participation. Magazine users were found, in an analysis of the 1956 national sample survey by the Survey Research Center at the University of Michigan, to·have the greatest familiarity with issues, to participate to a greater degree in the electoral process, and to be more "internationalistic" in attitudes. Next in order in each of these variables are newspaper readers, television viewers, and radio listeners.[34] Key also found that those who rank highest in media exposure, who use either three or four media for political information, tend to have a higher educational level and to be more involved in politics.[35] Jennings and Niemi have studied high-school students on a broad number of variables relating to political socialization. As regards media usage, they find that reliance upon the mass media for political news increases noticeably after high school. Further, there are considerable differences between students and their parents in that parents tend to pay greater attention to all four media.

> Although students watch a good deal of television, they pay attention to its news broadcasts much less regularly than parents. Daily attention to the newspapers is also much less frequent among the students, while the differences in the use of radio and magazine news are smaller but in the same direction. As with political interests, there are rather similar proportions of nonusers among students and parents. For the most part, increased media usage in adulthood means shifting from irregular to regular use.[36]

[33] *Ibid.* Does not equal 100% because of rounding.
[34] Key, *op. cit.*, pp. 347-50.
[35] *Ibid.*, pp. 348-49, 357-58.
[36] M. Kent Jennings and Richard G. Niemi, "Patterns of Political Learning," *Harvard Educational Review*, XXXVIII (Summer, 1968), pp. 450-51.

If we find these associations between mass media usage and political behavior, can we properly infer that the behavior is literally caused by the mass media? We have already suggested that there is a tendency either to emphasize media influence almost to the exclusion of other factors, or to discount the media almost entirely in accounting for political behavior. Hovland provides one of the more comprehensive reviews of the research on this topic.[37] As with his earlier research on interpersonal communication,[38] Hovland suggests that the communicator is at least as important as the content of the message he is sending. If the communicator, such as a radio or television personality or a newspaper reporter, is viewed as reliable, honest, sincere, and qualified to speak on the topic, the message is more likely to get through and to be accepted by the intended recipient. However, there is little evidence to suggest that perceived reliability of the source is at all related to the changing or modifying of opinions.[39] The communication itself has been examined for the nature of its appeal, emotional or rational, but research evidence on this point is inconclusive.[40] It is common to think of the demagogue working his audience up to fever pitch, using appeals of fear and hatred to get his message through. We can document such successes with ease, but there are numerous instances in which such appeals have only served to lose an audience. Thus, a speaker who insists on the presence of a genuine communist menace to our school system through sex education might very well get his message through to certain audiences. But, if he were to deliver the same message to other groups, he might be laughed off the stage. In other words, audiences themselves may be totally different and subject to entirely different types of appeals. In a similar fashion, audiences for the mass media can be stratified by any number of variables, such as age, education, sex, or region, to name a few. The mass media, to have a significant impact, must develop highly differentiated means of getting the attention of these various categoric groups in the first instance, and then finding the proper means of holding that attention and getting a message accepted. This is no easy task at all, and may contribute to a diminished effect of the mass media. We have pointed out how they are pluralistic in nature, addressed to a wide variety of audiences. But, to assume a continual broad-gauge effect of the media upon behavior and attitudes would be to infer that there is no pluralism in outlook, an assertion for which there is only dubious evidence.

[37] Carl I. Hovland, "Effects of the Mass Media of Communication," in Gardner Lindzey (ed.), *Handbook of Social Psychology* (Cambridge: Addison-Wesley Publishing Company, Inc., 1954), pp. 1062-1103.

[38] *Supra*, pp. 86, 227.

[39] Hovland, "Effects of the Mass Media . . .", pp. 1071-75.

[40] *Ibid.*, pp. 1075-77.

That the mass media have an important role to play in providing information about the political world to the citizen, and often mediating between the individual and the political system, there can be little doubt. However, the means by which they do this, with outcomes in terms of behavior and attitudes, is still a subject for continued research. The studies which exist on the mass media are often inconclusive at best.

UPPER-LEVEL ANALYSIS: COMMUNICATIONS AND THE POLITICAL SYSTEM

In the concern with building broad-gauge empirical theory, communications analysts such as Karl Deutsch have come the closest to providing a theory which is operational and serves the purposes of explanation and prediction. Almond has suggested some of the reasons why communication is such an important object of study at the system level.[41] For one, the various functions performed by and required of the political system are necessarily accomplished by the communications process. This alone would justify the attention paid to communications. But, on another level, communication is a function itself, and is not merely a vehicle for the performance of other functions. We can thus compare nations as to how the function of political communication is carried out, and with what effects. Suggested as a basis for comparison between political systems are the following criteria:

1. the homogeneity of political information;
2. the mobility of information;
3. the volume of information;
4. the direction of the flow of information.[42]

Conceptualization at this level can incorporate specifics such as those entailed in low- and middle-level analysis, and still led us to a greater generalizability.

In several works, Karl W. Deutsch has set forth and elaborated upon his basic scheme for communications theory. In these, he subsumes work done by various other theorists, notably Talcott Parsons.[43]

[41] Gabriel A. Almond, "Introduction: A Functional Approach to Comparative Politics," in Gabriel A. Almond and James S. Coleman, The Politics of the Developing Areas (Princeton: Princeton University Press, 1960), pp. 45-52.

[42] Ibid., p. 50.

[43] See especially Chapters 2, 3, 6, and 7 in Philip E. Jacob and James V. Toscano (eds.), The Integration of Political Communities (Philadelphia: J. B. Lippincott Company, 1964).

Borrowing heavily from cybernetics,[44] Deutsch postulates that control requires communication or the transmission of messages and information. Since politics is concerned with questions of power and control, Deutsch asserts that a necessary condition for examining these intangibles is an understanding of the central role of communications.[45] The fundamental assumption underlying the control approach, linking theory to substantive research, is that by viewing

> . . . nations and governments as communications systems, impersonal, verifiable evidence can be obtained to check general descriptive or qualitative assertions about nationalism, about sovereignty, and about the merger of states.[46]

By extension, we may also use this approach to examine the way(s) in which other systems and groups behave in the political world.

In this vein, Deutsch studied one of his suggested topics, that of nationalism, in light of communications.[47] He suggests that this topic, one which has absorbed political scientists for years, may be profitably broken down for study by determining the actual importance of such notions as "consciousness" or "will," concepts which frequently emerge in discussions of nationalism. These terms should then be operationalized and given empirical referents, so that they may be measured for relevance, as well as for the extent to which they actually reflect communications patterns. By so doing, Deutsch feels that it might be possible to

> . . . identify pathological or self-destructive developments in nationalism where they occur, and perhaps to predict them in their early stages, as well as to suggest approaches to policies that might tend to prevent nationalistic conflicts from leading to national and social destruction.[48]

Other aspects of nationalism are similarly operationalized and quantified by Deutsch, such as the process of national assimilation or differen-

---

[44] The term, as used by Wiener, derives from the Greek root which suggests "steersman" or "governor." See *Cybernetics*, p. 19.

[45] Deutsch, in Jacob and Toscano, *op. cit.*, pp. 49-51. A more elaborate description of the linkage between control and communications may be found in Deutsch, *The Nerves of Government*, pp. 75-142.

[46] Deutsch, in Jacob and Toscano, *op. cit.*, p. 49.

[47] Karl W. Deutsch, *Nationalism and Social Communications: An Inquiry Into the Foundations of Nationality* (New York: The Technology Press of the Massachusetts Institute of Technology and John Wiley & Sons, Inc., 1953). For a thorough critique of the means by which Deutsch imputes different meanings to "nationalism" and related concepts, see Walker Connor, "Nation-Building or Nation-Destroying?" *World Politics*, 24 (April, 1972).

[48] *Ibid.*, pp. 139-40.

tiation, and the efficiency of communications among a nation's people in order to determine to some degree a country's unity. Considerable data is brought to bear in this endeavor, and Deutsch uses it to summarize existing research on nationalism as well as to suggest further avenues of study for students of this particular problem. Of particular interest is his construction of a mathematical model of the processes of national assimilation and social mobilization.[49] This model is highly suggestive of trends to emerge later in political science which rely upon mathematics as well as statistics to assist in the task of prediction and explanation.

Deutsch does not dismiss statistics, however. In examining the system of world trade, he employs a statistical model to study the flow of imports and exports, although he suggests it might be applicable to transactions such as mail, telephone calls, and migration flows. Using the model, Deutsch and Savage found that they could predict world trade patterns and account for the impact of colonialism on trade patterns as well.[50] In another study, the suggested examples of mail, telephone calls, and migration are taken in the context of international and metropolitan levels of governance. For instance, the mail flow in Nigeria from 1929 to 1948, which increased by a multiple of eight, is taken to suggest a continual process of change in the country. Further, since there was a major shift in the flow of mail — from roughly half to only one-quarter going to other countries — Deutsch suggests that there is some evidence for believing that conditions of internal integration were being arrived at which were essential for independence.[51] Additional evidence for the decline and decay of central or inner cities may be examined by studying transactions within and between communities over a number of years. Deutsch suggests that the degree of integration of a metropolitan region may be related to the extent to which cities that are highly differentiated as regards income have worked out areas of agreement and cooperation.[52] In the same volume, Toscano applies a Deutsch-derived model to examine the Wilmington, Delaware, region by applying transaction flows as measures of political integration. These measures, taken together, are used to demonstrate the potential for integration in the region, and how one county in New Jersey is essentially divorced from other communities.[53] Thus, the models pro-

[49] Ibid., Appendix V. pp. 209-13.

[50] I. Richard Savage and Karl W. Deutsch, "A Statistical Model of the Gross Analysis of Transaction Flows," Econometrica, XXVIII (July, 1960), pp. 551-72.

[51] "Transaction Flows as Indicators of Political Cohesion," in Jacob and Toscano, op. cit., pp. 76-77.

[52] Ibid., pp. 93-95.

[53] James V. Toscano, "Transaction Flow Analysis in Metropolitan Areas," in Jacob and Toscano, op. cit., pp. 109-14.

duced by communications analysis can well serve the functions of explanation and prediction, as well as assist in the guidance of further research.

INTEGRATING THE LEVELS

It is fitting that one of the final works we examine in this text, which has been devoted to an examination of integrative approaches to political science, should be a clear example of this trend. Richard M. Johnson's examination of how Supreme Court decisions are communicated and implemented not only draws on several different facets of political science but from other disciplines as well.[54] His concern was with how the Supreme Court decisions abolishing prayer in the schools[55] were arrived at, transmitted, implemented and viewed at the local level. Thus, he is concerned not only with decision-making, but groups, attitudes and values, role expectations, and leadership as well, to name a few considerations. All of these variables are cast in the context of a communications network, in order that a consistent explanatory framework might be used. It is taken here as an example not only of interdisciplinary work by a political scientist, but because it effectively demonstrates how the various levels of communications that we have discussed in this chapter may be linked together. One of the most complex problems facing political scientists is that of linkage, or the means by which attitudes and decisions are communicated, complied with, or distorted. The linkage problem can be well-studied in a communications framework, and Johnson provides a valuable contribution toward understanding how decisions are arrived at, transmitted, and perceived by the citizenry-at-large.

Taking the Supreme Court as the highest level in the decisional process, comparable in effect to the political system which we earlier considered, he defines decision-making

> . . . in a relational sense. Activity is entailed not only on the part of those attempting to affect the behavior of others but on the part of those whose acts are to be affected. As for Supreme Court decision-making, it is compliant behavior on the part of others that gives substance to the Court's

[54] The Dynamics of Compliance: Supreme Court Decision-Making from a New Perspective (Evanston: Northwestern University Press, 1967).

[55] Engel v. Vitale, 370 U.S. 421 (1962); Abington School District v. Schempp, 374 U.S. 203 (1963).

determinations. If the Court announces a policy and no compliant behavior ensues, then there is no decision.[56]

Such a definition obviously implies a power relationship, and power is viewed as requiring communication in the first place.

Johnson hypothesizes that "pressures of a very specialized kind are brought to bear upon a wide range of actors motivating them to alter activity to make it consistent with rulings of the United States Supreme Court."[57] He examines the types of pressures upon policy implementers and those who are affected by the decisions of the Court. These pressures are explained as relating to cognitive consistency and dissonance,[58] or the means by which people attempt to bring their attitudes into some balance with their cognitions. This implies, however, that existing behavior patterns may ultimately have to be changed by some individuals as their perceptions of public policy or the Supreme Court could otherwise lead to noncompliance. How then are these changes brought about?

The Court is pictured as a highly-regarded source of messages, lacking in formal coercive power, but achieving a high degree of compliance nonetheless. The manner in which the Court "presents itself invoke(s) responses which are congruent with the substance of its policies."[59] The content of the messages or decisions is especially important, inasmuch as the Court lacks effective sanctions to ensure compliance. Reviewing the five major cases since World War II to come before the Court involving religion and the public schools, Johnson concludes that message cues were based upon the persuasiveness of the arguments presented. The Court relied as well upon effective symbols such as Madison and Jefferson.[60] Messages are transmitted to and through a large number of individuals, who will vary with the content of the decision. In the cases involving school prayers, communications recipients and channels included "state attorneys general, superintendents of public instruction, school superintendents, principals, teachers and school-board members."[61] All of these individuals have a host of roles to play, and their perceptions must be taken into account in determining whether compliance or noncompliance will result. Without becoming involved in other communications channels analyzed by Johnson, such as the media,

[56] Johnson, op. cit., p. 8.
[57] Ibid., p. 16.
[58] See Chapter Four, pp. 88-90, and Chapter Five, pp. 103-05, for discussions of cognitive consistency and dissonance as they relate to attitudes and political socialization, respectively.
[59] Johnson, op. cit., p. 42.
[60] Ibid., pp. 55-57.
[61] Ibid., p. 58.

the message or decision is eventually received at the local level, where it will be implemented or challenged. Johnson describes one such local environment, "Eastville-Westville," in terms of prevailing attitudes and norms, and the ways in which the prayer decisions were eventually accepted and implemented. Using a variety of techniques, including content analysis of the media and surveys of "influentials" as well as a cross-section of the community, he presents a comprehensive picture of a little-understood and complex phenomenon, that of linkage between government and citizen. The communications framework employed adds greatly to an understanding and appreciation of the processes involved in cutting through various levels of government and society in order to implement official policy.

SUMMARY AND CRITIQUE

Communications theory is one of the best examples of the ways in which political scientists, drawing heavily from other disciplines, have attempted to integrate theory and content at the most narrow and broad levels. Basic concepts have been defined and operationalized in a considerable body of literature and are incorporated in models for the generation of additional research and theory. In this sense, communications theory might well be the paradigm-in-development of which we spoke earlier.[62] In the narrowest sense, we can examine the means by which individuals receive and transmit information, how perception and socialization condition the process, and how this tends to integrate one into groups. Similarly, the group approach to the study of politics can be improved by turning to these same constructs for an enhanced understanding of how groups operate internally as well as with reference to other groups or the political system. Decision-making studies can also profit from the detailed questions posed by communications theory, as can systems theory as well. We have shown how communications analysis can be applied at various levels, such as interpersonal communications, mass media, or broad units of the political system, including the system itself. What remains to be done?

One of the most difficult problems facing those who would use communications analysis is that of meeting Deutsch's injunction that we treat the objects of study as impersonal processors of information. We have difficulty enough, for instance, in querying individuals as to their

[62] See pp. 33-35.

values, attitudes, opinions and beliefs, and attempting to make inferences about their perceptual processes from surveys and experiments. To
make inferences about the means by which individuals process, encode,
and decode information is even more demanding — if not impossible —
if carried to its logical extreme. For instance, the communications approach must deal with units of information. If we take a sentence as
our "unit," then we may ultimately be called upon to analyze something
in the area of 10^{50} possible sentences in the English language alone.
As Meehan points out, no formal mathematical structure could possibly handle that order of complexity.[63] Obviously, communications
theory cannot even hope to retreat to more readily understandable
constructs, more easily operationalized, and more susceptible to generalization. In this effort, political scientists will no doubt have to pay
greater attention to the findings and techniques of biologists and psychologists. For example, if we learn how the human mind physically
copes with problems and apply these findings to political behavior, we
may expect to make bold new strides in the science of politics.

As with systems analysis, we may criticize communications theory
for a tendency to be more mechanistic than is customary in studies of
human behavior. The impersonal view of individuals supposedly taken
by the communications approach may seemingly imply that humans,
in groups or alone, are nothing more or less than participants in a process
about which they have nothing to say — that they are indeed auto-
matons. Yet, no communications theorist has taken this point of view.
Indeed, Deutsch emphasizes that we cannot take artificial distinctions
between such entities as mechanisms and organisms as being necessarily real. Communications theory can show how individuals react to
demands placed upon them by others and by their environment.[64] This
hardly suffices to substantiate any charge that the communications
approach is as cold and impersonal as it might appear at first glance, or
that the charge is meaningful, for that matter.

The communications approach especially lends itself to operationalization, and the opportunity to quantify and to measure. In this respect,
communications theory can meet the criticism offered earlier by Eckstein
as regards the group approach, in that it does lend itself to testable
propositions, in which formal relations between variables can be meas-

[63] Eugene J. Meehan, *Contemporary Political Thought: A Critical Study* (Homewood, Ill.: The Dorsey Press, 1967), p. 329. The Estimate of 10^{50} is by V. H.
Yngve, and is cited by Mortimer Taube, *Computers and Common Sense* (New York:
McGraw-Hill Book Co., Inc., 1961), p. 29.
[64] *The Nerves of Government*, pp. 79-80.

ured in an attempt to describe cause and effect.[65] A good deal of the communications approach is concerned with so-called "indicators" of performance. For example, Deutsch's concepts of *lead*, *load*, *lag*, and *gain* may be operationalized within a given communications situation to indicate the relative efficiency and effectiveness of the system. Young warns that this might ultimately lead to "the dangers of false counting and distorted quantification in the search for performance indicators."[66] There is no doubt that this can very well happen, and indeed could be detected in already published research. But this danger is not limited to communications theory alone nor for that matter to any other approach taken by behavioral scientists. It is altogether possible that false quantification or an undue haste to lend an empirical referent to one's work could emerge in *any* scientific endeavor. The fact that a Lysenko could and did count missing tails on rats did not dismiss the validity of the entire field of genetics. When he was ultimately found out, his work was derided and dismissed, as it should have been. The same can happen to specialists in communications approaches to behavior as well. The ultimate test of any work is its acceptance by those who are professionally qualified to evaluate it. One need only turn to the "Communications to the Editor" section in any issue of the *American Political Science Review* to develop an appreciation of how grudgingly acceptance may be granted one's work by fellow political scientists. We may take Young's caveat, therefore, but not as having any special significance for communications approaches alone.

Young does offer a cogent criticism in this line, however, to the effect that by concentrating on processes, such as communications flows, one may well ignore the outcomes of those processes. This is, of course, entirely likely, but only to an extent which does not appear to offer any reason for undue concern. For instance, Young suggests that the content of communications may be at least as important, if not more so, than the actual number of messages.[67] This goes without saying, for a considerable amount of gibberish could otherwise be considered of greater significance than a single important "yes" or "no." However, the communications approach cannot be considered so mechanistic that it ignores content. If one is concerned solely with flows, then concepts such as distortion and noise would be thoroughly irrelevant to the communications analyst. In the examples we have used in this chapter of

[65] See Chap. Seven, p. 166.
[66] Oran Young, *Systems of Political Science* (Englewood Cliffs, N.J.: Prentice-Hall, Inc., 1968), p. 60.
[67] *Ibid.*

empirical applications of communications theory, we have seen nothing to warrant either charge of merely counting or ignoring content. Deutsch may have merely been counting, when he pointed out the great increase in mail flows within Tanganyika, for he certainly was not privy to the content of all the letters which the postal service carried as the colony approached nationhood. The outcome is accounted for by Deutsch, and indeed was predictable, because the communications flow, as one indicator, would have warranted an assumption of increasing integration of the community. For that matter, White House correspondents can and do make certain inferences about the conduct of our nation's affairs merely by scanning the list of visitors the president will receive in any given day. Johnson demonstrated ably that content can be used ably in a communications analysis of events, relating values, attitudes and communications patterns one to another to explain the outcome, namely enforcement of the Supreme Court's school prayer decisions.

We have faulted other approaches in earlier chapters, approaches which their adherents would have us believe offer us a genuine "theory" of politics. In each case we found the approaches wanting in one respect or another. Is communications analysis sufficiently given over to explanation and prediction that it may warrant the label of theory? In most respects it would appear to be just that. We have found that one can operationalize and relate variables which are at once broad and specific and avoid many of the pitfalls offered by other approaches. It is probably still too early to reach a definite statement that this approach meets all the requirements of theory, however. For one thing, all too little work has been done employing the approach, although it appears to be rapidly gaining favor. Another problem is that the variables considered by communications analysts may be exciting for the time, because they serve to fill in some of the gaps in research which heretofore existed. For instance, studies of political development can and may profit greatly by accounting for communications-related variables. However, this does not necessarily mean at all that studies of this type, or of other types, for that matter, are necessarily best cast in the communications framework. In other words, the communications approach may simply be offering us a new and more highly refined model, capable of generating more useful concepts and testable hypotheses.

A related problem is that of integrating earlier findings which did not use the concepts elaborated by Deutsch and those of his school, especially studies at the lower levels of communications such as those which describe primary group interactions. To cast these findings in a new light, and yet not misconstrue their meanings, will be a difficult but necessary task. Similarly, Deutsch and other communications theorists have given us a new and potentially useful means of examining interactions at higher levels, such as those involving the media, political parties, pressure groups, or other informal institutions which may act as intermediaries between the individual and the political system. It will also be necessary to determine to what degree we may profitably use such analysis, and whether we may abuse the tools provided us by communications analysis. In other words, can we possibly make too much of a good thing? In attempting to quantify relevant variables in a communications context, we must pay increasingly critical attention to the ways in which we operationalize and quantify, as well as determine the necessity or desirability of doing so at all levels and in all instances.

Finally, we must not limit ourselves to communications theory alone. North, an advocate of the communications approach, provides the necessary warning for those who see this as the final paradigm for political science.

> Currently, the communications approach — and appropriate, still developing techniques of measurement — looks extremely promising. At this point it would appear to be premature, however, to settle upon any single model, paradigm, pretheory, or particular set of tools. The most rewarding procedure seems to require, for the time being, at least, the encouragement of alternative models and alternative methods and techniques. . . . It is almost self-evident that communication approaches and general systems and decision-making approaches are complementary. In the long run several competing measurement devices are likely to prove reciprocally reinforcing in somewhat analogous ways.[68]

[68] North, in Charlesworth, op. cit., pp. 315-16.

Theory and Politics

11

INTRODUCTION

How does political science advance from approaches to theory to theory itself?[1] If we wish to develop theories of politics which both describe and explain political behavior, how might we best proceed? If we look to the natural sciences, we find researchers have focused on a problem of interest to them, pursuing its analysis and resolution by whatever approach is most fruitful. At some point in time, the connections between generalizations developed by studying specific research problems become apparent, and broader, more encompassing generalizations result. Rather than grandiose theorizing, the careful consideration of explicit problems, within a comparative context, would appear to be the more appropriate theory-building strategy. Obviously, the first step would be the repeated testing of narrow-gauge hypotheses in order to establish

[1] We have previously suggested that "a theory is a group of laws, usually rather few in number, from which others, usually a larger number, have actually been deduced and from which one expects to deduce still further ones. The laws that serve as the premises of these deductions are called axioms of the theory; those which appear as conclusions are called theorems." Gustav Bergmann, *Philosophy of Science* (Madison: University of Wisconsin Press, 1957), pp. 31-32.

scientific laws. From that stage, a focus might be placed on building so-called middle range theories; the combining of related generalizations into a set of generalizations of broader scope would be the strategy most likely to have the greatest pay-off for social science theory construction in the forseeable future.[2]

We have considered eight major varieties of approaches to the development of theory in political science. How can they be used in the study of specific research problems? What is the utility of each? It should be apparent that each cannot be used to study all problems; the appropriate theoretical approach is dictated by the nature of the research problem. Approaches such as systems and decision-making are more appropriate for studying the behavior of social systems, while attitude or personality would generally be more useful in analysis of a problem of individual political behavior. However, one can be interested in comparing political systems in terms of the distribution of attitudes among individuals who are its members. The political socialization of individuals may be studied because one is interested in the consequences for the political system of sub-cultural variations in the learning of support for the political regime and community, and thus the focus is on consequences for political stability or systems persistence. Obviously, the approach used is a function of the research problem. A limiting factor is the nature of the data which is available or can be collected for the purposes of hypothesis testing. Attitudinal data would not be available to study patterns of support for an extremist political position in an election held 100 years ago, but census data exists indicating residential patterns, and one can thus examine group patterns of voting.

By what criteria should we evaluate the various approaches to political analysis which we have considered? Several guidelines can be stated. The most general, of course, is the capability of the approach to contribute to the development of empirical theory which can explain and predict those events or processes which we wish to explain or predict. Within that context, several other criteria have been utilized in criticism of the various approaches. First, the necessity for well defined concepts, unambiguous yet appropriately comprehensive, has been noted. The concepts should be capable of being operationally defined, and the development of appropriate indicators has also been emphasized. Thus, while we emphasize formulation of hypotheses, emphasis must also be placed on data collection in terms of the relevant concepts. In addition, it should be possible to make inferences in testing propositions without referring

---

[2] Robert Merton, *Social Structure and Social Theory* (Glencoe: The Free Press: 1957), revised edition, p. 280.

to theory or concepts outside the approach being used. If that becomes necessary, then our approach needs to be reformulated.

Other criteria for evaluating an approach include its capacity to stimulate research. For example, little research has been based on David Truman's group theory of politics (*The Governmental Process*). Its heuristic value in stimulating empirical research and further theorizing has been limited; therefore one questions whether that approach is capable of making a significant contribution to the development of empirical political theory. Another criterion frequently expressed is that of parsimony, *i.e.*, an approach should explain as much as possible as simply as possible.

A distinction was made earlier between macro-theory and micro-theory. *Micro* refers to individual level, while *macro* refers to the study of larger units of social analysis. The argument can be presented that the primary focus of political science should be at the political system level, and therefore we should be concerned about individual behavior, such as voting in an election, casting a vote in a legislature, or rendering a legal judgment, only if it helps to explain differences in system behavior over time or variations between different political systems. Regardless of the support given to this view, we must acknowledge that we need to relate micro-level analysis to macro-level concerns.

An example of this problem is the relating of individual voting behavior to policy outputs and system processes. We could focus first upon such variables as individuals' interest in politics, sense of civic duty, sense of political effectiveness, party image, sense of identification with a party, and social group characteristics. These individual characteristics could then be related to generalizations about system level differences.

For example, Robert Alford in *Party and Society* focuses on the extent to which the connection between class position and voting behavior is reinforced or negated by loyalties based on religion or region.[3] By "region" Alford means sub-national territories which have the potential to engender loyalties and to become the focus of political conflict. These, rather than social class, may become the focus of political loyalty. The South in the United States, Wales and Scotland in Great Britain, and Quebec in Canada are examples of such regions.

To examine the class basis of voting Alford used party preferences in voting in national elections, as obtained from survey interviews conducted between 1936 and 1960 for the United States and for shorter time spans for Australia and Great Britain.[4] Occupation was used as a

---

[3] Robert R. Alford, *Party and Society* (Chicago: Rand McNally, 1963).
[4] *Ibid.*, p. 71.

measure of social class,[5] with occupation being dichotomized into two categories, manual and non-manual. This categorization is *objective class* as measured by the indicator of occupation and does not take account of the individual's perception of his social class, or the possibility of incongruence among different indicators or components of social class.

The author views policy differences between parties representing left or right tendencies, and he categorizes political parties as parties of the left or the right in each of the four countries studied. The measure of class voting, then, is the difference in support for parties of the left between non-manual and manual workers.[6] For example, if seventy-five per cent of the manual workers vote for parties of the left and only thirty-five per cent of the non-manual workers support left parties, the index of class voting would be forty. The level of class voting over time

	Per cent Supporting Parties of the Left
Manual Workers	75
Non-Manual Workers	35
Index of Class Voting	40

within each country and between countries is examined by Alford as is the level of class voting by region and by religion in the four countries studied. He found the highest level of class voting in Great Britain, followed by Australia, the United States, and Canada. The level of class voting in the United States has fluctuated over time, and was for the period studied lowest in the South. Class voting varied by religious affiliation, with class voting occurring least among Catholics.

Alford also examined the relationship between a number of other variables and levels of class voting. Several interesting patterns were found. For example, he concluded that localism and informal bases for political action are greater in the countries with lower levels of class voting, while the countries with higher levels of class voting also have mass-based and more bureaucratic parties. The degree of centralization of control over administration is positively associated with the level of class voting. Differences between social classes in the sense of political efficacy and levels of political participation are greater in countries with

[5] *Ibid.*, p. 74.
[6] Alford had to resolve several definitional problems. One was the treatment of non-wage earners who were included in the survey samples, such as retirees, housewives, and students. Another was to establish criteria for defining parties of the left which could be applied cross-nationally. A third was to determine what was the office for which the dependent variable of "party voted for" was to be measured.

low levels of class voting. Additionally, the non-rational, particularistic aspects of politics such as patronage, graft, and vote decision based on particularistic characteristics of candidates such as race or religion are more prevalent in countries with low levels of class voting.

Let us summarize what Alford has done. He has utilized information about individuals collected through surveys of samples of eligible voters to construct indicators of group behavior (patterns of voting by occupation, religion, and regional groups), and used that to analyze and attempt to explain differences in other aspects of political behavior at both the system and individual level. Of course, the generalizations are limited to the time span and countries studied.[7]

Care must be taken that an error in inference is not made when moving from one level of analysis to another. For example, one cannot infer that the relationship among individual characteristics is the same as that present in group data. Therefore, finding that counties with higher levels of blue collar workers were also the counties which were more supportive of a particular candidate in an election does not necessarily mean that the blue collar workers were the most supportive of that candidate. Other inferential fallacies are also possible. One is generalizing from individual relationships to collectivities such as a nation. Thus, one should not assume the nation with the most persons ranking high in achievement motivation will have the most rapid or highest level of economic development. Other inferential fallacies include the selection of data to substantiate one's preferred findings, and generalizing findings from one historical period, geographical situation, or environmental context to another which is not sufficiently similar. In the latter case, one cannot assume that all the relevant conditions prevalent in the first period, situation, or context are present in the second with which it is being compared. For example, one cannot assume that the conditions surrounding the undeclared war in Korea in the 1950s were precisely the same as the conditions antecedent and accompanying the undeclared war in Viet Nam in the 1960s.

Let us turn to a crucial aspect of political analysis. How can we use these various approaches to study policy and political problems of interest to us? To illustrate, we will examine their use or potential for utilization in the study of the following problems: (1) the variations found in the policies of a level or type of government; (2) the development of and change in party systems and voter alignments; and (3) political power and poverty in modern society.

---

[7] For a summary of his findings and inferences based on them see Alford, *Party and Society*, op. cit., Ch. 10-11.

COMPARATIVE POLICY OUTPUTS

How can one account for policy differences between units of government? What are the effects of such characteristics as mal-apportionment of the legislature, the absence of party competition, or a low tax base on state or local politics? Can the methods and theoretical bases used in studies of such questions in the United States be used for cross-national analysis or for studies of policy outputs in another country, such as Canada, Sweden, or India?

Political scientists have until recent years tended to assume that policy outputs, such as type and level of support for education, welfare, or transportation programs, were different between states like Mississippi and Ohio in part because Mississippi was a one-party state while Ohio tended toward vigorous two-party competition. Such assumptions have been challenged by a series of articles and books which have tended to indicate that variations in policy outputs of the states are in large part a product of the level and pattern of economic development of the state, rather than its political system or political process characteristics.

This research on policy patterns is based on systems theory. The model formulated by Dawson and Robinson was presented in this form.

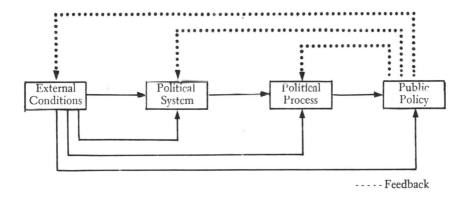

Figure 1[a]

[a] Richard Dawson and James Robinson, "Inter-Party Competition, Economic Variables, and Welfare Policies in the American States," *Journal of Politics*, 25 (1963), p. 266. By permission.

In their definition of concepts in the model, policy includes the goals or objectives of the political system, the means by which they are implemented, and the consequences of the means selected. Process is the interaction between subsystem components over time. The political system definition is based on Easton; the political system is the "group of functionally interrelated variables whose task is the authoritative allocation of values for a given society."[8] The explicit hypothesis stated to be tested by Dawson and Robinson was "the greater the degree of inter-party competition within a political system, the more liberal the social welfare measures that system will adopt."[9]

The next step in the research process was to specify the operational definitions of the concepts. The political systems examined by Dawson and Robinson were forty-six of the fifty states. Inter-party competition was viewed as having three components: the time span over which competition is studied, the significant offices for which the degree of competition is evaluated, and the way in which competition per se is measured. The time span selected for their study was the twenty-year span from 1938 to 1958, and the significant offices were the governorship, control of the upper house, and control of the lower house of the state legislature. Three separate measures of inter-party competition were used. States were ranked in terms of the percentage of popular vote for governor received by the predominant party in the state, and the percentage of seats held by the majority party in both houses. The three percentages were then averaged and each state assigned a rank on the basis of that average. For each of the three institutions, the percentage of the times that the majority party was in control was obtained, the three were averaged, and a rank assigned. The percentage of the time period that control of the three institutions was split between the two parties was computed and a rank order assigned. These three measures were the indices of inter-party competition.

To measure social welfare policies, nine measures of revenue and expenditure patterns for each state were ranked. Representative of those included are the percentage of the states' revenue derived from death and gift taxes, average per pupil expenditure for education, and average payment per recipient of aid for the blind. Three ordinal measures of external conditions were used: the rank order of each state on per capita income; the rank order of the percentage cmployed in occupations other

[8] Richard Dawson and James Robinson, "Inter-Party Competition, Economic Variables, and Welfare Policies in the American States," *Journal of Politics*, 25 (1963), p. 267.
[9] *Ibid.*, p. 270.

than agricultural, forestry and fishing; and the rank order of the proportion of the state's population residing in urban areas.

To test the hypotheses, rank order correlation measures were used
to examine the association between each of the measures of party competition and the measures of policies, between measures of external
conditions and of party competition, and between external conditions
and welfare policies. The relationship implied by their research findings
is presented in Figure 2.

Inter-party
Competition

Social Welfare
Policies

Figure 2

In other words, policy and party competition, according to Dawson and
Robinson, were both a function of external conditions.[10]

Now let us return to their original model. Does their hypothesis
state a relationship implied in the theoretical model? Granting that it
does, is inter-party competition to be viewed as a measure of the political
system or the political process? The authors indicate process is the interaction of the system's sub-components, while political system refers
to "that group of functionally inter-related variables whose task is the
authoritative allocation of values for a given society."[11] Obviously, one
intervening set of variables is left out of this analysis. In addition, a
complex system of interacting relationships has been left out of the
analysis, as feedback processes are ignored completely.

Have they adequately operationally defined and measured the concepts contained in their hypothesis? Why measure party competition at
an ordinal level when the variable can be measured at a higher level?
When one averages several separate measures of inter-party competition,
to what extent are the component phenomena being distorted? The
authors also assume that the three component parts are of equal weight
in contributing to inter-party competition; such an assumption is questionable.

The findings of Dawson and Robinson stimulated a number of
further studies of policy outputs and their relationship to environmental
and political characteristics of governmental units. These studies illus-

[10] *Ibid.*, p. 289.
[11] *Ibid.*, p. 267.

trate the problems of theory-building through careful, rigorous, and replicative hypothesis-testing. For example, most studies continue to be
based on an over-simplified systems model. Such a model incorrectly
identifies socio-economic variables as input variables.

Socio-Economic Characteristics	Conversion Processes	Policies

Figure 3

Inputs must be measured in terms of demands made, not in terms
of possible potential for demands and supports which may be reflected
by socio-economic characteristics of governmental units; indeed, one
must question if environmental conditions are adequately operationally
measured by such standard indices used as income levels, occupational
and urbanization patterns, educational attainment, and ethnic composition. In addition, significant intervening variables such as social structure, political culture, many aspects of institutional arrangements both
informal and formal, and elite attitudes, values, and perceptions are
ignored in the policy studies. Furthermore, systems models emphasize
the role of multiple feedback processes, yet feedback is virtually ignored
in the policy studies. With few exceptions studies of policy outputs
have also ignored the time dimension. Studies of change in policy over
time can help clarify the nature of the relationships between environment, system, process, and policy. For example, one study has examined
the relationship of socio-economic variables to policy outputs in the
states over a seventy-year span. Two relatively stable socio-economic
indices emerged, one reflecting industrialization and the other cultural
enrichment. However, these two indices varied in their relationship to
expenditure patterns during the seventy-year-period study, with the
industrialization measure fluctuating not only in magnitude, as did the
cultural enrichment variable, but also in the sign of the relationship.[12]

The linkages between theory, hypothesis, concept, data measurement, and inference are subject to other criticisms. Jacob and Lipsky
point out the inadequate operationalization of political system characteristics; among the system aspects which should be more extensively considered are the organization of the executive branch, the organization of
the legislature, the roles and strength of interest groups, intergovern-

---

[12] Richard I. Hofferbert, "Socio-Economic Dimensions of the American States:
1890-1960, *Midwest Journal of Political Science*, 12 (August, 1968), pp. 401-18.

mental linkages among federal, state, and local systems, and party system characteristics.[13] Additionally, the community power research has indicated that the same policy processes probably are not operating in all policy areas.[14] Studies of the budgetary process also indicate that budgetary changes are incremental, with major shifts occurring as a consequence of change in control of significant political positions, such as the assumption of office by a newly-elected president or governor who has a different set of policy priorities.[15]

As policy studies have evolved, measurement procedures have also changed. First, the operational definition of concepts has been such that concepts more frequently can be measured at the interval level.[16] A second measurement change has been to use a statistical technique, factor analysis, which permits constructing an index of a concept, such as welfare-education policy, out of a large number of separate measures.[17]

Other problems are presented by the statistical methods frequently used in data analyses. Causal inferences cannot be made from correlation and regression analysis of cross-sectional data. Indeed, state policies undoubtedly have causal consequences for state politics. For example, if a state votes special tax preferences to industry of such a level that the state achieves a competitive advantage over other states, it can attract industry and thereby increase its industrial development. This would probably also result in increased urbanization. Making causal inferences from correlational analysis of cross-sectional data is both statistically and logically fallacious. Methods do exist which can be used for deriving causal inferences; more sophisticated studies have made use of these.[18]

An additional problem in policy outputs studies, which probably contributes to the divergency of findings, is the failure to use a common definition of expenditure variables. Some studies have focused only on

[13] Herbert Jacob and Michael Lipsky, "Outputs, Structure, and Power: An Assessment of Changes in the Study of State and Local Politics," *Journal of Politics*, 30 (May, 1968), pp. 510-38.

[14] See, for example, Robert Dahl, *Who Governs?* (New Haven: Yale University Press, 1961).

[15] Otto Davis, M. A. H. Dempster, and Aaron Wildavsky, "A Theory of the Budgetary Process," *American Political Science Review*, 60 (September, 1966), pp. 529-47.

[16] See, for example, Ira Sharkansky and Richard I. Hofferbert, "Dimensions of State Politics, Economics, and Public Policy," *American Political Science Review*, 63 (September, 1969), pp. 867-79.

[17] *Ibid.* In addition, the statistical technique of causal modeling has been used to evaluate patterns of resource allocation over time in this area of research. See James C. Strouse, "Politics, Economics, Elite Attitudes, and State Outputs: A Dynamic Analysis Using a Block Recursive Model," unpublished Ph.D. dissertation, University of North Carolina, 1970.

[18] Strouse, *op. cit.*

state expenditures while others have included both state and local expenditures for such services as education. Critics have suggested that
both types of expenditure patterns should be considered.[19] Additionally,
the distribution of benefits is of significance in policy impact, but this
has not generally been considered in research efforts. For example,
is a state's gasoline tax revenue based on miles of existing state highways, which might tend to be of more benefit to rural counties, or is it
based on population density, which would benefit more the urban core
areas? Is the state aid to elementary and secondary education based on
need or on the local area's ability to match state monies? The distribution of expenditures or other policy outputs in terms of who benefits
from that policy has been neglected in the policy studies.

Environmental variables may set the boundaries within which expenditures or other policy outputs can vary, but the actual fluctuations
or policy alternatives which exist would be a consequence of other
factors. For example, the tax (revenue-raising) structure of a state is a
most significant and politically potent element of a state's policy outputs. The income levels and distribution of them, amount and structure of real and personal property, and retail sales set boundaries, but
the extent of the state's reliance on any one of these for revenue is a
political choice. Socio-economic characteristics establish boundaries;
political choices determine the mix used.

Other criticisms have been made of the comparative state and local
policy studies. Dyson and St. Angelo have pointed out that the incrementalism of expenditure increases which Sharkansky has found in state
expenditure patterns is both logically and statistically invalid. The
existence of a correlation between expenditures at Time 1 and expenditures at Time 2 is not adequate evidence of an incremental strategy
among public decision-makers. The assumption is that decision-makers
allocate funds to state agencies as an increment over what the agency
received the preceding year. What is needed is precise analysis of year-to-
year changes in state expenditures and not the gross analysis of changes
every five- or ten-year period. A state's relative capabilities and its actual
allocations may vary considerably from year to year. In other words,
incrementalism must be established, not assumed, and established by
analysis of year-to-year changes in allocations to particular agencies or

[19] James Dyson and Douglas St. Angelo, "Persistent Methodological and Theoretical Problems in Analysis of Policy Outputs," paper presented at the Southern
Political Science Association Meeting, Miami Beach, Florida, November 8, 1969, pp.
5-6, 10-11. The failure to control for the impact of federal aid in certain areas of
state expenditures, such as mass transportation, highways, education and welfare, also
results in a distortion of the evaluations of the impact of state economic and political
system variations on patterns of state expenditures.

programs. Additionally, a pattern of incrementalism is descriptive of a process of change, but does not of itself explain major changes in expenditure levels. Dyson and St. Angelo concluded from their research that changes in environmental variables were not related in either a strong or persistent fashion to changes in outputs, raising further questions about conclusions about incrementalism in state policy outputs.[20]

The studies of policy outputs have relied almost exclusively on what are generally called aggregate data. This term is applied to data collected for population aggregations, such as census data or budget and revenue data for the states. A crucial question must be raised: are aggregate data adequate for testing the systems models underlying the comparative policy outputs studied? Apparently some researchers have reached the conclusion that they are not, for they have moved to incorporate into their research other types of data. These are of two types: demand measures based on sample survey studies and data drawn from survey studies of elite perceptions, attitudes, values, or behavior which can be used to measure process variables or to evaluate intervening variables.[21]

While policy includes the type and quality of programs which a governmental unit operates, policy studies have tended to rely too heavily on revenue and expenditure patterns as indicators of the kind and quality of programs. No doubt this has been done partly because of the problem of measuring program characteristics. How, for example, can one measure state differences in civil rights programs? One proposed solution is to measure them as one would a set of attitudes, treating the absence of a particular program as a negative response to an attitude item. The resulting configuration can be examined to see if it forms a pattern and, if so, to see what variables are associated with the pattern found.[22] Undoubtedly the importance of various factors in accounting for policy differences between governmental units is also a function of the type of policy being evaluated. Revenue and expenditure patterns may vary more with economic development or tax base, while other forms of policy, such as election laws, protection of civil rights, uses of police power, or permissible forms of local government, would vary more with political system or political process variables.

Sharkansky has argued that distinctions should also be made be-

---

[20] *Ibid.*, p. 25.

[21] Strouse has incorporated measures of elite attitudes into his analysis of expenditure patterns. See Strouse, *op. cit.*

[22] This method has been used in the analysis of states' civil rights laws by Donald J. McCrone and Charles F. Cnudde. See their "On Measuring Public Policy" in Robert E. Crew, Jr. (ed.), *State Politics* (Belmont, Calif.: Wadsworth, 1968), pp. 523-30.

tween public policy, policy outputs, and policy impacts. He distinguishes among them in this fashion:

> Public policy represents actions taken by the government; policy outputs represent the service levels which are affected by these actions; and policy impacts represent the effect which the service has on a population.[23]

The environment, according to Sharkansky, represents the "social, economic, and political surroundings"[24] which both supply the impetus for public policy and are affected by its impact.

Other examples can be cited. Suppose that a state government over time fails to enact policies demanded by a particular group. If the issue is salient to the group and its members become sufficiently aroused, the group might support candidates of another political party, leaving the coalition of the political party they have customarily supported. For example, Catholic white collar workers who normally support the Democratic party in a northern industrial state have lobbied unsuccessfully for years with the Democratically controlled legislature for state aid to children attending parochial schools. A number of Republican candidates take a position on the issue supportive of the Catholics' position, and gain substantial and continuing support from Catholic white collar workers. These Catholics gradually come to consider themselves Republicans. In effect, policy outputs have affected the political process by resulting in party realignment. This can, of course, occur on the national level, and has occurred during historic disaffection with national policies and conditions. In such a case, either state and national party policy conditions may coincide, or a new party is created, or the trend may begin in one region of the country and spread to others over a period of time.

While our primary focus has been on outputs at the state level, others are possible. One can compare between cities, between states and cities, and between governmental units and different countries. Such analyses could contribute to explanation of the relative effects of variations in environment, demands, and governmental processes and institutions on policy outputs.

Note that we started with a systems approach to the study of comparative policy outputs, but as research has continued other approaches have been used in conjunction with systems theory. The

[23] Ira Sharkansky, *Policy Analysis in Political Science* (Chicago: Markham Publishing Company, 1970), p. 63.
[24] *Ibid.*

movement from theory to hypothesis statement and testing has been accompanied by a number of problems, many as yet unresolved, in concept definition, operational measurement, data analysis, and appropriate inference. The appropriateness of various theoretical approaches to the study of policy patterns can be adequately evaluated only when these problems are resolved and further research conducted.

PARTY SYSTEMS AND VOTER ALIGNMENTS

Another example of the use of different approaches in examination of a particular problem is provided by the study of party systems and voter alignments. A number of different questions have been raised in focusing on this problem.

How can we best describe and explain the development and activities of political parties? What factors could account for the differences in party systems which exist in various developed nations? What variables can explain differences in the participation rates, party types, and party systems of the many nations which have come into being since World War II? How can we account for changes in the American party system?

A number of different approaches have been used with varying degrees of success to explain the evolution of party systems. One set of analyses of party system development and voter alignments combines the use of Parsons' structural-functional analysis, group theory, and attitudinal analysis. Parsons asserted that four functions must be performed by any social system; adaptation, integration, goal attainment, and pattern maintenance.[25] Four sub-systems perform these functions, and six types of interchanges exist. Stein Rokkan and S. M. Lipset argue that the party system's evolution is a consequence of three of these interchanges, the essential ones being those between the integrative and goal attainment sub-systems, the integrative and pattern maintenance sub-systems, and the pattern maintenance and goal attainment sub-systems.[26] The first involves patterns of competing parties, the second

[25] Stein Rokkan and Seymour Martin Lipset, "Cleavage Structures, Party Systems, and Voter Alignments: An Introduction," in S. M. Lipset and S. Rokkan (eds.), *Party Systems and Voter Alignments* (New York: The Free Press, 1967), pp. 1-64, Stein Rokkan, *Citizens, Elections, Parties* (New York: David McKay Company Inc., 1970), Ch. 3.
[26] Rokkan and Lipset, *op. cit.*, pp. 6-9.

membership in various groups in society and the readiness of these groups to be mobilized, and the third representative processes.

They see the process of nation-building as presenting four institutional problems, or "thresholds," which must be overcome in the development of a modern nation-state. The first of these, legitimation, refers to effective recognition of the right to criticize, oppose, petition, and demonstrate against the regime. The second, incorporation, refers to granting to political oppositions the right to participate in the selection of representation equal to that of establishment-supporting groups. Representation, the third threshold, is overcome when those who oppose the regime obtain the right to serve in the legislature. The final threshold, majority power, refers to overcoming the immunity of the executive from legislative influence on executive decision-making. Both the timing of the overcoming of these barriers and the height of the barriers are viewed as having considerable influence on the nature of the party system. For example, a nation with low barriers on the legitimation and incorporation thresholds but high barriers on the representation and majority thresholds tends to have a competitive party system with high payoffs for successful alliances and the separation of executive and legislative power. This is descriptive of the American party system. Low thresholds for legitimation and incorporation, a high barrier on the representative dimension, and a barrier of medium height on legislative influence over the executive describes a system perhaps illustrated by the government of Great Britain.[27]

Using these theoretical approaches and focusing on the development of political parties in Western European nations, Lipset and Rokkan suggest that the coalition structure of party systems is a consequence of the timing, sequence, and intensity of effects of four critical conflicts in the process of nation-building. These four conflicts were those between the dominant and one or more subject cultures; the church, either national or extra-national (Catholic) versus the interests of the state; the conflict between the primary elements of the economy, such as agriculture, and the secondary economy (industry); and lastly, the conflict between workers and employers which was a final outgrowth of the industrial revolution. The authors assume that nation-building was a three-phased process in Western Europe, the first phase being the efforts of a nation-building elite to penetrate and standardize peripheral areas of disputed control between the state and the church interests. Conflict in the society ensued from such efforts. The second phase found a variety of alliances being formed to support and to oppose these efforts

[27] *Ibid.*, p. 27.

at centralization. The outgrowth of those efforts at national integration was a shifting focus to goal attainment, with efforts focused on gaining some measure of political control in order to achieve specified ends. Accompanying these efforts may be reforms in and extensions of the right to vote, changes in other electoral procedures, and extensions in the subject areas in which the national legislature exercises the law-making power. The nature of Western European party systems is, then, a function of the timing of various conflicts and the barriers to the injection of conflicts into the political system.[28]

Lipset and Rokkan assert that the conflicts between center and periphery and between church and state characterize the national revolution, while the conflicts between urban and landed interests and between employers and workers characterize the industrial revolution. They argue that the key conflict in the development of party systems in Europe was that between the nation-state and the church, while in most countries the key conflict in modern times has been between workers and employers, or in the adaptive sub-system. Another conflict has been in the goal attainment sector of society, primarily focusing on an attack on the elites of the society. One might view the rise of National Socialist and Fascist parties in those terms.[29]

The analytical scheme developed by Lipset and Rokkan has been used to analyze the development of party systems in Western European countries. However, the authors have not provided operational definitions of their key variables, thus impeding application of this analytical approach in studying the development of non-Western European party systems. The utility of the scheme is also limited by the failure to consider the functions of parties and political movements other than serving as vehicles for the expression of conflict.

Another approach to analysis of the development of party systems focuses explicitly on structural characteristics alone. Such factors as expansion of the suffrage, the complexity and divisiveness of the social structure, the existence of a unitary as opposed to a federal political system, the structure of legislative and executive power, and the nature of the electoral laws are viewed as determining the number and type of political parties and the ease with which new parties can arise within a political system.[30]

Analysis of party systems and voter alignments in the United States has utilized both group and attitudinal approaches. The attitudinal

[28] *Ibid.*, pp. 33-43.
[29] See Rokkan, *op. cit.*
[30] Leon Epstein, *Political Parties in Western Democracies* (New York: Praeger, 1967), Ch. 2.

studies have focused on evaluations of the character and extent of attachment to specific political objects, such as political parties and specific
office holders or candidates for office. The frequency with which certain
issue stands are held, as well as their saliency and intensity, are also
utilized. This focus on the beliefs and attitudes of individual citizens as
the basis for analyzing voter alignments has been utilized in a series of
major electoral studies conducted by researchers at the Survey Research
Center, University of Michigan. The key variables in their analysis are
those of a voter's sense of affiliation with a political party (party identification), his image expressed in terms of likes and dislikes of the various political parties in the system (party image), his concerns with issues
and policy preferences (issue orientation), and the voter's preferences
for a particular candidate or set of candidates (candidate orientation).
A number of other attitudinal characteristics, such as sense of political
effectiveness, trust in others, sense of responsiveness attributed to different levels of government, and sense of civic duty, are also utilized to
explain the patterns of voter alignments and levels of political participation. Concepts and propositions of group theory are also used, with the
distribution of the dependent and independent variables in the voter
populations being studied.[31] The relationship between historical events,
their possible attitudinal consequences for groups in the population, and
for voter alignments are also considered in some studies.[32] However,
for most research prior to the 1950s these inferences are not based on
data derived from survey research.

The earlier survey research on voting behavior, conducted by sociologists, focused on the group basis of political behavior. Research examined the political affiliations, voting turnout, and direction of the vote of
various categoric groups, using categories such as age, sex, region of the
country in which the voter was raised, occupation, income, education,
ethnicity, and religion. Small group theory also served as a basis for
analysis, focusing attention on patterns of communication, opinion leadership, and giving of voting cues.[33]

[31] See, for example, Angus Campbell, Philip E. Converse, Warren E. Miller, and
Donald E. Stokes, *The American Voter* (New York: John Wiley and Sons, 1960);
Angus Campbell, Gerald Gurin, and Warren E. Miller, *The Voter Decides* (Evan-
ston: Row, Peterson and Company, 1954); Donald R. Matthews and James W.
Prothro, *Negroes and The New Southern Politics* (New York: Harcourt, Brace, and
World, 1966); Angus Campbell, Philip E. Converse, Warren E. Miller, and Donald
E. Stokes, *Elections and The Political Order* (New York: John Wiley and Sons, Inc.,
1966).

[32] See, for example, Gerald M. Pomper, *Elections in America* (New York: Dodd,
Mead & Company, 1968); V. O. Key, Jr., *Southern Politics* (New York: Random
House, Vintage Editions, 1949).

[33] See, for example, Paul Lazarsfeld, Bernard Berelson, and Hazel Gaudet, *The*

Certain problems exist in the attitudinal analysis of voter align-ments. One, of course, is that behavior and attitudes may be incongru-ent. For example, a person may identify himself as a Republican, but consistently support the Democratic party's candidates. Secondly, the electoral laws and competitive nature of the various states may distort the patterns of party affiliation. The existence of a closed primary in a state may warp party registration into the majority party and hence party identification is not reflective of presumed relevant attitudes. Some evi-dence exists that an individual may have different identifications at the state or local level and national levels, with six per cent of the voters so indicating in the 1958 election.[34] One limitation in attitudinal studies is that the data base is available only for a limited number of countries and for only more recent times. Thus, data-based research utilizing an attitudinal approach cannot be used for research into the origins and development of party systems.

Can Easton's system approach be used in the analysis of party sys-tems and voter alignments?[35] Does such an approach permit one to incorporate a variety of political, social, legal, and personal variables to account for variations in party systems which could not otherwise be integrated into an explanatory system? An examination of the political systems of the American South can illustrate the usefulness or lack of it of a systems approach. We can raise two questions: What criteria are provided by Easton for what are the change-producing inputs into south-ern political systems? What testable hypotheses are presented about the relationships of types and levels of inputs and outputs — in this case, party systems and voter alignments?

Easton views parties as structural mechanisms for handling stress created by conflicts within the society. Where competition is per-mitted by the regime, maximum inclusiveness in the parties is encour-aged by the party system. Electoral rules are considered a device for facilitating inclusiveness or exclusiveness of parties and their contribu-tions to reduction of support stress.[36] However, no testable hypotheses

---

People's Choice (New York: Columbia University Press, 1948); Bernard Berelson, Paul Lazarsfeld, and William N. McPhee, Voting (Chicago: University of Chicago Press, 1954); Lester Milbrath, Political Participation (Chicago: Rand McNally, 1965), Ch. 5.

[34] Philip E. Converse, "On the Possibility of Major Political Realignment in the South," in Campbell, Converse, Miller, and Stokes, Elections and the Political Order, op. cit., p. 219.

[35] See Ch. 9 for a discussion of Easton's systems analysis.

[36] For a discussion of the effects of the legal, social, and political impediments to political participation in the South and the types of political systems extant in the South in the mid-1940's, see V. O. Key, Jr., Southern Politics, op. cit.

are presented, operational definitions of key concepts are absent, and making inferences about relationships on the basis of Easton's systems analysis is not possible. One can, independent of Easton's conceptual framework, hypothesize that legal, economic, and political factors could limit or structure the inputs of supports and demands into the political system. Thus the use of literacy tests and the poll tax as well as economic sanctions kept black registration low in the South. Another device used to exclude blacks from political participation was the white primary; the primary was treated as an activity of a private club, and the club had the right to limit participation to those it wished to admit as members. Other limiting factors on the input of demands into the southern political systems were presented by the commanding positions of southerners in the congressional and senatorial power structures. The chairmen of key committees controlling legislation which could effect changes in the structure of southern politics tended to be southerners. Another key element in excluding federal intervention was a rule in effect until 1936 which required that the nomination for president in the Democratic nominating convention be by a two-thirds majority; that rule gave an effective veto power over any candidate to the southern delegations. These legal and political barriers to participation in the South began to be dissolved in the 1930s and 1940s; the white primary was overturned by the Supreme Court in 1944, the Twenty-fourth Amendment to the Constitution prohibiting the payment of a poll tax as a pre-condition for voting became effective in 1964, and the use of literacy tests as a discriminatory device to keep black citizens from registering to vote was successfully attacked by the Voting Rights Act of 1965. The filibuster as a means of keeping civil rights legislation from coming to a vote in the Senate was overcome for the first time in 1964 during the process of enacting the Civil Rights Act of 1964. The ability of southern congressional and senatorial committee chairmen to use their powers to prevent passage of civil rights legislation has been inhibited by either writing legislation in such a fashion that it could be sent to a committee with supportive members and chairmen, or in the Senate by sending legislation to a committee with instructions that it be reported out by a specific date. An additional inhibitor, the need for southern states' votes in the electoral college, ceased to be a factor when Franklin Roosevelt and other Democrats succeeded in obtaining an electoral college majority without the support of all the southern states. Thus the legal and political factors which worked to keep the federal government from intervening in southern politics on behalf of the civil rights, including the right to participate in politics, of black citizens had all been struck down by the late 1960s, the legal and political devices used by state and local governments in the South to prohibit black participation in politics had been negated by federal law or Supreme Court decision, and supports and demands could be effectively and directly inputted into the political system by blacks through electoral and political party activity.[37]

The input of demands by black citizens was not only inhibited by the legal devices which prevented or inhibited their registering to vote, but demand input was also inhibited by the existence of malapportionment in southern as well as most other state legislatures. The bias in the southern systems tended to favor the more rural counties, and, according to one researcher, it particularly favored the counties with the highest proportion of black citizens.[38] In just those counties was the concern greatest for keeping the black man out of the political system. Because the maintenance of racial segregation and exclusion of the black from full participation shaped southern politics, the economic basis for voting alignments prevalent in the rest of the country were de-emphasized here. Competition between the two parties, based largely on economic issues, was suppressed in the South, as party competition would encourage broadening of the electorate, while racial segregation would be better served by an exclusionary approach to politics. Hence, southern politics had a different focus, and a different pattern of voter alignment. Conflict occurred within the Democratic party. In the absence of a party appeal in the general election with a focus on economic issues, how was conflict structured in southern politics?

V. O. Key reported that several different patterns of southern politics existed. One was personalism, a division of the Democratic party in a state into one dominant faction, with a changing coalition of interests and individuals opposing the dominant faction. The dominant faction generally centered around one individual, such as Huey Long of Louisiana or Eugene Talmadge of Georgia. A second pattern was that of multifactional politics in the Democratic party; in this pattern coalitions are highly unstable, forming and regrouping in succeeding elections. Politics in these states had a friends-and-neighbors quality, with voting support being based on personal acquaintance or name familiarity. Such familiarity was found to be related to residing in or near the home county of the candidate supported, hence the label of friends-and-neighbors politics. A third pattern of southern politics was that of bi-factionalism; in three southern states (Virginia, Tennessee, and North Carolina), Key

---

[37] An excellent summary of the various laws and decisions which effected these changes is contained in *Revolution in Civil Rights* (4th edition, Washington: Congressional Quarterly Service, 1968).

[38] V. O. Key, *op. cit.*, footnote 12, pp. 308-09.

found a dominant faction with a minimum amount of issue basis, and some semblance of Republican opposition. Thus in Virginia the Byrd machine was opposed by a shifting coalition of interests based on either ambition or issue opposition. Also present in these states was an active, but generally unsuccessful, Republican minority. Thus, prior patterns of political conflict structured a continuing pattern of party system characteristics, based on the presence or absence of personalities, issues, and other party opposition.[39]

Key concluded that the alignments of voters in the South could be explained in part by the emphasis on one issue — race — rather than on another — economic issues — with the latter dominating the politics of the non-South and serving as an aligning dimension for competitive two-party politics. In addition, the alignment in the South was maintained by political and legal devices excluding a minority group from participation. When the political and legal devices were overcome, the minority entered into political participation. Voting registration of black citizens increased from 250,000 in 1940 to 3,112,000 in 1968 or from five per cent of the black voting age population to sixty-two per cent in 1968. As the South continues in its industrialization and urbanization, the basis for inputs of demands present in other areas of the country will probably also become more prevalent in the South, and the neutralization of race as the issue around which southern party politics is structured will occur. The structuring of southern politics on the same bases as in other areas of the country is also being influenced by Supreme Court decisions striking down discriminatory practices existing throughout the United States — those practices including de jure school segregation and racial discrimination in housing, transportation, employment, and public accommodations. The enforcement of such decisions in the short run may increase the impact of the issue in politics, as demands to overturn decisions or not enforce them are presented by various groups. However, in the long run such decisions destroy the basis for an exclusionary and uniquely southern party politics, and bring to the front in the South the same issues as in other areas of the country, whatever the dominant economic or social issues might be.[40]

The striking down or terminating of southern laws and practices which excluded the black from southern politics could be conceptualized as inputs from the environment, with the outputs of the larger political system (the United States) being inputs into the southern

[39] Ibid., passim.
[40] Joe R. Feagin and Harlan Hahn, "The Second Reconstruction: Black Political Strength in the South," *Social Sciences Quarterly*, 51 (June, 1970), Table 2, p. 47.

political systems. The consequences have probably been the beginning of a restructuring of southern politics, creation of more open access to southern political systems, new patterns of demands, and a further re-shuffling of the patterns of conflict and of voter alignments.[41] We might expect changes to occur at different rates in southern political systems or perhaps different patterns of participation and voter alignment to result from different types or rates of barrier reduction, but no testable hypotheses are provided by Easton concerning the relationship between patterns of measured changes in inputs and measured changes in outputs (party systems and voter alignments).

Easton's systems theory has not contributed significantly to the analysis of party system development and change. The absence of operational definitions of key concepts and testable hypotheses in Easton's systems theory results in the conclusion that the so-called theory is not a theory. The relationships between reductions of barriers to participation, increased political participation, and changes in southern political systems as a consequence can be stated and tested without recourse to Easton's conceptual apparatus. The shifts in party systems and voter alignments can also be conceptualized as involving changed perceptions, cognitions, and attitudes on the part of actual and potential political participants. Patterns of reference group identification and group interaction change, and new party alignments occur. Eastonian conceptual apparatus contributes little to the analysis. The specific types of demands and supports which result in party alignment changes are not suggested by Eastonian analysis, and no criteria for selection of relevant variables are presented. If an Eastonian-based analysis of inputs of demands and supports to southern political systems is the focus, could not one just as easily concentrate on economic patterns of development, urbanization, and changes in mass media distribution and consumption as on changes in political and legal barriers to participation? In summary, Easton's systems approach does not adequately identify relevant variables, suggest and define useful concepts, provide operational definitions of the concepts which are elaborated, nor provide testable hypotheses for research.

---

[41] Samuel Lubell has argued that rather than eliminating race as a basis for southern politics, the combination of court decisions, new laws, and social conflict may have the consequence of making desegregation the issue basis for politics throughout the country. Thus, rather than the South acquiring northern political patterns, the North would acquire southern political patterns. See Samuel Lubell, *The Hidden Crisis in American Politics* (New York: W. W. Norton & Company, Inc., 1970).

CONCLUSION: POLITICAL ANALYSIS AND PRACTICAL POLITICS

But, so what? By now the reader has been exposed to a host of different and elaborately worked-over concepts, hypotheses, and analytic frameworks. Is there any practical use for all of this? Or is political science becoming increasingly ivory-towered, losing contact with reality, and slipping into a jargon and verbiage unique unto itself, with its own arcane mysteries fathomed only by the initiates? One could argue that a verbal anesthesia has been developed by political scientists, using terms which are not all in the lexicon of the layman. For instance, *rotated factor matrix, regime affect, stochastic models,* and *cognitive dissonance* are not terms which are bandied about in normal cocktail conversation, let alone the various news media which focus upon politics. Criticisms of the increasingly scientific approach to politics come from all sides, and most evidently come from within the discipline as well. One example focuses upon just such verbiage as we have described. Many of these criticisms are thoughtful and insightful, although it must be pointed out that every discipline, whether justified or not, develops its own jargon and key-words. We would be remiss if we did not refer the reader to the poem by the prominent student of international relations Inis L. Claude, Jr., "Questions for a Political Science Recruit,"[42] which concludes:

> Come now, can you operationalize,
> Quantify and conceptualize?
> Can your output be machine-read?
> Have you a code in your head?
> Are you adept at research design —
> Brother, can you paradigm?

Such not altogether tongue-in-cheek criticisms aside, we find that there are indeed some very practical usages for the scientific approach to political science. But, before we discuss some of the ends to which analysis of the variety we have been describing in this text may be put, we must first issue our own caveat.

The reader is no doubt familiar by now with any number of individuals who cannot understand either why one would study political

---

[42] *P. S.,* III (Winter, 1970), p. 47.

science in the first place, or how and why (if they are aware of it at all) the scientific approach to politics may be used. One can gain insights into politics from any number of sources, and many persons might even claim that politics is an avocation with them. Without claiming that the state of our knowledge has advanced as far as that of medicine, the political scientist must constantly be subjected to any number of would-be analysts, just as doctors are frequently asked by their patients to prescribe certain medicines, as if those same patients were skilled diagnos-ticians. In other words, everybody is his own "seat-of-the-pants" political scientist, just as many of us are our own doctors, armchair psy-chologists and fine arts critics. There is little if anything that one can do about this, for we certainly cannot claim, as political scientists, ulti-mate and superior wisdom on all things political. Similarly, the question as to why political science may be taking on the trappings of the natural sciences and what the consequences of this may be can and often does lead into a discussion, on both sides, which is something less than ra-tional and illuminating. We prefer instead to suggest that the argu-ments advanced in Chapter Two may suffice in this regard, and point to some of the results of the scientific approach to politics.

One major area in which empiricism has been shown to have applic-ability is that of policy planning. The governments of this or any other nation wish, in rational settings, to ensure success for these plans. In their development, plans will be subjected to the most careful scrutiny as to possible costs, benefits, and implications. Indeed, this is one reason why documents such as the United States Census are so valuable for government planning experts. If one were to be developing an all-out attack on the problems of the inner city, for instance, census data would be required at a minimum to understand how many people might be affected, the number of inadequate housing units, the extent of unem-ployment, illiteracy, and disease rates, to name a few. In short, it is better to argue from data than from mere conjecture. Planning would also want to take into account the likely outcomes — what has hap-pened when such programs have been attempted elsewhere, even if only part of the program has been tried? Were the desired results achieved, and if not, why? Again, data of this nature can be used not only to plan more effectively, but to enable policy-makers to better predict what might happen, through the use of explanatory variables. An example of this might be the study of the impact on attitudes and behavior of a massive Office of Economic Opportunity anti-poverty program. The study, conducted by a group of political scientists from the State Uni-versity of New York at Buffalo, has been funded in an attempt to discern the various payoffs to such a program.[43] Of related interest is the study of the means by which the 1963 Community Health Center Act was implemented in several metropolitan areas,[44] in which the need for developing measures of effectiveness is set forth. For that matter, planning of community programs should obviously try to take into account existing attitudes in the "target" community, before they attempt to impose programs without some preparation as to how the programs might be received. Sears studied black attitudes in Watts after the 1965 riots. He found that compared to results for white respondents to his survey, there was a greater disaffection with the government, and lowered feelings of political efficacy. Although there was no notable tendency toward "revolution," the riots apparently led to a greater pragmatism in the community, particularly in terms of the necessity of getting more blacks into positions of governmental responsibility.[45]

Planning with the assistance of empirical research need not be limited to domestic policies alone. A great deal has been said of late concerning what is known as "deterrence theory," or the means by which one or more nations seek to deter another nation or group of nations from entering into armed conflict. Russett has examined this problem, using data gathered by a consortium of Yale political scientists.[46] He focused on all cases over a three-decade period where a major power threatened to attack a small ally of another powerful nation, seeking to establish those factors which will or will not make deterrence a credible policy. Using objective measures of importance to the major power, such as the minor nation's Gross National Product as a percentage of the major nation's G.N.P., economic and political interdependence, and

[43] At this writing, the results of the study are still fragmentary and largely unpublished papers delivered at annual meetings of professional associations. They include: Lester W. Milbrath, "The Nature of Political Beliefs and the Relationship of the Individual to the Government" (Midwest Political Science Association, Chicago, Ill., May 2-3, 1968); Milbrath, "The Impact of Social Change Problems Upon the Poor" (American Political Science Association, New York City, September 2-6, 1969); Everett M. Cataldo, Richard M. Johnson, and Lyman A. Kellstedt, "Political Attitudes of the Urban Poor: Some Implications for Policy Making" (American Political Science Association, Washington, D.C., September 3-7, 1968).

[44] See Robert H. Connery et al, The Politics of Mental Health: Organizing for Community Mental Health in Fragmented Metropolitan Areas (New York: Columbia University Press, 1969); also, Charles H. Backstrom, "Social Indicators: Local Community Response to National Programs" (unpublished paper prepared for delivery at the annual meeting of the American Political Science Association, Washington, D.C., September 3-7, 1968).

[45] David O. Sears, "Black Attitudes Toward the Political System in the Aftermath of the Watts Insurrection," Midwest Journal of Political Science, XIII (November, 1969), pp. 515-44.

[46] Bruce M. Russett, "The Calculus of Deterrence," Journal of Conflict Resolution, VII (June, 1963), pp. 97-109.

the extent of major nation/smaller nation military cooperation, he tested several extant hypotheses concerning deterrence. The results of his studies are not couched in any terminology which could be confusing to government policy-makers, or others who are not initiated into the "mysteries" of political science. To the contrary, he shows that there is no single factor, such as strategic balance, which is "essential to deterrence. But as more are present the stronger mutual interdependence becomes, and the greater is the attacker's risk in pressing onward."[47] The importance of this article, for foreign policy-makers, lies not only in its clear findings and in the implications for alliance or deterrence strategy. Rather, it also shows the distinct advantages of an empirical approach, using both the inductive and deductive reasoning processes, in order that hypotheses may be legitimately tested. For instance, the reader may be familiar with Herman Kahn's *On Thermonuclear War*,[48] a significant document in the making of foreign policy in the 1960s, which is primarily inductive in approach, offering a grand strategy for numerous things, deterrence included. While the work itself may be highly significant, the question to which we may address ourselves must necessarily be, is it credible? Like deterrence theory itself, can the work be accepted on its face, or should it be tested? Where it is tested, Russet has shown that it is wanting in validity, at least in part.

In recent years, we have seen the development of numerous "forecasting" or prediction devices in domestic elections. Examples of these might be the "Vote Profile Analysis" developed by pollster Louis Harris, or the National Broadcasting Company "projections" on election eve. While these may be interesting to the viewer, who will be able to get final returns later in the evening anyway, they are of limited utility to the candidates, except for calming or increasing election day jitters. What the candidate most needs is accurate guidance in the planning of his campaign, guidance which will give him the maximum number of votes, hopefully enough to win. This must obviously come very early in the campaign, so that necessary adjustments in tactics and strategy can be made, if necessary. In 1959, the Democratic Advisory Council engaged a group of political scientists from the Massachusetts Institute of Technology for just that purpose. They formed a private corporation known as "Simulmatics"[49] and set about simulating the 1960 presidential election long before it took place, for the guidance of Democratic plan-

---

[47] *Ibid.*, p. 109.
[48] (Princeton, N.J.: Princeton University Press, 1960.)
[49] This group's work served as the basis for a rather sensationalized novel by Eugene Burdick, *The 480* (New York: McGraw-Hill Book Co., 1964).

ners.[50] They used poll data which was not at all current, based upon voter preferences and perceptions as of 1958, on fifty-two so-called "issue-clusters." Voters were divided in 480 groups, based upon regional and socio-economic characteristics, and their reactions were "simulated" on computers, using a statistical model to "predict" the election, several months before it was held. They ranked thirty-two states, excluding the South, on the basis of how well Kennedy would do in the election. Democratic planners were especially interested in the extent to which Kennedy's religion would affect his chances. Taking this factor into account, by examining voter perceptions of the religion issue, their results were far better than the state-by-state polls which were being taken during the campaign. Specifically, the simulation's results had a correlation of .82 with the actual results as compared to a much lower correlation (.53) between poll forecasts and the election returns.[51] Bear in mind that this was done using data which was two years old at a minimum. After the election, when those in the Simulmatics project were not under the pressure of deadlines, they "postdicted" the election, and found that their results were amazingly close to what actually happened, as Kennedy got 322 electoral votes in the simulation, only eight more than he actually received.

> The mean deviation of the postdicted Democratic percentage of the party vote from the actual is but 9/10 of 1 percent in the 32 states of the North and but 6/10 of 1 percent for the country as a whole.[52]

The applicability of theoretical models and empirical political research would seem to be obvious, at least for those who can afford to pay the costs involved. It must be pointed out, however, that simulation need not be limited to elections alone, and is dependent upon the nature of the problem involved and the availability of data.

Simulating winning elections may call for resources which are beyond the means of the average individual, however. Is there any practical use to which the reader of this text might put some of the recent developments in political science? We believe that this is entirely possible, and turn now to how one may directly influence policy, and at a level

---

[50] See Ithiel de Sola Pool, Robert P. Abelson, and Samuel L. Popkin, *Candidates, Issues, and Strategies: A Computer Simulation of the 1960 and 1964 Presidential Elections* (Cambridge: The M.I.T. Press, 1964), especially Chapter I on which the following discussion is based.

[51] *Ibid.*, pp. 56-57. A correlation of .82 is quite high, in that the upper limit is 1.00.

[52] *Ibid.*, p. 109.

which does not call for a great deal in terms of resources. In recent years, the journals have contained the results of some significant research employing the role and system approaches, focusing on attitudes, perceptions, and behavior in city councils. While the idea of a city council may not send shivers up one's spine, the fact is that they are local, omnipresent at least to the extent that almost all cities in the United States have one, and they do have a good deal to say about the making of local policy. Indeed, in the confronting of urban problems, city councils are a logical starting point for those who would become involved. What has political science had to say which might be helpful to those who would attempt to use pressure tactics on such a body?

A major study has been conducted over the last several years, employing survey research, involving interviews with all incumbent councilmen in the eighty-four cities in the San Francisco Bay area. From this study, and some of the reports which have been published, we may draw some useful information and suggestions as to tactics which might be followed. The authors initially point out that "there has been remarkably little cumulative knowledge about the components of group influence on policy outcomes."[53] Their preliminary report on this question is based on information from twenty-five cities. They hypothesize that the success of interest groups is highly dependent upon predispositions which the councilmen might hold, and that access to these individuals is in large part a function of just those predispositions. When asked why some groups could be influential in the policy process, eighty-four per cent of those answering the question responded on the basis of some characteristic connoting "respect," such as intelligence, or good name of the group, or the common sense displayed by the group. It should also be pointed out, for the benefit of the cynical, that only thirty-one per cent mentioned a characteristic based upon objective strength, such as the wealth or voting power of the group.[54] On the basis of their attitudes toward pressure groups, the councilmen are classified as "Pluralists," "Tolerants," and "Antagonists." The "Pluralists," those who most highly valued group contributions to the legislative process, saw interest groups as contributing needed information as well as having the potential to mobilize support for proposals before the council. However, roughly seventy-five per cent of the legislators could be described as either neutral or hostile to interest group activities, and the authors suggest that:

[53] Betty H. Zisk, Heinz Eulau, and Kenneth Prewitt, "City Councilmen and the Group Struggle: A Typology of Role Orientations," *Journal of Politics*, XXVII (August, 1965), p. 618. The following discussion relies upon this article, pp. 618-46.
[54] *Ibid.*, p. 628.

It does not appear to matter greatly, in terms of the behavior we are describing, whether the councilman is neutral
and relatively unaware, or hostile and highly aware, of the
groups. *Unless groups are both salient and valued,* the political actor in the local community makes little effort
to modify his behavior on their behalf.[55]

As an aside, it might be pointed out that these and other orientations,
including those of state legislators, are not necessarily inbred and a
product of early socialization experiences. To the contrary, they are
apparently acquired as a result of personal experience in the context of
the particular legislative body in which he operates, as well as his constituency and party.[56] What may be gathered from this? We may, for
the time, assume that pressure activity offers no guarantee of success
unless certain preconditions are met, in the eyes of the councilmen, for
they have to deal with their fellows as well as others, and may ultimately be held accountable to someone other than the interest group
attempting to secure some given end.

A major problem affecting those who would contend with the
problem of the metropolis is the sheer proliferation of governments which
may be involved in the process of instituting meaningful change. Further, the governments may reflect entirely different life styles on the
part of their constituent members, and may also pursue policies which
are contradictory with those of others in the metropolis. Using a broad
variety of data relating to policy development in the Bay Area, Eulau
and Eyestone found once again that councilmen's perceptions play a key
role in the process. The authors find that:

There is in the councils of a metropolitan region such as that
around the San Francisco Bay a satisfactory level of agreement on what the problems are that cities in different stages
of development face, and there is very high agreement on
what the city's future should be like. There is less agreement,
as one might expect, on the specific policies that should
be adopted to obtain the goals that are envisaged . . .[57]

It would appear that a tactic which might be employed in the Bay Area,
and especially in those areas where the consensus is not as high, would be

[55] *Ibid.*, p. 645. Italics in original.
[56] Kenneth Prewitt, Heinz Eulau, and Betty H. Zisk, "Political Socialization and
Political Roles," *Public Opinion Quarterly,* XXX (Winter, 1966-67), pp. 569-82.
[57] Heinz Eulau and Robert Eyestone, "Policy Maps and Policy Outcomes: A
Developmental Analysis," *American Political Science Review,* LXII (March, 1968),
p. 143.

to develop a multiple approach to metropolitan problems. This approach should be concerned not only with what *ought* to be done, but with what *can* be done. Such an approach would have to account for the numerous preferences and biases among city councilmen throughout the region, in an attempt to find some common ground within each council as well as intra-regionally. But, to what extent is such a campaign likely to succeed, even if it could find the necessary common denominators? This would appear to be in part a function of the type of community involved, and some conventional wisdom is thrown out by the council project researchers in the process. For instance, in larger cities, councilmen were more susceptible to interest group activity than were their counterparts in cities which were both smaller and more homogeneous.[58] A suggested strategy for influencing representative bodies on this as well as other problems is offered.

> It appears that members of the public dissatisfied with their representative assembly can intrude into its deliberations and force attentiveness in two ways at least, (1) by playing a role in determining who is selected to the representative body, and (2) by defeating incumbents when they stand for re-election. . . . When, however, citizens do not exercise that control, allowing the assembly more or less to determine its own members and seldom unseating an incumbent, they thereby permit the representative group the privilege of defining for itself the goals and programs of the community.[59]

This is, of course, the rather conventional approach to electoral accountability which has been taken by many who exhort the public to "turn out the rascals" when the job is not being done. But, does it all work quite that simply? Not so, one of the project members suggests, as there are any number of individuals in office who will leave office voluntarily, and may therefore prove to be unresponsive to normal electoral pressures. The reasons why councilmen, or other office-holders for that matter, might leave office without being instructed by the electorate to do so are many and complex. But, most important for those who would affect the course of their government, there is a tendency in such circumstances for those who left office to be replaced by similar men, who will be in essential agreement as to what the public priorities may

[58] Kenneth Prewitt and Heinz Eulau, "Political Matrix and Political Representation: Prolegomenon to a New Departure from an Old Problem," *American Political Science Review*, LXIII (June, 1969), pp. 427-41.
[59] *Ibid.*, p. 441.

or may not be.[60] Methods of influencing such individuals cannot have their root in elections, and may have to lie elsewhere. The assumption is that pressure activity, of the sort we have discussed earlier, may very well be the only means by which the public can have its voice heard and acted upon, although this remains moot.

From this short review of the practical aspects of political science, as well as from the various critiques of approaches which we have offered in earlier chapters, it is obvious that our discipline offers no final answers at this time, if ever final answers can be given. But, we are certainly not at an impasse. A decade ago ground was just being broken in most of the areas we have discussed. This text could not have been written with the linkages of theory and method which we have attempted to impart. A genuine excitement in the discipline is the realization that we are constantly probing, testing new hypotheses and new techniques as well as challenging old ones, in areas of inquiry never before considered amenable to empirical research. The development of scientific knowledge in any discipline proceeds by theory-building and hypothesis-testing, and that is true in political science as well. It is true that we have problems in organizing our research across such diverse fields as international relations, voting behavior, comparative governments, and public administration. But, the increasing relevance of political science bodes well for the future of the discipline. As knowledge accumulates and is further aggregated into a coherent whole, we can be better prepared to comprehend the subtleties of politics, to predict the consequences of alternative actions, and perhaps even contribute to the making of better public policy.

[60] Kenneth Prewitt, "Political Ambitions, Volunteerism, and Electoral Accountability," *American Political Science Review*, LXIV (March, 1970), p. 14.

Index

Index